GunDigest
SHOOTER'S GUIDE to
RIFLES

D1563122

WAYNE VAN ZWOLL

Published by

Gun Digest® Books, an imprint of F+W Media, Inc.
Krause Publications • 700 East State Street • Iola, WI 54990-0001
715-445-2214 • 888-457-2873
www.krausebooks.com

To order books or other products call toll-free 1-800-258-0929
or visit us online at www.gundigeststore.com

ISBN-13: 978-1-4402-3072-1
ISBN-10: 1-4402-3072-2

Edited by Jennifer L.S. Pearsall
Cover Design by Al West
Designed by Jim Butch

Printed in USA

ACKNOWLEDGEMENTS

any people contribute to any book—not just editors and production staff, but those who've put the author in the position to write. I must credit first the writers before me who chronicled and explained. And entertained. Words that lie dead and stale have no affect, no matter how true or significant their message. Learning to write well takes much time and work, and also mentors with talent—people like Warren Page and Jack O'Connor, Russell Annabel, Jim Corbett and Ben East. Here's to John Jobson, John Hunter, and John Madson, Peter H. Capstick and Peter Matthiessen, the wordsmithing of Ted Trueblood and Robert Service—all of different backgrounds and writing styles, all gifted.

The industry people behind this work are legion, from inter-viewees who became friends, like Don Ward and Scott Downs, Dave Emary and Lex Webernick, Chris Hodgdon and Torb Lind-skog, to editors at more than 25 magazines and publishing houses who've delivered my work to readers. Accomplished riflemen Gary Anderson, Lones Wigger, and David Tubb have shared their tech-niques, improving my own scores as I relayed those tips. Talented riflemakers Al Biesen and Gary Goudy have showed me how they crafted rifles that have come to define "classic." David Miller and Kurt Crum, Gene Simillion, D'Arcy Echols, Patrick Holehan, and others leave me agape at their artful sculpting of steel and walnut.

This book's scope and details, and the many years behind its production, make even a partial list of contributors laughably in-complete. I won't attempt one. Missing a few names is less ac-ceptable than omitting many. I didn't write this book alone. I'm indebted to all who helped—most of all, perhaps, to Earl Wick-man, who decades ago opened his basement range to a skinny kid star-struck by rifles.

— *Wayne van Zwoll*

CONTENTS

CONTENTS

Wayne van Zwoll has been shooting, competitively and in the hunting field for 45 years and has published 14 books and more than 2,000 magazine articles and columns on hunting and shooting. Wayne qualified for the final Olympic tryouts in the English Match and has won two state prone championships. He has coached marksmanship for many years, taught Hunter Education in five states, and won several awards (including the John T. Amber) for his writing on the shooting sports.

A book on rifles is like a book on automobiles, farming, or world history: incomplete. After 35 years publishing on rifles, I'm falling behind. The slice of the topic I can cover in depth gets ever thinner, because the whole keeps growing!

So, this *Shooter's Guide to Rifles* isn't an all-there-is-to-know-about-rifles book, rather, it's a distillation of what I've come to consider the most important things about rifles, or, more accurately, what I know that seems important. It is, by some measures, comprehensive. It's crammed with stuff, some of which you'll find nowhere else. It tells about the people who designed our most significant rifles and the chance events that brought them success. It takes you to the hunting field and to arenas where extraordinary marksmen shot their way into history books. You'll see the rifle as a weapon, but also as art and explore the way rifles are built. Detailed advice on shooting technique from the most accomplished riflemen will help you hit!

This book covers rifle ammunition and ballistics, as well, so you can better choose cartridges and loads for hunting or competition. You'll read how to get a fail-safe zero, extend your effective shooting range, and overcome adverse conditions afield. Bewildered by technical terms like "leade" and "headspace?" You can rely on this book's glossary. You'll learn about scopes and reticles, too, and gear that can give you center hits with dead-on holds at extreme range. Notes on rifling tell why this elementary component is anything but simple!

Because I've used rifles on game from fox squirrels to African elephants, and because many rifle enthusiasts are also hunters, you'll trek to the mountain in this book. Hunting rifles scarred from the bush carry tales of adventure, and you'll read some of those here. Beyond the battle square, rifles enabled pioneers to strike out into dangerous places. Rifles remain the passport to adventure for millions of big game hunters world-wide. Once limited to ranges measured in feet, the rifle has extended accurate, lethal reach to well over a mile. Its story is fascinating. Come along!

— *Wayne van Zwoll*

DEATH IN THE AIR

Staying safe when hunting or fighting was hard when your reach was limited to that of your hand, or perhaps a club. Throwing rocks afforded a margin of security, but rocks had no effect on big animals. Spears proved more lethal. The bow added reach, as it released with explosive force and great accuracy the power stored slowly by muscles drawing the string.

The bow dates back at least 15,000 years, to early Oranian and Caspian cultures. With it, Persians conquered the civilized world. Around 5,000 B.C., Egyptian archers helped free that culture from Persian domination. By 1,000 B.C., Persians were flinging arrows from horseback. Short recurve bows, for easier use from the saddle, arrived as early as 480 B.C.

The bow may have come to England by way of the Vikings, but the Welsh had it very early on. At the Battle of Hastings, in 1066, Normans drew their English foes onto the field with a false retreat, then drove arrows toward

oncoming troops, winning the day. English archers came to prefer a one-piece bow "deeply stacked"—that is, thicker and not so broad in cross-section as the flat, sinew-backed bows where bow-worthy timber didn't grow. A long draw—to the cheek, not the chest—gave the English longbow its name, though staves commonly stood taller than the archers.

In battle, the Viking/Norman tactic of hailing arrows into distant troops held sway. Attackers could thus be discouraged from charging to engage with sword and spear. Advances toward well-positioned archers resulted in terrible casualties, even as armor evolved to defeat the feathered shaft. Steel-tipped arrows from powerful bows could drive through an oak door, and they perforated light metal; also the armor-wearied foot soldiers who wore it. English bowmen aimed for the joints and for the head of any man so foolish as to shed his helmet on a hot day. They deliberately targeted horses during a cavalry assault, not only to cripple and kill, but to make the steeds unmanageable and spill their riders. Open ground gave entrenched archers a lethal advantage.

Laws tailored to the bow soon appeared. Royal statutes dictated that anyone earning less than 100 pence a year had to own a bow and arrows—and yield them to inspections! Conscripts were required to practice. Deer poachers in Sherwood Forest, subject to hang-

The bow and arrow directed the course of history in Asia and Europe. At Crecy, in 1346, and Agincourt, in 1415, English archers loosed many thousands of arrows from longbows to defeat the French. On America's western frontier, the bow remained popular among native tribes long after firearms became available. Bows and arrows could be fashioned on the trail; they could be carried easily and shot rapidly from horseback. At pistol range, the feathered shaft often proved more accurate, and as deadly!

ing by their own bowstring if caught, earned a pardon if they served the king as archers—many did. A contingent of these men gave an historic account of themselves at Halidon Hill, in 1333. Their arrows killed 4,000 Scots, at a cost of only 14 English dead. At Crecy (1346) and Agincourt (1415), England's archers famously vanquished the French.

While English yew wood served archers well enough, it couldn't match that from Mediterranean lands for purity and straightness. Some of the best bows derived from Spanish wood. After the longbow gained its fearsome reputation, Spain forbade the growing of yew, lest it find its way to England and thence into battle against Spanish troops. Desperate for staves, the English schemed their way around this sanction, requiring that some staves be included with every shipment Mediterranean wine!

Bow wood deteriorates with age and weather. While the yew longbow endured as one of the most important implements of its time, surpassing even the hard-hitting crossbow as a weapon, it was hardly ever embellished. When bows sustained damage or lost their cast, they were discarded as firewood. Only a few examples remain, the most notable recovered, in 1841, from the wreck of the ship Mary Rose sunk, in 1545.

Native tribes in North America fashioned bows from yew in the Pacific Northwest, but also from hardwoods; ash and hickory in the East, Osage orange in the Midwest. The bows varied in length, profile, and cross-sectional shape. Most were flatter than the English longbow. Compressible horn on the bellies and elastic sinew on the backs improved cast. Before horses became available on the plains, native bows there averaged nearly five feet tip to tip, almost as long as bows used by forest tribes east of the Mississippi. Mounted warriors came to favor staves as short as 40 inches, like those used by Northwest tribes. Arrows from eastern woodlands were long and beautifully made, with short feathers. Ac-

curacy was the top priority, because one shot was all that could be expected. On the prairie, though, where hunters rode alongside bison and loosed several arrows quickly at short range, precision mattered less. Also, arrows driven through bison seldom survived. Fletching was long because the crude shafts needed strong steering and because the feathers spent little time against the bow handle before the shot. Raised nocks helped horsemen feel the arrow by pinching it at the string. Albeit the biggest arrowheads might seem best suited to the heaviest game, Indians knew better. Most heads for bison, deer, and elk were slender, to better penetrate. Arrows for small animals had heads big enough to quickly arrest the arrow.

The Sioux and other natives on the plains pushed the bow as much as they pulled the string. This technique permitted quick shooting with short but powerful bows. The mounted Indian normally drew to the chest and well shy of the arrowhead; a 24-inch arrow might be pulled 20 inches. That draw stacked enough thrust to drive arrows through bison! The effectiveness of the arrow, the ease of finding bow- and arrow-making materials, and the speed with which repeat arrows could be launched kept the bow popular among mounted warriors well past the arrival of firearms. "Bigfoot" Walker, the Texas Ranger who, in the late 1830s, helped Colt's develop the massive Walker handgun, respected the plains Indian and his bow. "I have seen a great many men in my time spitted with 'dogwood switches'... [shot] faster than you can fire a revolver, and almost with the accuracy of a rifle at the distance of fifty or sixty yards."

Farther East, the first muskets had little to offer red men skilled with bow and arrow. Powder and ball had to be bought or stolen. Loading the flintlock was slow, and the mechanism proved unreliable in wet weather. Heavy and unwieldy, these guns delivered poor accuracy. They made a frightful noise and spewed thick smoke that obscured the target. Both brought unwanted attention to the shooter … .

CHAPTER 1

FIRESTICKS!

Clumsy, unreliable, and slow to load, they turned armies with noise, smoke, and mystery.

Flint gripped in the jaws of the flintlock's hammer strikes a frizzen, knocking it forward to shower sparks into priming powder cradled in a pan. That flame races through a touchhole to the main charge.

In 1249, nearly two and a half centuries before Columbus reached the Americas, English friar and philosopher Roger Bacon described a wondrous new substance. It had appeared in fireworks generations earlier, in the Orient.

The explosive "Chinese snow" was hardly gunpowder as we know it. Bacon's first compound would have made an inefficient and unreliable propellant. But, in those days, there were no gun barrels; the idea of bottling gas pressure from burning powder to force a projectile through a tube had yet to be explored. Not until the early fourteenth century would firearms appear in England, following experimental work on propulsion by Berthold Schwarz.

The first guns developed in Europe were heavy tubes that required two attendants. Swiss called these firearms *culverins*. The *culveriner* held the tube, while his partner, the *gougat*, lit a priming charge with a smoldering stick or rope. *Culverins* were clumsy and inaccurate and often misfired. Still, the noise and smoke could unnerve an enemy armed with spears or pikes or even bows. *Culverin* muzzles were also fitted with ax heads, to make them useful when ignition failed. Eventually these firearms were modified so one soldier could load and fire them

Early rifles were handmade and costly. They became canvases for artists. This flintlock shows deep, full-coverage engraving — German, probably.

unassisted. Mechanical rests helped shooters steady the heavy barrels. A forked brace adapted from fourteenth-century artillery supported the *petronel*, a hand cannon held against the breast for firing. Braces fashioned for saddles allowed cavalry to fire these cumbersome weapons.

In 1327, Edward II used guns during his invasion of Scotland. Eleven years later, French chemists changed the composition of gunpowder from 40-percent saltpeter, and equal proportions of charcoal and sulfur to 50-25-25. The English later settled on a mix of 75-percent saltpeter, 15-percent charcoal, and 10-percent sulfur. That composition became established as blackpowder, until the development of guncotton, in 1846.

Powder manufacture in the U.S. probably started at Milton, Massachusetts, near Boston. At the beginning of the Revolution, enterprising colonists had made or captured 40 tons of blackpowder! But the need was great, and new powder mills became a priority. By war's end, American forces had 1,000 tons on hand. By 1800, the nation's powder mills were producing 750 tons annually.

While stationary guns aimed at a massed enemy could be fired without regard to tim-ing, soldiers on the move couldn't wait for a wick to burn down to the charge. They needed a device to ignite the powder right away. The first lock was a crude lever by which a long, smoldering wick was lowered to the touchhole in the barrel. This wick was later replaced by a shorter wick or match lit from a cord kept smoldering atop the barrel. The shooter eased a serpentine cock holding the match onto the cord. When the match caught fire, he moved it to the side and down to the touchhole. (A trigger came later.) The matchlock took several forms, the Spanish *arquebus* among them. *Arquebusiers* carried smoldering wicks in perforated metal boxes on their belts. But preparation didn't ensure discharges. In 1636, during eight hours of battle at Kuisyingen, one soldier managed only seven shots! At Wittenmergen two years later, seven shots came off relatively fast—in four hours.

Eliminating that balky wick became the goal of sixteenth-century German gun designers. Result: the "monk's gun," with a spring-loaded jaw that held a piece of pyrite

(flint) against a serrated bar. To fire, the shooter pulled a ring at the rear of the bar, skidding it across the pyrite to produce sparks. The sparks fell in a pan containing a trail of fine gunpowder that entered the touchhole. This design led to another, in Nuremberg, around 1515. The wheellock featured a spring-loaded sprocket wound with a spanner and latched under tension. Pulling the trigger released the wheel to spin against a fixed shard of pyrite held by spring tension against the wheel's teeth. Sparks showered into the pan. Wheellocks were less affected by wet weather than were matchlocks. They were faster to set and gave quicker ignition.

The actions of pyrite and steel were reversed in the *Lock a la Miquelet,* named after *miquelitos* (Spanish marauders) in the Pyrenees. Oddly enough, this design appears to have Dutch origins. It would evolve to become what we know as the flintlock. At the pull of the trigger, a spring-loaded cock clutching a piece of flint swings in an arc to strike a pan cover or hammer. The cover flips back to expose the pan, which holds priming powder. Sparks shower into the pan, igniting the powder, which conducts flame into the barrel's touchhole to fire the main charge. The cock later became known as the hammer, and the hammer a frizzen. Flintlocks were less expensive to build than were wheellocks and, in time, proved more reliable.

White smoke from a blackpowder charge in a flintlock envelopes a shooter. Note smoke over the frizzen, the vertical steel shield kicked forward to expose the pan.

Matchlock, wheellock, and flintlock mechanisms had a common weakness, exposed priming that in wet or windy weather could render the gun useless. Too, a weak spark might even fail to ignite dry priming, and a gap in the trail of pan powder to the touchhole might yield only a "flash in the pan." Sparks struck *inside* the barrel would solve many problems!

PYRITE TO PERCUSSION

Early in the eighteenth century, chemists found that fulminic acid (an isomer of cyanic acid), produced shock-sensitive salts. In 1774, the chief physician to Louis XV wrote about the explosiveness of mercury fulminate. Englishman E.C. Howard discovered, in 1799, that adding saltpeter produced a shock-sensitive but stable explosive. "Howard's powder" may have contributed to the work by Scotch clergyman Alexander John Forsythe who, in 1806, became the first on record to ignite a spark in the chamber of a firearm. Two years later, Swiss gunmaker Johannes Pauly came up with a paper percussion cap in a cartridge inserted from the breech. A spring-loaded needle pierced the cap, detonating the fulminate.

As internal combustion at last seemed practical, a host of inventors rushed to redesign firearms. In 1818, Englishman Joseph Manton built a gun with a spring-loaded catch that held a tube of fulminate to the side of the barrel and over the touchhole. When the hammer crushed the fulminate, breech pressure blew the tube away. The Merrill gun, 14,500 of which sold to the British government, featured this mechanism. The London firm of Westley Richards followed, in 1821, with a percussion gun firing fulminate primers in a flintlock-style pan. The pan cover, forced open by the falling hammer, exposed a cup of fulminate. Two years later, American physician Dr. Samuel Guthrie conceived a more convenient fulminate pellet. In the final sift, though, most credit for the metallic percussion cap must go to Joshua Shaw, of Philadelphia. In 1814, Shaw, a sea captain, was denied a patent for a steel cap because he was British born and not a U.S. citizen. He persevered with a pewter cap, then one of copper. Development of a hollow nipple provided a tunnel that funneled sparks to the chamber. In 1822, Shaw patented his own lock. Congress awarded the 70-year-old inventor an honorarium for his work—24 years later!

Shooters were reluctant to adopt percussion ignition. In the early nineteenth century,

This caplock, an English back-action sidelock with fine engraving, has Damascus barrels fashioned by wrapping steel strips around bore-size mandrels.

chemistry was still viewed with suspicion, and fulminates were chemicals. Some early caps didn't spark reliably. Too, percussion guns were rumored to kick harder, while delivering a weaker blow downrange. Even Britain's Col. Hawker, a firearms authority, measured his praise of percussion ignition: "For killing single shots at wildfowl rapidly flying, and particularly by night, there is not a question in favour of the detonating system, as its trifling inferiority to the flint gun is tenfold repaid by the wonderful accuracy it gives in so readily obeying the eye. But in firing a heavy charge among a large flock of birds the flint has the decided advantage." Governments, perhaps predictably, stuck with the proven pyrite for infantry arms.

As percussion caps progressed, in baby steps, toward universal acceptance, guns changed in other ways. The superior accuracy of rifled bores had been clearly demonstrated in shooting matches as early as 1498 (in Leipzig, Germany) and 1504

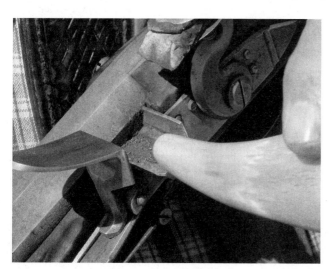

Powder from a horn charged the barrel from the flintlock's muzzle. Finer powder was used to prime the pan and carry ignition through the touchhole into the barrel.

Loose powder and patched ball have given way to polymer-tipped jacketed bullets (here Hornady's) in sabot sleeves and convenient cylindrical pellets (here Pyrodex, a blackpowder substitute).

The patch (usually linen) around a round ball "took" the rifling and made loading easier than pushing a groove-diameter ball home.

the French-style flintlock developed early in the eighteenth century. From it evolved the *jaeger* (hunter) rifle. Initially, the *jaeger* had a 24- to 30-inch barrel of .65- to .70-caliber with deep rifling. Double set triggers were common. The stock had a wide, flat butt and a rectangular patchbox. To conserve lead, frontier gunsmiths started making *jaegers* with bores .50-caliber and under. A pound of lead, they found, would yield 70 .40-inch balls, but only 15 that were .70-inch in diameter. Gunmakers made barrels longer to improve accuracy, replaced the *jaeger's* sliding patchbox cover with a hinged lid, and trimmed the stock to reduce weight and bulk. A crescent buttplate fitted it to the shooter's upper arm.

While most of these changes came at the hands of German immigrant riflesmiths in Pennsylvania, the elegant firearm that emerged became known as the "Kentucky rifle." To speed loading, shooters cradled undersized balls in greased patches that took to the rifling. British troops charged their Brown Bess muskets as fast, but they couldn't match the reach or accuracy of American rifles. Strangely, crack *Jaeger* troops on the British side still loaded their rifles with tight-fitting round balls. Colonists whipped the *Jaegers* almost as handily as they defeated British regulars. The cleaning action of the lubed patch and its protection of the bore against lead fouling benefited hunters, as well as soldiers.

(in Zurich, Switzerland). But rifled barrels were costly to make and slow to load. So, when the Pilgrims landed, they carried the still common smoothbores, heavy and unwieldy, with .75-caliber barrels six feet long. Early on, they failed in battle against Indians carrying bows and arrows.

Armed conflict in the New World did not follow traditional European patterns. Instead of a large phalanx slow moving and clearly visible, the enemy was a single antagonist, mobile, agile, and hidden by vegetation. Accuracy mattered! Also, the enormous balls hurled by British muskets consumed too much valuable lead. Hunters as well as militiamen in nascent America came to favor

CHAPTER 2

BEYOND THE CUMBERLAND

Its roots in Germany, the American rifle evolved in the Alleghenies, then headed west.

West lay the plains, then the Rockies, tall and timbered—and unexplored. Mountain men dared not blink.

Commercial manufacture of rifles came to America just 40 years after the Declaration. It was not imported, but homegrown on New York's Mohawk River. Eliphalet Remington's project, in his father's forge on Staley Creek, began as had many rifles of the day. He chose a rod for the barrel, then, pumping the bellows, heated it to cherry red. He hammered it half an inch square in cross-section, wound it around an iron mandrel, then brought it to white-hot temperature, sprinkling it with Borax and sand. He held one end with his tongs and pounded the other on the stone floor to seat the near-molten coils. After it cooled, Lite, as he was known, checked the .45-caliber tube for straightness and hammered out the curves. Then he ground and filed eight flats, because octagonal barrels were popular. Lite paid a Utica gunsmith four double *reales*— about a dollar in country currency, when $200 a year was a living wage—to rifle his barrel. That took two days. Returning home, Remington bored a touchhole and forged a breech plug and lock parts. He shaped them with a file, then brazed the priming pan to the lockplate. He used uric acid and iron oxide, a preservative called "hazel brown," to finish the steel. With a draw knife and chisel, Lite shaped a walnut stock, smoothed it with sandstone, sealed it with beeswax. He made the screws and pins, too. Then he tested his new rifle at a local match. He placed second. Impressed, the winner asked how he could buy a Remington rifle … .

BIGGER MEDICINE

The march of settlements west of the Ohio Valley affected rifle design. Charges fired from slim Kentucky rifles killed deer and turkeys with dispatch, but proved ineffective on bison. Neither were long barrels and slender stocks suited for life on the prairie, where shots might be taken on horseback. As Daniel Boone probed the Cumberlands in the late 1700s, gunmakers were already beefing up rifles for use on the frontier, where hunters could ill afford a rifle down for repair; the nearest gunsmith might be hundreds of miles away. The "mountain," or "Tennessee," rifle had a bigger bore and a heavier stock than a typical Kentucky rig, and iron furniture.

This transition in rifle design occurred as Gen. W.H. Ashley, head of the Rocky Mountain Fur Company, came up with the rendezvous as a way to collect furs from trappers in the West. Among the many Easterners seeking his fortunes in St. Louis, gateway to the West and operations base for mountain men, was Jacob Hawkins. In 1822, his brother Samuel closed a gunshop in Xenia, Ohio, to join Jake. The two started

The Kentucky rifle could kill western deer, but the plains also held buffalo and grizzlies. Rifles with bigger bores evolved in shops like that of the Hawken Brothers of St. Louis.

building rifles under their original Dutch name, Hawken.

As Youmans, from North Carolina, had become renowned for his Tennessee rifles, the Hawken brothers would all but define the plains rifle. It had a shorter, heavier barrel for horseback carry. The full-length stock gave way to a half-stock, typically maple and often without a patchbox. The thick-walled barrel with a big bore accepted powerful charges. Until 1840, the standard mechanism was a flintlock. While the Hawkens fabricated their own, they also used Ashmore locks. Double set triggers remained a popular feature. The typical Hawken weighed just under 10 pounds, with a 38-inch, .50-caliber octagonal barrel of soft iron. Hawken barrels featured slow-twist rifling. They proved less susceptible to fouling than did the hard-steel, quick-twist barrels common to English rifles of the day. Hawken bores retained traces of bullet lube and delivered superior accuracy with

Lead bullets with grease grooves followed the patched round ball. They added inertia and accuracy. This is a modern rendition, Thompson/Center's Maxi-Ball.

patched balls. Henry Lehman, James Henry, George Tryon, and other gunmakers also built rifles with the Hawken look and features.

Charge weights for plains rifles typically ran 150 to 215 grains. Hunters reported kills at ranges to 300 yards with Hawken rifles. That was long shooting then! In 1920, Horace Kephart reported finding a new Hawken rifle in St. Louis, writing for the *Saturday Evening Post* that it "would shoot straight with any powder charge up to a one-to-one load, equal weights of powder and ball. With a pure lead round ball weighing 217 grains, patched with fine linen so that it fitted tight, and 205 grains of powder, it gave very low trajectory and great smashing power. Yet the recoil was no more severe than that of a .45-caliber breech loader." Bore sizes of Hawken rifles increased as lead became easier to get and the commercial shooting of buffalo became more profitable. In 1849, when the California Gold Rush began, you could buy a Hawken rifle for $22.50.

That year, Jake Hawken died of cholera. Sam kept the shop open. In 1859, he made his first trek to the Rocky Mountains, where many of his customers had used his rifles. After a week's work in Colorado mines, he headed back to Missouri. In his absence, son William Hawken ran the business. William had earlier ridden with Kit Carson's mounted rifles. On September 23, 1847, during the Battle of Monterey, he and a group of 42 frontiersmen fought to hold a bridge over San Juan Creek. Vastly outnumbered, the Americans emerged with only nine ambulatory men. William was among the wounded.

Sam Hawken eventually hired a shop hand, German immigrant J.P. Gemmer. Capable and hard-working, Gemmer bought the Hawken enterprise, in 1862. He may

In country once trapped by mountain men, Wayne killed this mule deer with a modern muzzle-loading rifle. He tracked it to get the shot and used iron sights.

Harris Holland, a tobacconist, started a gunshop in 1837, at age 31. With nephew Henry, he built it in to one of the world's most famous makers of firearms.

have used the "S. Hawken" stamp on some rifles, but marked most "J.P. Gemmer, St. Louis." Sam Hawken outlived Jim Bridger, Kit Carson, and many other frontiersmen who favored Hawken rifles. When he died, at age 92, the shop was still open for business! It closed, in 1915, half a century after Winchester's first successful repeating rifle, 20 years following the introduction of smokeless powder.

ROCKET BALLS!

Loading rifles from the muzzle was not only slow, it couldn't be done easily from horseback or when crouched behind low cover. But until the advent of metallic cartridges, loading from the breech got little traction. While firearms with a hinged breech date to at least 1537, flint ignition shackled them. The percussion cap put inventors back on that path. Beyond the ignition question, their main challenge was to build a breechloader stout enough to withstand heavy powder charges, and one that would also function while hot and dirty.

The first American breechloader to win popular acclaim was developed by John Harris Hall, in 1811. Six years later, the U.S. government issued a few of these rifles to soldiers. But the Hall failed in service. It was weak and crude, a flintlock firing paper cartridges. The use of paper to enclose a charge dated to at least 1586. These cartridges had no priming, and guns were still loaded from the muzzle. Shooters bit or ripped off the cartridge base to expose the charge. The paper burned to ashes upon firing.

Replacing pyrite with the percussion cap did away with the biting and tearing, because the cap's powerful spark could penetrate thin paper. Around 1835, Johann Nikolaus von Dreyse put a primer on a bullet held inside a paper hull. A long striker penetrated the charge to pinch the pellet against the bullet. The von Dreyse "needle gun" earned a great following. About 300,000 were built for the Prussian army over the next 30 years. (Incidentally, the "needle gun" mentioned by writers in the late nineteenth century was not always the von Dreyse. Another rifle so named was the .50-70 Springfield that became the 1873 .45-70 "Trapdoor" U.S. service rifle. That gun's long breech block housed a needle-like striker.)

Meanwhile, Eliphalet Remington paid $2,581 for the gun firm and services of William Jenks, a Welsh engineer who'd designed a breechloading rifle. Remington adapted the Jenks rifle to use Edward Maynard's percussion lock, which advanced caps on a strip of paper. J.H. Merrill would later improve the Jenks rifle. In government tests, its tallow-coated cardboard cartridges fired reliably, even after a minute's submersion in water. By 1847, Stephen Taylor had patented a hollow-base bullet with an internal powder charge held in place by a perforated cap that admitted sparks from an external primer. The next year, New York inventor Walter Hunt developed a similar bullet. What made Hunt's "rocket ball" most interesting, however, was the rifle to fire them. Hunt's "Volitional Re-

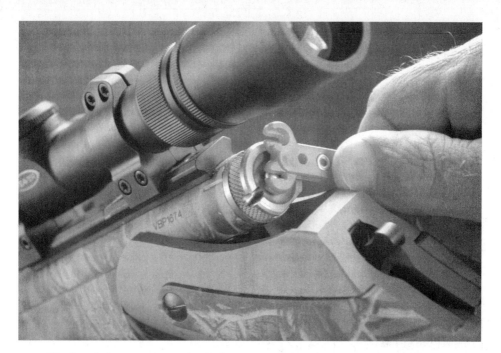

Modern blackpowder rifles, like this Thompson/Center, are patterned after breechloaders, with in-line ignition protected from weather. Here a hunter uses a plastic tool to seat a primer.

peater" had a tubular magazine under the barrel and used a pillbox mechanism to advance metallic primers. Alas, the action, cycled by a finger lever, was prone to malfunction.

Lacking the funds to promote or improve his rifle, Hunt sold patent rights to fellow New Yorker and machinist George A. Arrowsmith. In Arrowsmith's shop, Hunt's repeater came under the hands of the talented young Lewis Jennings. In 1849, after receiving patents for Jennings' work, Arrowsmith sold the Hunt rifle for $100,000 to railroad magnate and New York hardware merchant Courtland Palmer. With Palmer's financial backing, designers Horace Smith and Daniel Wesson addressed the feeding issue from the ammunition side. They took cues from a metallic cartridge patented in 1846 and 1849 by the Frenchman Flobert. But rather than placing a ball atop a primer, Smith and Wesson modified a rocket ball to include a copper base that held fulminate. They adapted these cartridges to pistols, too. In 1854, Courtland Palmer invested $10,000 in new tooling to bankroll a partnership with his employees and a firm that would become known as Smith & Wesson.

Sales of both rifles and pistols disappointed Palmer. In 1855, a group of 40 investors from New York and New Haven bought out Smith and Wesson and Palmer to form the Volcanic Repeating Arms Company. They chose one of their own as director. Shirt salesman Oliver F. Winchester moved the firm from Norwich to New Haven. When sluggish sales sent it into receivership, in 1857, Winchester bought all assets for $40,000. He reorganized the enterprise into the New Haven Arms Company. Benjamin Tyler Henry came on as chief mechanic. In 1860, Henry earned a patent for a 15-shot repeating rifle chambered to .44 rimfire cartridges. Underpowered, unreliable, and prone to leak gas, it was nonetheless coveted by hunters as well as soldiers, because it could be recharged with a flick of the hand. The brass-frame Henry would father Winchester's first lever rifles, the 1866, 1873, and 1876. Confederates called the Henry "that damned Yankee rifle you loaded on Sunday and fired all week."

CHAPTER 3

ONE CARTRIDGE AT A TIME

Firepower came at a price.
Manifest destiny followed the echoes of powerful single-shots.

The last half of the nineteenth century produced more progress in gun design than any other 50-year period in history. Many inventors threw their energy into repeating rifles, but young Christian Sharps decided to build a better breechloading single-shot. Sharps, a New Jersey native, had worked under John Hall at Harpers Ferry Arsenal. In 1848, he received his first patent for a vertically sliding breech block. Fitted to an altered 1841 Springfield, the prototype withstood pressures from the most potent loads. After a halting introduction that cost him sales, Sharps was bailed out by businessman J.M. McCalla and A.S. Nippes, a gunsmith. Two decades later, five years before Christian Sharps succumbed to tuberculosis, the Sharps Rifle Manufacturing Company introduced the New Model 1869, its first rifle for metallic rounds. The New Model 1874 appeared the following year. It would become an iconic American rifle, erasing the great

The Farquharson action, named for the Scot who invented it, was patented in 1872. It was very strong and sized to chamber big cartridges. Ruger's No. 1 evolved from it.

buffalo herds doomed by railroads, cattle, hide and meat markets, and the government's efforts to bring the Plains Indian to heel.

While many buffalo hunters plying their trade in the 1870s favored Remington's Rolling Block, many others thought the Sharps superior. George Reighard was one. In a 1930 edition of the *Kansas City Star*, he explained how he shot bison:

I furnished the team and wagon and did the killing. (My partners) furnished the supplies and did the skinning, stretching and cooking. They got half the hides and I got the other half. I had two big .50 Sharps rifle with telescopic sights ... .

The time I made my biggest kill I lay on a slight ridge, behind a tuft of weeds 100 yards from a bunch of a thousand buffaloes

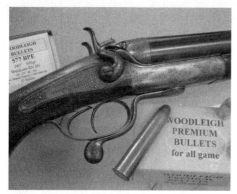

This lovely brute, a Boswell-built .577, shows the elegant lines of British percussion rifles. It has fluid steel barrels, but loads are properly kept to blackpowder pressures.

that had come a long distance to a creek, had drunk their fill and then strolled out upon the prairie to rest, some to lie down ... . After I had killed about twenty-five my gun barrel became hot and began to expand. A bullet from an overheated gun does not go straight, it wobbles, so I put that gun aside and took the other. By the time that became hot the other had cooled, but then the powder smoke in front of me was so thick I could not see through it; there was not a breath of wind to

carry it away, and I had to crawl backward, dragging my two guns, and work around to another position on the ridge, from which I killed fifty-four more. In one and one-half hours I had fired ninety-one shots, as a count of the empty shells showed afterwards, and had killed seventy-nine buffaloes ... .

The Sharps Rifle Company collapsed, in 1880. Its hammerless Model 1878 rifle never caught on, and the firm had no repeater to put against Winchester's 1873 and 1876 lever-actions. A military budget constrained by peace contributed to the firm's demise. Ironically, so did the lethal efficiency of market hunters with Sharps single-shots. The plains had been shot clean; no one needed a buffalo gun. By the early 1880s, so many bison had been killed that human scavengers would glean more than three million tons of bones from the prairie.

Still, the single-shot rifle was not dead. Long after the Civil War, many hunters still

The strongest early American breechloaders had dropping-block mechanisms as on this Lyman rifle, a modern rendition of the Sharps.

John Moses Browning was born in 1855. He attended school until age 15 but built his first gun at 11. He would become, by most standards, the greatest firearms designer the U.S. has ever produced.

In far-off British colonies, hunters after tough, dangerous game with early cartridge guns relied on heavy bullets driven by huge charges of blackpowder. This relic dwarfs a .30-06.

used muzzleloaders—both of necessity and by preference. Clearly, breechloading cartridge arms would drive rifle development, but the future of repeaters was less assured. It would land in the lap of a frontier lad with a genius for gun design to decide.

A GUNSMITH FOR THE GREAT SALT LAKE

In 1834, Jonathan Browning had moved his family 400 miles to Quincy, Illinois, a bustling town on the banks of the Mississippi. By age 35, he'd begun to fashion firearms. The recent invention of the percussion cap had spawned the revolving cylinder. But boring and indexing required tooling Jonathan didn't have. He devised a simpler mechanism and called the rifle his "slide gun." It featured a rectangular bar that slid from side to side through a slot in the frame. Five chamber cavities in the bar held charges. A thumb-lever advanced the bar to line up each chamber in succession, and the lever pushed the bar against the barrel to seal gas. Browning's rifle had a triggerguard that served as its mainspring. The hammer swung up from underneath.

In 1842, Jonathan and his family moved again, this time 43 miles north to Nauvoo, Illinois, a town founded three years earlier by Joseph Smith and his following of Mormons. Jonathan set up a gun shop on the first floor of a two-story brick house. He joined the Mormon movement; however, many people wanted to obliterate it. On June 25, 1844, Joseph Smith and his brother Hyrum were killed by a mob in Carthage, Illinois. The Mormons held together under Brigham Young and planned an exodus for spring 1846. Preparations were cut short by hostile neighbors, however. Forced across river ice in February, months ahead of schedule, the refugees endured grim conditions that claimed lives. In June, they halted near Kanesville (now Council Bluffs), Iowa. Soon thereafter, a U.S. Army officer rode into camp to request 500 volunteers to help fight a war with Mexico. This no doubt

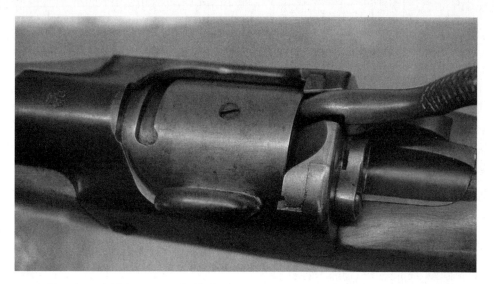

During the middle 1800s, gunmakers worldwide tried to design practical breech-loaders. This one came from Steyr, an Austrian firm. Josef Werndl, its inventor, once worked for Colt.

seemed ironic to the Mormons, who'd pleaded for government help in Nauvoo. Still, Brigham Young had plenty of volunteers, but he refused to let Jonathan Browning leave, as gunsmiths were valuable! In fact, Jonathan was then directed to stay, to supply other Mormons and send rifles west.

Thinned by time and hardship to 143 trekkers, Brigham Young's band of Mormons reached Salt Lake City on July 24, 1847. Five years later, Jonathan Browning came with his family to settle in Ogden (named after the Hudson's Bay Company explorer Peter Skene Ogden). Jonathan bought a plot and, with $600 he'd hidden under the floor of one his six wagons, built a house. By this time Jonathan had 11 children. He would take a second wife in Ogden and father 11 more, one of them, John Moses, born in 1855.

Though he had to help at a tannery his father built in 1862, John obliged his mother by attending school—until age 15, when the schoolmaster told him to quit: "You're done. You know as much as I do."

John was, by all accounts, precocious. As a 10-year-old he'd built his first gun, a flintlock made from a scrapped musket barrel and a board he shaped with a hatchet. John fashioned a crude pan and screwed it to the board, which he wired to the barrel. He stuffed the barrel with a charge of powder and rough

shot, then heated a batch of coke on the forge and put it in a perforated can. "Let's go hunting!" he called to brother Matt, directing him to swing the perforated can on a string to keep the coke alight. When at last they found some prairie chickens dusting, John aimed and Matt stuck a smoldering splinter through the touchhole. John found himself on the ground under a cloud of smoke—and the birds lay dead.

Jonathan Browning the elder listened to the tale that evening.

"Can't you make a better gun than that?" he chided.

John broke his gun into pieces on the forge.

Like his father, who soon lost interest in the tannery, John had a way with guns. By the time he was out of school, John knew he wanted to design guns as well as repair them. He didn't have to move to do this. The West was a land of promise, and two railways had just been joined at Promontory Point, 50 miles from Ogden. By 1878, when John turned 23, cartridge rifles had appeared. Without drafting tools, John sketched a single-shot action. He hand-forged the parts, filing them to dimension. A foot lathe Jonathan had brought by ox cart from Missouri helped with the rest. The finished gun was not only functional, but, with massive parts and simple construction, perfectly suited to the frontier. John wrote to New York's, Schoverling, Daly and Gates: "Please tell me how to patent a gun." His first patent request followed, May 12, 1897. Shortly thereafter, his father died, leaving him the head of two households.

McAUSLAND'S BIG FIND

With brothers Matt, Ed, Sam, and George, John Browning erected a 25x50 shop on a 30-foot lot at the edge of Ogden. Fortuitously, Frank Rushton, an English gunmaker touring the West, stopped by and showed them how to install and run the machinery needed to turn their shop into a factory. John put his single-shot into production, with Ed running the mill and Sam and George rough-filing receivers. Matt made stocks. Frank helped with barreling and attaching sights.

At $25, John Browning's rifle sold well. Just a week after opening a retail counter, the brothers had sold all the rifles they'd finished in three months! John ordered more steel, while Matt spent $250 to expand the retail store. But shortly, burglars made off with everything of value, including the prototype of John's rifle. Slowly the business recovered, with John and Matt as partners and Frank Rushton stayed on until an early death. John designed another dropping-block action and then, in 1882, fashioned a repeating rifle. While waiting for that patent, he started on another. In less than a year, while managing a factory, John Browning had designed, patented, and produced two repeating rifles!

In 1883, Winchester salesman Andrew McAusland happened across a used Browning single-shot rifle. At that time, Winchester lever-actions dominated the sporting rifle market. But they wouldn't handle the popular .45-70 cartridge. McAusland showed the rifle to Winchester president Thomas G. Ben-

Bison once numbered many millions. Market hunting reduced herds to remnants after the Civil War. Sport hunters led by the likes of Theodore Roosevelt brought them back. Limited hunting now keeps bison to levels consistent with available habitat. This New Mexico sportsman used an iron-sighted Marlin.

nett—who lost no time traveling to Ogden and what was billed as the biggest gun store between Omaha and the Pacific. He found a shop the size of a small livery manned by a half-dozen striplings barely out of their teens. But Bennett was no fool. He found John and came straight to the point.

"How much for your rifle?"

One rifle?

No, *the* rifle. All rights.

"Ten thousand dollars," said John coolly. It was a huge sum, in 1883.

Bennett countered at $8,000, paid $1,000 as a deposit, then, six hours after arrival, began his six-day train trip back to New Haven.

During the next month, John Browning pulled all stops to hike production of his single-shot rifle. After Winchester paid the promised $7,000, Bennett wrote Browning to remind him to stop building what was now a Winchester product. John, red-faced, complied. The rifle debuted in Winchester's 1885 catalog and was named for that year. The original Browning design, with high rear receiver walls, was barreled for powerful cartridges favored by buffalo hunters. Browning's rifle was stronger than the 1873 Trapdoor Springfield. Its breech block slid vertically like that of the Sharps, but a slim profile made for easier carry. Winchester also fielded a slender "low-wall" 1885, with improved loading access for smaller rounds.

CHAPTER 4

REMINGTON'S RUGGED ROLLING BLOCK

It humbled the Irish and bloodied the plains—and sustained America's oldest gunmaker.

Until John Browning designed what would become the 1886 Winchester (here with original lead and modern jacketed bullets), only single-shot rifles would handle the powerful .45-70 and .50-110.

As the South staggered, bloodied and diminished, from the blue haze of Gettysburg, the Army of the Potomac also found itself in shreds. President Lincoln's spare, humble address urged healing. For men who'd lost their past and their future, simply forgetting proved challenge enough. Many headed west for a new start. Some carried little more than they had during the war: provisions, a canteen, a rifle.

Eliphalet Remington II had expanded his Ilion, New York, factory to fill what would amount to nearly $30 million in Union firearms contracts. In nearby Utica, he converted the Hamilton Hotel into a factory that would eventually produce 200 pistols a day. He built 18,000 Maynard percussion locks and installed them on old 1842 flintlock muskets. By war's end, the company was finishing almost 1,000 rifles every day. Its ammunition production totaled nearly 10 million cartridges!

The war proved longer than anyone had predicted. Eliphalet "Lite" Remington did not survive it. Within a month after Stonewall Jackson's brigade routed the Union Army at Bull Run, on July 2, 1861, the 70-year-old industrialist lay stricken with what his doctors called "inflammation of the bowels." It may have been appendicitis.

Closed for the funeral, the Remington factory resumed production under sons Philo, Samuel, and Eliphalet III. Orders for military weapons came thick and fast until war's end. Then, suddenly, in April 1865, employees at Ilion sat by silent, heavily mortgaged machines. Remington mitigated the effect of cancelled contracts with a new breechloading rifle, but Joseph Rider's refinements of Leonard Geiger's split-breech mechanism had been rushed. The rifle fared poorly in 1865 Army trials against the Peabody, Henry, and Sharps. By early 1866, Rider had corrected the flaws. The Rolling Block rifle followed.

A strong, simple gun, the Rolling Block had a rotating breech block that sealed a cartridge in the chamber. The hammer hit a striker in this block, firing the round. A shooter thumbed the hammer to full cock, then rolled back the breech block by thumbing its right-hand tab. After inserting a round, he pushed the breech block forward, aimed, and fired. Breech block and hammer, of high-tensile steel, interlocked at the instant of firing to arrest the thrust of the case. Easy to maintain and almost foolproof, this mechanism was so quick to load that a practiced shooter could fire 20 rounds a minute! It was strong, too. In one test, a .50-caliber Rolling Block was loaded with 40 balls and 750 grains of powder, filling 36 inches of a 40-inch barrel. Upon firing, "nothing extraordinary occurred."

The rifle was tested, in 1866, when a band of 30 cowboys led by Nelson Story herded 3,000 cattle through Wyoming. Story had just bought new Rolling Blocks at Fort Leavenworth. With them, he and his men repulsed an Indian attack near Fort Laramie. Forbidden to go beyond Fort Kearney, Story waited two weeks, then, tired of the delay, he quietly moved his herd north on October 22, 1866. Hostile Sioux, led by Red Cloud and Crazy Horse, swooped out of the hills. The cowboys fired carefully, but barrels became so hot they had to douse them with water from canteens. The Sioux expected a pause

John Browning sold his first commercially successful rifle to Winchester—and followed with 40 more designs in the next 17 years. Remington's Rolling Block had stiff competition!

in the deadly volleys, but none came. They retreated and stopped to look back—only to find the Remingtons also reached much farther than their own rifles!

Twice more on the drive Story and his cowboys blunted Indian attacks. By the time they reached Montana, the cowpunchers were low on ammo, but had lost only one man. A few weeks after Story left, Capt. J.W. Fetterman and a detachment from Fort Kearney were ambushed by Sioux. Every soldier was killed. The next year, Fort Kearney was resupplied with fresh troops armed with breechloading rifles.

In 1866, Samuel Remington replaced Philo as company president. Sam had great success selling Rolling Block rifles to European heads of state, many of whom enjoyed hunting. Prussia didn't pan out, though. There, amid great pomp, the man who would become Kaiser Wilhelm I of Germany pulled the trigger on a dud cartridge. Angrily, he rode away.

FLAGSHIP FOR AMERICA'S GUNMAKER

By 1870, the Remington Arms plant covered 15 acres of floor space. The monthly payroll totaled $140,000, an impressive sum at a time when dinner at a good restaurant cost 25 cents. To meet deadline on a French contract, production peaked at 1,530 rifles a day. Remington cataloged several sporting rifles early in the decade (one for $8), but the Rolling Block remained its top seller. Its strongest competition came from Winchester's lever-action 1873, which, in .44-40, proved a reliable repeater and offered more power than its predecessor, the 1866 (in .44 Henry). Still, the 1873's short, relatively weak mechanism wouldn't handle potent rounds like the .45-70. The Rolling Block did and with great accuracy. Following a hunting expedition in 1873, George Armstrong Custer enthused, "With your rifle I killed far more game than any other single party ... at longer range." Alas, at the Little Big Horn, in June 1876, Custer's troops carried converted

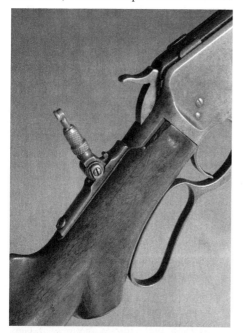

Shooters adapted some features of the single-shot buffalo rifle to lever guns. This 1892 Winchester wears a folding tang sight, for more precise aim.

Springfields, while attacking Sioux used rifles by Sharps, Winchester, and Remington.

The Rolling Block was a favorite tool of buffalo hunters. Buffalo hides in the late 1800s sold for up to $50, and skilled hunters could earn $10,000 a year. Brazos Bob McRae claimed 54 buffalo with as many shots at a single stand with his .44-90-400 Remington and its Malcolm scope!

The reach and accuracy of such rifles led to their use as long-range target guns. In 1874, Remington engineer L.L. Hepburn began work on a match rifle similar to those shot by the Irish in their then-recent victory at Wimbledon. The Irish had subsequently challenged "any American team" through an ad in the *New York Herald*. Each team would comprise six men firing at 800, 900, and 1,000 yards, 15 shots per distance. The newly formed National Rifle Association, along with the cities of New York and Brooklyn, each put up $5,000 to build a range for the match on Long Island's Creed's Farm, provided by the State of New York.

Remington's target rifle, a .44-90 hurling 550-grain conical bullets, appeared in March of 1874. In September, a favored Irish team firing muzzleloaders bowed to the Americans and their Remington and Sharps breechloaders. The tally: 934 to 931, with an Irish crossfire. Subsequent matches in 1875 and 1876 were won more decisively by the U.S., the Remington "Creedmoor" rifles posting the highest scores.

Rolling Block rifles in military form—with full stock, three barrel bands, and a bayonet—sold to hunters, as well as to many foreign armies. In fact, off-shore military sales accounted for most Rolling Block production. Many thousands were shipped in .43 Egyptian and .43 Spanish calibers. Meanwhile, the U.S. Army stuck with the 1873 Springfield, perhaps because the tooling was already at hand.

In 1878, military-style Rolling Blocks listed for $16.50, sporters for $30. Eventually chambered for modern bottleneck cartridges like the 7x57 Mauser, early Rolling Blocks were bored for blackpowder favorites of the day. Most popular among buffalo hunters were the .44-77, .45-70, and .50-70. As was the practice then, Rolling Block rifles came with many options. You could order rifles as light as 8½ pounds and as heavy as 15. Standard barrel length was 26 inches, but you get any length to 34 inches for 50 cents an inch. A single set trigger was a bargain at $2.50. Rifles built especially for competitive shooting, with heavy barrel, tang sight, set trigger, and checkered stock, cost considerably more than a base model; 130 years ago, Creedmoor-type Rolling Block rifles *started* at $100!

The Rolling Block Sporting Rifle became a favorite of buffalo hunters. Military versions sold to foreign armies. Target models helped beat the Irish at the Creedmoor matches, in 1874.

Meanwhile, another company had matured on the frontier. Like Eliphalet Remington, Marcellus Hartley had roots in New York's Mohawk Valley. Well educated, he proved an able businessman. At age 27, in 1854, he and two partners formed Schuyler, Hartley and Graham, Importers and Manufacturers of Guns, Pistols and Fancy Goods. The company rode out the financial panic of 1857. By 1860, it was the biggest gun distributor in the country, so President Lincoln turned to Hartley to find more rifles for the Union army. Armed with £80,000 government-backed credit, Marcellus bought 30,000 guns his first week in Birmingham, England. "Please send another £100,000!" he implored. Hartley acquired thousands more rifles, undercutting and scuttling contract offers from the Confederacy.

BERDAN, BALLOONS, AND BANKRUPTCY

After the war, Marcellus Hartley bought a Connecticut firm that loaded rimfire cartridges for the Spencer rifle, along with a similar plant in Massachusetts. In 1867, he incorporated the Union Metallic Cartridge Company, in Bridgeport, Connecticut, with Schuyler and Graham, Charles H. Pond, and Robert J. White.

U.M.C. lost money at first. But then A.C. Hobbs came along. Hobbs was a gifted mechanic who once accepted a challenge from the British Government to open a lock devised for the Bank of England. After 51 hours of continuous work, he succeeded. Hartley put Hobbs in charge of manufacturing. Then, Col. Hiram Berdan, renowned for his Sharpshooters in the Civil War, broached an idea for stronger cartridge cases. Instead of blowing priming compound into a folded rim, Berdan suggested a percussion cap held in a pocket in the center of the case head. Two flash holes on either side of a fixed anvil would admit the spark. This became the first practical centerfire design, superior in some ways to the Boxer cartridge developed in England about the same time.

Hobbs worked furiously to build machinery to make the new cases, while Hartley sought military contracts. He signed one that promised 10 million rounds to Turkey, another with the Russians for two million. In 1867, U.M.C. had one tiny plant run by 30 employees. Four years later it was boxing 400,000 cartridges a day. The ammo proved reliable and consistent. The battleship *Maine* showed it to be waterproof, as well. Thirteen years after sinking in Havana harbor, in 1898, the *Maine* was brought up. The U.M.C. cartridges in her hull were sent to Bridgeport for testing, and not one failed!

Among the largest orders received by U.M.C. was from the French Army, desperate following its defeats by the Germans at Metz and Sedan, in 1870. Under Premier Leon Gambetta, France defended its beloved Paris, now besieged by German troops. The defenders' only hope was to acquire American rifles and ammunition. Gambetta approached William Reynolds, the Paris representative for Schuyler, Hartley and Graham who had stayed despite the danger. "We need a hundred thousand rifles and 18 million rounds of ammunition," Gambetta pleaded. "Here's a draft on Lloyd's for the money."

Reynolds, a practical man, asked, "How do I get out of Paris? It's surrounded!"

Without blinking an eye, Gambetta replied, "Get a balloon."

In a balloon made of silk gowns pieced by French seamstresses and paid for with $1,250 in gold, Reynolds prepared to leave. But Gambetta commandeered the balloon for a quick trip to the front, forcing Reynolds to wait for another. When he finally lifted off, Reynolds was ducking the snap of bullets from German lines. He landed in a field near Ville Roy, his order intact.

Marcellus Hartley would eventually control E. Remington & Sons. But, by then, just as the Sharps had shot its way out of demand, so, too, had the durable Rolling Block. For three decades near the end of the nineteenth century, peace denied Remington military orders. The company scrambled to market with agricultural tools and sewing machines. It almost salvaged sagging fortunes with a new device called, by its inventor, the "Type Writer." In 1872, a sharp young Remington executive, Henry Benedict, urged Philo Remington to buy the manufacturing rights. He did. But the

Most hunters these days favor repeating rifles. Here Wayne totes a lever-action Model 94 Winchester, developed by John Browning in the twilight years of the single-shot.

new machine sold poorly (it cost $125!), so, in 1886, Remington sold its typewriter business to Benedict for $186,000. That decision denied the company untold millions.

Remington's slide into bankruptcy began in the 1870s. A rifle designed by James Lee during that decade was later built by Remington. Lee got manufacturing rights back after 1886, when creditors put the Ilion giant into bankruptcy. The British adopted Lee's brilliant magazine and other features of his rifle in the famous Short Magazine Lee Enfield (SMLE), a battle rifle that would see action in two world wars. Early in 1888, Marcellus Hartley and Thomas Bennett (Oliver Winchester's son-in-law) bought E. Remington & Sons for $200,000. Hartley worked hard to revive it, recruiting bright inventors to Ilion. In 1892, Arthur Savage came there to work on a hammerless lever-action gun with a spool magazine. But, by 1912, U.M.C. would earn $15 million in gross receipts, 30 times Remington's revenues.

CHAPTER 5

GERMAN GENIUS

No rifle action has earned such worldwide acclaim.
Was it as simple as a door-latch?

B orn in 1838, in the Swabian village of Oberndorf, Peter Paul Mauser did not succeed right away as a gun designer. His first project went nowhere. But he and brother Wilhelm persevered to submit a viable infantry arm to the Prussian army. In 1872, the single-shot 11mm Mauser Model 1871 was accepted as the country's official infantry arm. Its rugged turn-bolt action derived, legend has it, from Paul's inspection of a door latch.

Other governments took notice. Paul and Wilhelm were quickly informed, however, that the Prussian army would pay them only 15 percent of what they'd been led to expect for design rights. Also, these rifles were to be built in government arsenals, not by the Mauser brothers. The pair still needed work. They wound up with a contract to produce 3,000 sights for the Model 1871. A Bavarian order for 100,000 sights eventually led them to build a Mauser factory, in Oberndorf.

Soon thereafter, the Wüerttemberg War Ministry awarded Paul and Wilhelm a contract to build 100,000 *rifles*. To do this, they immediately formed a partnership with the Wüerttemberg Vereinsbank of Stuttgart to buy the Wüerttemberg Royal Armory. On February 5, 1874, it became Mauser Bros. and Co. The sprawling armory, which had begun life as an Augustinian Cloister, shipped the last of the Model 71s in 1878, six months ahead of schedule. Production of sights and an order of 26,000 rifles for China kept the brothers busy, while Paul invented a single-shot pistol and a revolver. Neither succeeded. After Wilhelm died young, in 1882, Mauser became a stock company.

In 1889, Fabrique Nationale d'Armes de Guerre (FN) was established in Liege to produce Mauser rifles for the Belgian government. The FN project followed development of the Model 1889, Paul's first successful smokeless rifle. The 1889 incorporated elements that established Mauser as the dominant gun designer on the Continent. During the next six years, he overhauled the rifle to make it even better. One of the most important changes, a staggered-column fixed box magazine, came along in 1893. By 1895, Paul had developed an action that would be perfected as the famous Model 1898. Shortly after its acceptance by the German Army on April 5, 1898, the Mauser 98 became the most popular military arm to that point in history. Exported to many countries, it would be built in many more. France, Great Britain, Russia, and the U.S. designed and produced their own battle rifles, but none surpassed the 98 in function or reliability.

After World War II, the Mauser firm was renamed "Werke" (works) replacing "Waffenfabrik" (arms factory). Mauser's business shifted toward the sporting trade. The U.S. agent, A.F. Stoeger, Inc., of New York, assigned numbers to the various Mauser actions. By the end of the Depression, there were 20 configurations in four lengths: magnum, standard, intermediate, and short. The short, or "kurz" version featured a small receiver ring and was factory barreled for only three cartridges, the 6.5x50mm, 8x51mm, and .250 Savage. Magnum and kurz actions were made strictly for sporting use. Mauser did not adopt the Stoeger num-

The slot on the rear bridge allowed soldiers to quickly charge the Mauser 98 with the rounds held in a disposable clip. Note the thumb cutout in the receiver wall.

bers one through 20, but collectors still use these designations.

While surplus military Mausers sold on the heels of war at ridiculously low prices, commercial versions always came dear. In 1939, a Model 70 Winchester cost $61.25, while a Mauser sporting rifle listed at $110 to $250. Square-bridge actions cost more, and left hand Mausers commanded a $200 premium.

Though in today's era of detachable box magazines shooters pay this design little attention, Paul Mauser's magazine may top the 98's massive extractor as his star achieve-

The 1898 Mauser bolt has a massive extractor claw to prevent double feeding. The left lug is split for the mechanical ejector. Positive function, in and out!

ment. He figured that a staggered column would enable him to fit the most cartridges in the belly of a rifle action. But how to shape the box? Each cartridge needed support— from the box on one side, from the next cartridge or the follower underneath, and on the other side. He determined the stacking angle should be 30 degrees; viewed from the end, the primers of three cartridges touching each other would form the points of an equilateral triangle. D'Arcy Echols, an accomplished contemporary riflesmith who openly marvels at Mauser's work, explains that the magazines were made for specific cartridges.

"Mauser didn't fashion one box for many hulls, like major gun companies do today to save money. What makes Mausers feed so reliably is their cartridge-specific magazines. You have to admire the guy who came up with the formula."

The numbers are easy to crunch: Multiply the cosine of 30 degrees (.866) by the cartridge case head (or belt) diameter, then add head diameter to that product. For example, a .375 H&H Magnum case is .532-inch across

The third or safety lug on the Mauser 98 bolt is visible here between the gas flange (left) and signature long-spring extractor.

the belt. So .866 x .532 = .460 + .532 = .992. Theoretically, that's the correct rear box width for any cartridge deriving from the .375 case. But most cartridges are not straight. They taper. To provide adequate support, a magazine must taper, too. At the point of shoulder contact (or, on a case without a neck, close behind the crimp), the same formula delivers proper *front* box width. A .458 Lott, for instance, has a front measure of .480-inch; .866 x .480 = .415 + .480 = .895, the correct inside width of the box at the case mouth. A box designed for one cartridge will work for others only if they share front and rear diameters *and* have the same span between them. Overall cartridge length should be nearly the same, as well.

If you subscribe to Mauser's reasoning, magazine interchangeability is limited. A 7.65 rifle rebarreled to .270 requires a longer magazine, of course, but also one slightly wider up front. A 7.65 box is .801-inch wide at the shoulder of a .270 round. A properly engineered .270 magazine is .822-inch wide at that point. Put a .270 in a 7.65 box, and the triangles between cartridge centerlines get steep up front; the rounds tend to cross stack. Bullets emerge from the box craning their necks. A jam may result.

DETAILS TOO EASY TO MISS

Paul Mauser knew that not all cartridges have straight sides and that some rimless rounds might contact the box between base and shoulder. So he relieved the box sides from just ahead of the cartridge base to just behind the shoulder. He paid equal attention to magazine followers, tapering each to fit the box and shaping the top surface "just so." The width of the follower's lower shelf is matched to the case, with a 61-degree step between the upper and lower shelf. To make the next to last cartridge feed, the top shelf is high enough to support that round without lifting it off the last cartridge in the stack. The follower slopes like a ramp to accommodate cartridge taper and keep rounds level in the box.

Paul engineered considerable side clearance into his followers. Says protégé D'Arcy Echols, "It's common to see floorplates machined to hold Mauser magazine springs tightly. At first I made a couple that way myself—I figured Mauser's machinists were just sloppy in cutting spring slots .180-inch too wide at the rear of the floorplate. Was I ever wrong! Those springs are *supposed* to wiggle back and forth on the plate as cartridges are stripped off the top. If you don't let the spring shuffle, it twists, and the follower tips or gets cocked sideways." D'Arcy Echols makes his followers .060-inch narrower than their boxes so they can wiggle a bit. A follower that allows too much play, however, will bang the front of the box during recoil. And, while length may be the least critical follower dimension, a short follower will dive in front. A long one can bind.

The bottom rim of the 98 Mauser's bolt face is milled flush with the center of the face so the case head can ride up into the extractor claw. This permits controlled round feed. Important to infantrymen, early snaring of the case head precluded double loading—the inadvertent stripping of another round from the magazine after the bolt had run one into the chamber. This would, naturally, cause a jam. Controlling feed from the initial travel of the bolt forward also prevents spilling the cartridge if you cycle the action with the rifle tipped steeply to the side.

Bracketing the ejector groove on a 98 bolt face are two cartridge support lugs. The lower of these is angled to guide the rim of the cartridge case as the magazine spring pushes it up. Because a staggered cartridge stack is not constricted at the top into one column that pops the uppermost round into the middle of the action, this lower lug is important. It must herd cartridges from both sides of the magazine toward the center of bolt travel and coax the case rim into the extractor claw. Once there, the case is held against the claw by both lugs. The angle, bearing surface, and thickness of the lower lug determine how easily the case will step across

the bolt face, yield to the extractor, and stay centered as the bolt slides home.

D'Arcy Echols says that the cartridge should spring the extractor claw a measure

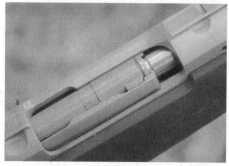

The Mauser claw has carried over into many rifles. Here a Ruger 77 Hawkeye controls a .375 Ruger cartridge from follower to chamber.

Winchester's Model 70 was designed with the Mauser-style extractor. The ejector was also mechanical, though it did not require a split lug.

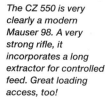

The CZ 550 is very clearly a modern Mauser 98. A very strong rifle, it incorporates a long extractor for controlled feed. Great loading access, too!

Buzz Fletcher built this svelte rifle on an 1898 action. It's chambered in .256 Newton. A 98 requires lots of work, but under skilled hands makes a lovely sporter!

of about .004-inch for a tight fit. "Trouble is, there's that much variation among various brands of the same cartridge. Weatherby cases manufactured by Norma have extractor grooves that average .010-inch deeper than the grooves in Weatherby cases by Remington and Winchester." The result is that a Mauser-style extractor designed to properly fit a Norma hull will prove to be too tight for the others and may prevent the case head from climbing all the way up

For hunting dangerous game, the Mauser extractor is widely considered a must. Wayne shot this leopard in tall grass at 11 paces with a Montana rifle so equipped.

the bolt face until chamber contact with the case body forces it. An extractor fitted to a Remington or Winchester rim won't hold a Norma round as securely because there's no tension on the claw. In neither instance do you get truly controlled feed, no matter what shape the extractor!

Incidentally, Mauser purposefully did not design his extractor to jump over the rim of a round loaded directly into the chamber by hand. But there's roughly .030-inch extra clearance broached in the right lug raceway of the receiver ring, should single loading become a necessary function. You just pinch the extractor spring toward the bolt body as you seat the bolt. The extractor claw, which subtends about 20 percent of the rim's arc, makes the jump. To prevent sticky cases from slipping from the extractor's grasp, Mauser undercut the extractor tongue and its groove in the bolt body so that an extra tug during extraction puts the claw deep into the extractor groove.

Paul Mauser obviously didn't engineer the marvelous 98 on a Saturday afternoon. His ingenuity and insight—and perseverance in this project—are evident to any rifleman who looks closely as he cycles the action.

CHAPTER 6

THE DEER RIFLE: AMERICAN ARCHETYPE

From saddle to sledge, lever guns endured the frontiers
and earned the fierce loyalty of riflemen.

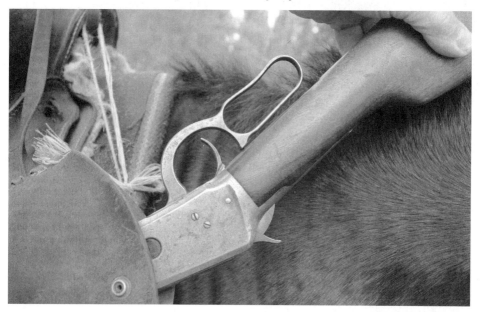

The lever-action rifle did not arrive to kill eastern whitetail deer or fill scabbards in the Rockies. It didn't come to serve hunters at all.

"... Where is the military genius [to] modify the science of war as to best develop the capacities of this terrible engine—the exclusive use of which would enable any government ... to rule the world?" In an appeal to the U.S. Government, Oliver Winchester so described his Henry rifle. In another age, it might as easily been written of the bow. Or the atomic bomb. Wielded by Union troops, the Henry was to Confederates a "rifle you loaded on Sunday and fired all week." It

Winchester's Model 94. At home in the scabbard or on the stump at the deer crossing, it's most popular in .30-30. More than six million have been made!

could spew a stream of 15 bullets with barely a blink between shots.

The brass-frame Henry would spawn Winchester's Models 1866, 1873, and 1876. The 1866 had a receiver loading gate and a wooden fore-end, both lacking in the Henry. But it still fired Henry's anemic .44 rimfire round, whose 28 grains of blackpowder pushed a 216-grain bullet 1,025 fps. The Model 1873 chambered the .44-40 (.44 WCF), Winchester's first centerfire cartridge. Its 40-grain charge drove a 200-grain bul-

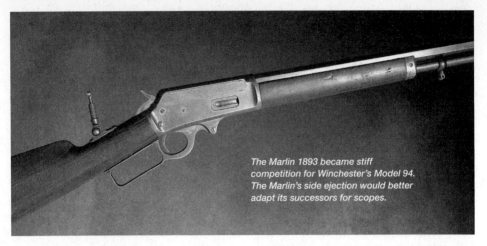

The Marlin 1893 became stiff competition for Winchester's Model 94. The Marlin's side ejection would better adapt its successors for scopes.

let at almost 1,200 fps. When .44-40 rifles sold to the walls, Colt's began chambering the round in its single-action revolver. That 1878 decision drew cheers. Now shooters on the frontier could stock one load for both rifle and pistol. The .44-40 had enough punch for big game, more than enough for bandits.

The Model 1876 Winchester, introduced at the 1876 Philadelphia Centennial Exposition, shared features of the 1873, but its bigger action took the .45-75 WCF round. It lasted just a decade. That iron-framed repeater might have been Winchester's last, had not one of its salesmen stumbled upon a second-hand rifle during his travels west. Of obscure manufacture, the dropping-block single-shot showed clever thinking. He showed it to Thomas Bennett, company president and Oliver Winchester's son-in-law. So began a 17-year relationship between John Browning and New Haven's firearms powerhouse. Browning would deliver more than 40 designs during that period, 11 between 1884 and 1886 alone! Not all went to production, but Bennett bought them all, to keep them from the competition.

When Bennett offered $50,000 for a stronger lever-action to replace the Model 1876, Browning fashioned one with the vertically sliding lugs that gave his single-shot (Winchester's Model 1885) such strength. It became the Model 1886. Soon after it appeared, Bennett requested a short-action version. He

offered John $10,000 " … if you deliver in three months, $15,000 if you can finish in two." John is said to have replied, "The price is $20,000. I'll get it to you in 30 days. If I'm late, it's free." He delivered early.

The compact Model 1892 became an instant hit. Chambered in .44-40, .38-40, .32-20, and .25-20, it earned a worldwide following. Rifle-length magazines held up to 17 rounds, and lightweight carbine versions of the 92 scaled as little as 5½ pounds. The carbines stayed in Winchester catalogs until 1941. Counting the half-magazine variants Models 53 and 65 (circa 1924 and 1933), more than 1,034,000 Model 92s shipped. Meanwhile, the Model 1886 became the repeating rifle for hunters hurling heavy bullets at the biggest game.

Winchester's fine Model 71 in .348 had more power than necessary for deer. It became a hit in elk country. Production spanned only 22 years, 1935 through 1957.

The Model 1894 followed. "Saddle gun" in the West and "deer rifle" in the East, it vaulted to the top of sales charts. Also Browning-designed, the 94 chambered several mid-length cartridges, notably the .30 WCF, or .30-30 Winchester, the first successful smokeless round for sporting rifles. Loaded then with 160-grain bullets at 1,970 fps, it has more horsepower now. In 1924, a half-magazine version of the 94, the Model 55, appeared. It gave way, in 1933, to the Model 64. The 94 in its various versions lasted 112 years before falling from Winchester's book in March 2006, when the New Haven plant closed. It remains the most popular lever rifle of all, with more than six million produced! The 94 has been copied by other makers, recently Mossberg; late-model Winchesters are instantly distinguishable from those built before 1964.

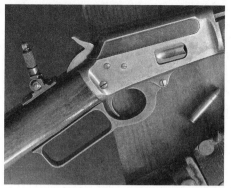

The short-action Marlin 94, for the likes of the .32-20, was not a powerful rifle, but at the end of the nineteenth century, such potent rounds as the .30-30 simply were not considered necessary for deer!

A MECHANISM WORTH IMPROVEMENTS

During the 1890s, as Winchester scrambled to maintain its dominance, John Marlin and Arthur Savage earned patents for other

The Winchester Model 71 was a costly rifle to build. Idaho outfitter Ron Ens appreciates the balance and gunny feel of this Deluxe 71 bored out to .450 Alaskan.

The Model 94 appeared with modified trigger, checkered stock, and angled ejection late in life. In .307 and .356 Winchester, it also got more power.

lever-action designs. Both came up with fine rifles. Marlins had solid-top receivers and side ejection. Savage's hammerless Model 1895 had a rotary magazine that permitted use of pointed bullets. While these rifles owed some of their success to Winchester chamberings, Savage soon trotted out its own .303, with a 190-grain bullet moving as fast as the .30 WCF's 160-grain.

Winchester upped the ante with a more potent lever rifle, again from its Utah gun wizard. Announced in June 1896, the Model 1895 tipped its hat to smokeless powders and cartridges with pointed bullets and high breech pressures. It was the first successful lever rifle with a vertical magazine. The single-column fixed box was charged from the top. Capacity

The Marlin 336, introduced before WWII, is still with us. This early, smooth-cycling rifle in .32 Special wears a receiver sight for quick aim in timber.

depended on the cartridge. The Model 1895 was initially offered in .30-40 Krag, .38-72-275, and .40-72-330. The .236 U.S. Navy made the charter list, but rifles for it were not manufactured. In 1898, the .303 British joined the roster, followed in 1903 by the .35 Winchester and the next year by the .405. Then came the .30 Government 03 (in 1905) and .30 Government 06 (1908). Teddy Roosevelt liked his 1895 in .405, claiming the rifle "did admirably with lions, giraffes, elands, and smaller game" on safari. The U.S. Army bought 10,000 Model 95s in .30-40 Krag for the Spanish-American War. Russia secured nearly 300,000 in 7.62mm Russian before our troops entered WWI. The 1895's military tenure was truncated by the 1898 Mauser and 1903 Springfield bolt-actions.

By 1900, three of every four guns used by American sportsmen were of Browning design. They were all Winchesters. That year, Thomas Bennett and John Browning had a falling out over a self-loading shotgun. The firm's line of lever-actions had few empty slots; Winchester would wait 35 years before introducing another lever gun. The Model 71 descended from and replaced the 1886. Chambered for the big, rimmed .348 Winchester, the 71 came in rifle and carbine, standard and deluxe versions. Alas, steep production costs and the trend to bolt-action rifles strangled this elegant rifle in just two decades. It dropped from the line in 1958, after a run of about 47,000.

If, during the days following the Great War, you owned a lever-action that wasn't a Winchester, it was likely a Marlin. John Mahlon Marlin was 18 years old in 1853, when he apprenticed as a machinist in Connecticut. He agreed to work for no wages for six months, after which he'd earn $1.50—a week! His aptitude showed first in derringer-style pistols, then Ballard rifles. The first successful Marlin lever-action was the top-ejecting Model 1881 in .40-60 and .45-70. It sold for $32. The subsequent 1889 spit empties to the side and had a more reliable carrier. It followed the Model 1888, designed by L.L. Hepburn for the .32-20, .38-40, and .44-40. Hepburn's 1893 was built for longer cartridges: the .32-40 and .38-55, then the .25-36, .30-30, and .32 Special. By the 1920s, Marlin's 93 rivaled Winchester's 94 in popularity.

"A new gun especially for American big game" appeared, in 1937. The Marlin 1936 had a "solid frame, 20-inch round tapered special smokeless barrel [with] Ballard-type rifling, visible hammer, case-hardened receiver ... . Seven shots in caliber .30-30 and .32 Special." All variations cost $32. Just a year later, the Model 336 replaced the Model 36. The obvious difference was a round bolt "encased in the area of the locking bolt by a solid bridge of steel in the receiver." The extractor was new, too, and the 36's flat mainspring gave way to a coil spring. The 336 and 1895 (same receiver, but for .45-70-size cartridges), changed little after WWII, albeit new chamberings and configurations have added versatility. Hornady's recent .308 and .338 Marlin Express cartridges, and its LEVERevolution ammunition, have revived interest in Marlin's great rifles. Minute-of-angle groups paired with the solid, "gunny" feel of lever-actions bred in the nineteenth century make a heady combination. Bullet trajectories lever-rifle shooters could once only dream of—and power to match—now give bolt-gun reach to Marlin's line.

CHAPTER 7

THE SAVAGE 99:
A LEVER GUN TO LAST

He explored the Outback, grew coffee, and built a torpedo.
Then he designed the iconic Model 99.

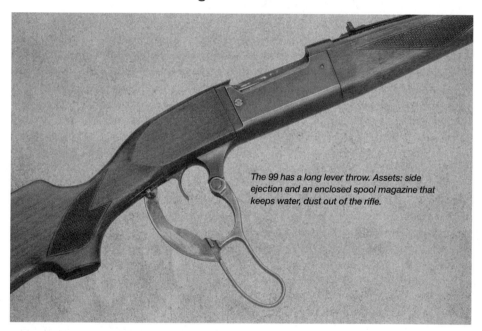

The 99 has a long lever throw. Assets: side ejection and an enclosed spool magazine that keeps water, dust out of the rifle.

As this is written, the Savage Model 99 has been discontinued for just more than a decade. It remained in production for a century, because it has those indefinable qualities that make it an extraordinary rifle. A lever-action slim and flat and saddle-ready, it cheeks like a wish and points like a wand. But unlike the tube-fed, exposed-hammer rifles of Wild West fame, the 99 carries reserve cartridges in a machined-steel receiver. There's no outside hammer, and the bolt locks against the receiver itself, not against rails.

The Savage 99 appeared when labor costs were much lower. "Today," say Savage engineers, "the machining and final fit would make it too expensive to sell." More's the pity.

Arthur William Savage was born May 13, 1857, in Kingston, Jamaica, where his father, a Special Commissioner from England, established schools for newly freed slaves. Unlike frontier gunsmiths of the nineteenth

The Savage 99 rifle derived from earlier designs that didn't make the cut as infantry arms. As a sporting rifle, the 99 lasted nearly a century.

century—Lite Remington and John Browning—Arthur Savage got a fine education in England and the U.S. After university, he sailed for Australia, where he met and married Annie Bryant and managed a cattle ranch. The young couple started a family, soon to include eight children. One of their four sons was born in a wagon during an overland trek.

Savage proved an able stockman. Over the next 11 years, he built a cattle empire and sold it. With the money he bought a Jamaican coffee plantation. While building that business, he turned his hand to designing firearms and explosives, collaborating on what would become the Savage-Halpine torpedo. It sold to the Brazilian government after the U.S. Navy demurred.

Though the close of the nineteenth century brought hard times to several gun companies, Arthur Savage pursued a new rifle. He was just 35, in 1892, when he fashioned the

Savage No. 1, a hammerless lever-action operated with the near (or little) finger. An ingenious rotary magazine held eight cartridges. The rifle had a 29-inch barrel, a musket-style stock. Then living in the U.S., Savage submitted his repeater to U.S. ordnance trials at Governor's Island, New York. It lost to the Norwegian-designed Krag-Jorgensen bolt-action, which became the U.S. service arm.

Convinced of the merits of his rifle, Savage reconfigured it for sportsmen. He reduced magazine capacity to five for a trimmer profile, shaped the lever to accept three fingers. Patents awarded him early in 1893 described a prototype model in .32-20. Savage followed with his own smokeless round that outperformed not only the rather anemic .32-20, but the more powerful and popular .30 WCF (Winchester Center Fire, or .30-30, as it's better known). In April 1894, he formed the Savage Repeating Arms Company in Utica, New York. Rifle production began the next year. Marlin Firearms Co. of New Haven, Connecticut, supplied tooling and built the first Savage rifles, their magazines lengthened for the new .303 Savage round. Dubbed the Model 1895, Arthur Savage's lever-action was truly hammerless. In lock-up, its bolt abutted the web of steel forming the rear of a forged receiver.

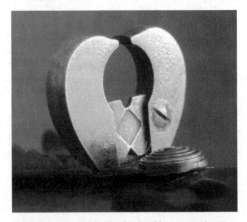

Early 99s wore sights like this buckhorn, popular at the time, but not a very good option. This style open sight obscured much of the target.

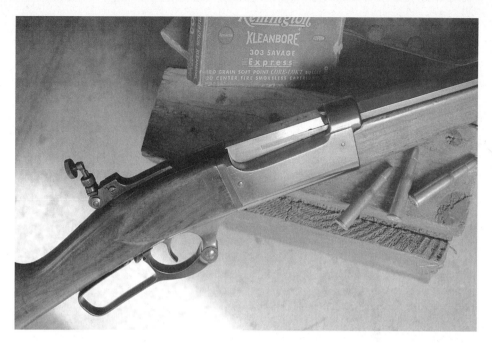

The .303 Savage, a smokeless round developed in 1895, was the charter chambering in the Savage 99. About 6,000 rifles were made between 1895 and 1899, when Savage modified the action.

Because the 1895's mechanism was almost totally enclosed, it protected shooters better than other lever guns in the event of case failure. Unlike Winchester and Marlin lever-actions, it had no hammer slot, no separate loading port. The shooter thumbed cartridges through the ejection port, designed so spent cases flew to the side and out of the sight line. As scopes gained favor, that side ejection became an even bigger asset.

The 1895 had a coil mainspring, the first ever on a commercial lever gun. Coil springs were more durable than leaf springs, standard on the competition. A through-bolt held buttstock to receiver, a more secure arrangement than wood screws in tang extensions. The rotary magazine was shielded from water, debris, and impact by the receiver. A window on its forward left side showed the cartridge count. Unlike tubes, this spool magazine had no contact with the barrel, so it didn't impair accuracy. Because cartridge weight stayed between the hands, balance was unaffected by the number of rounds in reserve. Perhaps most importantly, Savage's spool also permitted safe use of pointed bullets; stacked end-to-end in the tube magazines other makers

employed, cartridges could fire upon recoil unless bullet tips were flat or round.

237 YARDS OFF IN A STRONG WIND ... .

The cartridge Arthur Savage developed for his new rifle looked and performed like the best of its competition—in fact, a little better. The .303 Savage resembled the .30 WCF, or .30-30, with a rimmed, generously tapered case and a long neck. But its 190-grain bullet had more punch. The .30 WCF was first loaded with a 160-grain bullet at 1,970 fps. The .303 Savage launched 190s at about the same speed. (Incidentally, these were .308-diameter bullets, not the .311s of the .303 British, Great Britain's service round.) Designed for smokeless powder, the .303 Savage listed a blackpowder loading until 1903 (the same year the company also discontinued a target load with paper-patched bullet). The .303 Savage wooed hunters worldwide. One from British Columbia claimed 18 kills with a box of 20 cartridges, including two grizzlies in the tally. Harry Caldwell, who dedicated his life to mission work in China, used a Savage rifle in .303 to shoot tigers. In its 1900 catalog, Savage ran an excerpt from a letter by an Alaskan hunter who applied his .303 with lethal effect on a whale—that tale may have choked off further testimonials!

Still, W.T. Hornaday, author of *Campfires in the Canadian Rockies*, wrote, "I have just [shot] one bull moose and two bull caribou, all killed stone dead in their tracks with one of your incomparable .303 rifles. I shot the moose at a distance of 350 yards ... [and my guide] killed a very fine large mountain sheep [with] the first shot 237 yards off and in a very strong wind ... . [The] barrel is small and [has] no long magazine to catch the wind ... ."

Savage's Model 1895 was cataloged with 20-, 26-, and 30-inch barrels in .303 only. About 6,000 rifles were built between 1895 and 1899, when Savage modified the action. The subsequent Model 1899 became available in .30 WCF a year later. In 1903, the .25-35, .32-40, and .38-55 joined the list (all were dropped in 1919). So similar was the new rifle to its predecessor that, for $5, Savage offered to convert the earlier version with a new bolt and bolt components, hammer, sear, and hammer indicator. The indicator was a small bar at the top front of the bolt. In a cocked rifle, the bar was up. Not long into production of the Model 1899, the bar was replaced by a pin that protruded from the top rear of the receiver.

Many hunters are unaware that the 1899 (and the later 99), has a rebounding firing pin. Besides assisting ejection, this feature allows for de-cocking and safe carry with a round in the chamber. To de-cock, simply lower the lever a couple inches, just past its resistance, then pull the trigger as you close the action. The cocking indicator will lie flush with the top of the receiver, showing the rifle is not cocked. To cock without extracting or ejecting, just lower the lever the same distance,

then close. As Arthur Savage designed his rifle to cock near the end of lever travel, cycling is easier than with traditional lever guns. Primary extraction also occurs with the loop close to the grip, where fingers have their greatest leverage.

The Model 1899 appeared in many forms. Barrel lengths of 20 to 28 inches were mated to several stock profiles. Barrel contours had letter designations: "A" for round, "B" for octagonal, "C" for half-octagonal. The 1899-F saddle-ring carbine with 20-inch barrel proved especially popular. Savage announced the CD Deluxe and H Featherweight, in 1905. The Model 1899-D, a .303 with musket stock and bayonet, died in 1905, though a batch of D rifles appeared in 1915. In 1907, a take-down rifle appeared. In 1913, the hot new .250-3000 cartridge replaced the .25-35, chambered in the 22-inch barrel of the 1899-A since 1903.

The .250-3000 was the brainchild of Charles Newton, an attorney who spent most of his career designing rifles and cartridges. This new case had the same base diameter as the .30-06, but was shorter. Newton suggested a 100-grain bullet at 2,800 fps; Savage chose an 87-grain bullet at 3,000 fps—*blistering* speed in those days. That claimed velocity became part of the cartridge name. Later, the round was called simply the .250 Savage. Factory loads with 100-grain bullets are now standard. Newton also gave Savage the .22 Hi-Power, or "Imp" cartridge. It debuted in the Model 1899-CD rifle, in 1912. A 70-grain .228-inch bullet clocking 2,700 fps seduced hunters; but the Hi-Power couldn't guarantee kills on heavy game. Its place in the 'chuck pastures was later snatched by the .22-250. The .22 Hi-Power would vanish by World War II.

To diversify its business after the Great War, Savage bought the J. Stevens Arms Company, of Chicopee Falls, Massachusetts. Joshua Stevens, who'd died, in 1907, at age 92, had built from his 1860s gun shop a

Cartridges for lever-action Savages, in chronological order from left: .32-20 (prototype rifle), .303 Savage, .30 WCF (.30-30), .25-35, .38-55, .250 Savage, .300 Savage; .308, .243, .358, .284, and .375 Winchester. Not shown: .32-40 (dropped in 1919), .22 Hi-Power (dropped, in 1941) and .22-250 (in 99-C only, from 1977).

powerful enterprise that sold affordable but well-made firearms to millions of hunters and target shooters. Savage's 1920 purchase of Stevens was the first of several acquisitions. Also in 1920, the Savage Model 1899 became the Model 99. The mechanism didn't change much, and early production offered five styles. Letter designations excepting the "A" remained—but they appeared on different rifles. The new 99-D was a welter-weight take-down, not a military musket! New use of old letters would continue. The original 99-E, circa 1920 to 1933-'34, was Savage's "Light Weight" with a schnabel-style fore-end. The 99-E, arriving in 1961, had a rounded, press-checkered hardwood stock—"E" then meant Economy. The 99-A came for a time, in 1926-'27, to supplant the original 1899-A. It re-emerged in different form, in 1971.

CELEBRITY ENDORSEMENTS

From the start, Savage lever rifles and their ammunition were touted for their accuracy. The 1903 catalog showed a 10-shot, 100-yard group measuring $^{15}/_{16}$-inch. Smokeless powder, claimed Savage, improved accuracy, produced higher velocities with smaller charges, reduced fouling, and cut recoil by 45 percent! Surely that last assertion raised eyebrows, but the drum-beat to smokeless lured shooters from rifles engineered for blackpowder rounds. The Savage 1899, not incidentally, ran on smokeless.

Endorsements from famous outdoorsmen

helped sell 99s. In 1901, Savage got a letter from Teddy Roosevelt describing his Model 99 as "the handsomest and best turned out rifle I have ever had." T.R.'s affinity for Winchester 1886 and 1895 lever-actions are better known, but he adored his Savage!

Roy Chapman Andrews, explorer for the American Museum of Natural History, carried a Savage. He called the .250-3000 "The most wonderful cartridge ever developed." On his third Asian expedition, in 1920, Andrews relinquished his 99 for a bolt-action Model 1920 Savage. But another hunter on that trek, Harry Caldwell, brought his 99.

The .300 Savage cartridge arrived in 1920, along with the 99's debut. Designed to perform in the same class as the .30-06, it operates at about 47,000 psi, roughly 5,000 psi higher than average pressure from a modern .30-30 load. Still, the case measures only 1.871 inches, and the .30-06 mikes 2.494. The .300's limited capacity puts it 250 fps behind the .30-06. But legions of hunters bought Savage 99s in .300. They used the stubby round to down elk and moose, as well as deer. In Model 99 barrels rifled 1:12, the .300 remained the rifle's

most potent chambering until the .308 Winchester appeared, in 1952.

During World War I, the Savage Corporation had partnered with Pennsylvania's Driggs-Seabury Ordnance Company to produce Lewis machine guns. In the second World War, the entire Savage-Stevens line turned to the manufacture of military weapons. At peak production, Savage was turning out 8,500 guns a month on 1.2 million square feet of factory floor in four facilities! Its payroll grew to 13,000—10 times the peace time total. By war's end, the firm delivered more than 2.5 million firearms. Half of these were Thompson submachine guns. Savage also built 330,000 Lee-Enfield rifles for Great Britain, after the huge losses at Dunkirk. Then, following the Lend-Lease Act, Savage agreed to double production of the SMLE to 60,000 per month. By mid-1944, the company had manufactured a million of these iconic rifles.

Arthur Savage did not see the end of the second World War, but during the preceding two decades, he had no doubt reveled in the popularity of the .300 Savage among hunters. New versions of the 99 rifle had appeared while he dabbled in other enterprises. He prospected for oil, ran a tire company, and managed a citrus plantation in California.

Arthur Savage died, in 1941, at age 84. Five years later, Savage Arms consolidated its firearms production at Chicopee Falls and closed the original Utica facility. It also trimmed the line of Model 99 rifles down to the 99-EG and the beefier 99-R and 99-RS. The EG, a svelte, well-balanced rifle with 22- and 24-inch barrels and schnabel fore-End, had been exceedingly popular before the war. The RS was simply a deluxe R, with a Redfield receiver sight and a 7/8-inch sling in QD swivels. All three rifles were of solid-frame design and chambered only in .250 and .300 Savage. Prices: $89, $101, and $121.

Passing the million-rifle mark in the 1950s, Savage's 99 added short-action cartridges introduced by Winchester that decade, the .308, .243, and .358. The .284 joined the list in 1964, the .375 Winchester in 1980. During the 1960s and '70s, eight new versions of the 99 appeared, including DE and PE engraved presentation rifles (1965) and a 75-year anniversary rifle (1970). All told, the Savage 99 has been sold in 14 chamberings, including, briefly, the quick-stepping .22-250. Catalogs have listed 31 versions, as many as 10 at a time, plus a take-down 99 with a .410-bore shotgun barrel.

The 99 mechanism has endured few changes during its long life. The two most noticeable arrived in the 1960s. In 1961, the lever safety was moved to the tang, and, in '65, a detachable box magazine replaced the spool. Stock changes included a switch from walnut to beech; checkering progressed from hand-cut to pressed (in '65), then to machine-cut. A minor change that set the 99 apart from other rifles of its generation was the addition of scope-mount holes, beginning in 1950.

While bolt-action rifles have become more and more economical to manufacture, the same is not true of the 99. The Savage design requires hand fitting—a costly step complicit in the 99's demise. In the early 1990s, Savage tried to save the rifle by shipping parts to a Spanish gun firm, which investment-cast receivers and shipped barreled actions back to Savage for stocking. That didn't last.

Savage's first catalog, circa 1900, listed Model 99s for $20, with engraving from $5, checkering from $2. A Lyman tang peep sight (or wind-gauge globe front sight), cost $3.50. Sling and swivels added $1.50. Custom stock dimensions could be special-ordered, but, in 1905, Savage admonished buyers that, "… deviation from (standard dimensions) requires the stock to be cut from the solid block by hand. This is expensive work and there is an extra charge of $10 … ." The last Savage 99, described in 1997 editions of *Shooter's*

The Model 99 is a collectable rifle—sadly, most of the best and scarcest are now in collections. Books like this one apprise aficionados of the 99's heritage, exploits.

Bible and *Gun Digest*, retailed for $650. It had a 22-inch barrel in .243 or .308, plus a detachable box magazine. That year the company also fielded its 99-CE, or Centennial Edition, in .300 Savage only. A thousand were built. List price: $1,660.

POSTSCRIPT: A BOLT-ACTION TO GROW ON

Introduced in 1958, the Savage 110 followed the Remington 721/722 by a decade, Winchester's Model 70 by two. Like the Remingtons, it was an inexpensive rifle (original price was $110), but sturdy, reliable, and accurate out of the box. A barrel nut made headspacing easy. The bolt-face extractor and ejector, with judicious use of stampings and alloys, kept the rifle affordable, even as walnut gave way to less expensive woods and hand checkering vanished. The 110 remained essentially unchanged for many decades. It also remained quite popular. Many hunters liked the tang safety, and the reputation of the 99 certainly didn't hurt this Savage.

Within the past few years—or since the 99's demise—myriad new versions of the 110 have made headlines. The company has adopted a two-digit label for the short action, a three-digit for the long. The numbers 11 and 16 designate chrome-moly and stainless steel, respectively. Ditto 111 and 116. But there are other numbers, like the 14 and 114, for the walnut-stocked Classics. These (with the entry-level Savage Axis and Stevens 200), have thrived in a competitive market. One of the most appealing of the current crop of Savage bolt guns is a 5½-pound rifle with checkered walnut. Called the "Lightweight Hunter," it shows detailing and finish well above average for working-class deer rifles. I snared a .243 for testing.

This rifle is based, not surprisingly, on the current Savage Model 11. One recent refinement is a bolt-release plunger in the guard. It replaces the right-side lever of early 110s. You must still pull the trigger while depressing the plunger to free the bolt. Bolt removal is a must before disassembly, because the plunger obscures the forward guard screw—which is also the rear action screw (a wood screw secures the rear of the guard). Leave the bolt in and you'll almost surely bump the trigger as you wrestle with the plunger. The rifle now muzzle-up, the trigger and bolt release agree to let the bolt plummet onto the comb nose. But this proved to be my only irritation with the Lightweight Hunter, and it's one you now needn't endure.

The Lightweight Hunter's pillar-bedded walnut is nicely contoured, with a slender grip, generous comb flutes, a bold, classic comb nose, and ruler-straight buttstock lines, top and bottom. The thick, black Decelerator pad shows perfect fitting. The fore-stock at the receiver is quite trim (bulk here has become distressingly common on mid-priced rifles). Up front the stock tapers gracefully. Shorter by a couple inches than the stock on my Savage M14 Classic, it wears the forward

Wayne fires a 99, one of his favorite lever rifles. Its stout, rear-locking action bottled high pressures from the .243, .308, .358, and .284.

swivel stud only a ½-inch shy of its place on the 14, so it's still in a useful spot for sling use. The fore-end has four pairs of bottom cut-outs, ostensibly to pare ounces. They're neatly done. So is the machine-cut checkering in attractive panels fore and aft. Belly hardware fits closely its stock recess. I'm delighted the buttstock was not lopped to reduce weight or adjust the balance. Length of pull is a standard 13½ inches.

Savage has lightened the action by machining the tubular receiver flat on the sides, then making recess cuts on the bridge and left receiver wall. Spiral flutes on the bright-polished bolt body (blackened in the grooves), eliminate more metal. The floating bolt head helps ensure proper cartridge alignment and contact. The right-hand lug clutches the extractor. It complements a plunger ejector. The detachable box magazine is easy to load, and (three cheers!) you can top-load it in the rifle. The top cartridge is centered. There's nothing new about the sandwiched "washer" recoil lug, but the barrel nut is smooth, not grooved.

AccuTrigger, standard on Savage's flagship rifles, adjusts from about six pounds

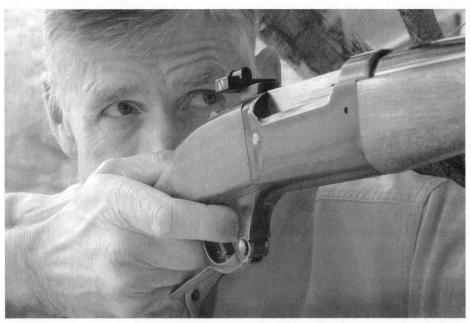

Many consider lever-actions appropriate only for close-quarters work in thick cover. But with new chamberings, and improved bullet designs on older cartridges, the lever is equally at home on the open range these days, as demonstrated by the author and this fine pronghorn he took.

down to less than one. It's safe at all weights, because the central blade must be depressed to permit sear release. Light trigger pull with a clean break helps you shoot any rifle more accurately, but especially bantam-weights. Trigger pull on my Lightweight Hunter registered 2½ pounds, just about ideal for a hunting trigger, in my view.

Savage has retained the 110's hallmark tang safety, but improved it. The thumb-switch on current versions is larger, with more aggressive serrations for easier manipulation with gloves. It also has three positions. With the tab fully retracted, bolt and trigger are locked. A middle detent allows you to operate the bolt. Forward is "fire." Like the AccuTrigger, the safety works well and adds practical value to the rifle.

Savage chambers its Lightweight Hunter in .223, .243, .260, 6.5 Creedmoor, 7mm-08, and .308. In the long-action version, pick .270 or .30-06. All rounds are fed from a steel detachable box that fits flush, holds four rounds, feeds reliably from the center, and drops conveniently into your hand when you press a forward release tab. The box can be top-fed while in the rifle—a very nice touch.

The slim 20-inch barrel of the Light-weight Hunter gave me pause. But this rifle balances well; it doesn't feel muzzle-light.

It could use another inch of barrel. As I like my rifles with a slight tilt forward, a couple of additional ounces would suit me. On the other hand, the Lightweight Hunter is quick to point and surprisingly easy to steady with a Weaver K2.5 in low rings.

You're going to tell me now that I've no business running accuracy tests with a 2.5X scope. I'll concede that more magnification can help shrink groups. But hunting with a big, powerful scope atop a 5½-pound rifle makes no sense. Besides, targets of appropriate size can give you tight groups with glass of modest power. I once drilled a .17-inch group with a 3X, and have shot many half-minute clusters at 4X.

At the range, I found the Savage Light-weight Hunter a solid performer with several loads. It gave me a ¾-inch group with Hornady's 85-grain InterBond and averaged well under 1½ inches with most bullets. Even for coyotes it has deadly precision to 250 yards, point-blank range with a 200-yard zero.

I like this new Savage better than I thought I would. It's a feather-light rifle that points like a wish, but steadies itself obediently. It feels good, cycles without hiccups, and shows more care in finishing than many more costly bolt guns. It wears walnut well and shoots as accurately as I can from a slinged-up prone position.

CHAPTER 8

WINCHESTER'S M70: THE RIFLEMAN'S RIFLE

Call them snobs, those who worship the pre-'64 Model 70. But don't assume they're wrong.

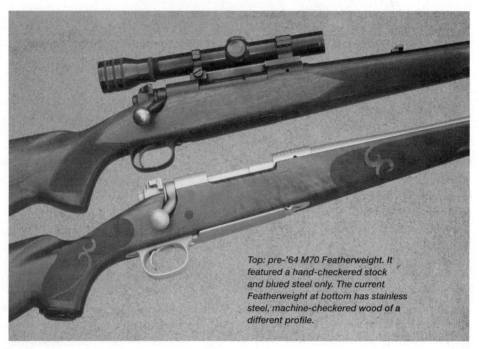

Top: pre-'64 M70 Featherweight. It featured a hand-checkered stock and blued steel only. The current Featherweight at bottom has stainless steel, machine-checkered wood of a different profile.

Winchester's Model 70 ascended a relatively short ramp. The firm's first successful bolt rifle, the Model 54, was but a decade old, when the 70 was conceived.

The 54 followed the .45-70 Hotchkiss, abandoned soon after its introduction in the 1890s. In 1897, the Lee Straight Pull appeared, only to nosedive six years later. During WWI, Winchester built Pattern 14 and Model 1917 Enfield rifles for British and American troops, a task that would catalyze efforts to develop a bolt-action hunting rifle.

By 1922, Winchester designers had pruned the weaknesses of the Lee, Hotchkiss, and Enfield.

The 54's coned breech derived from the 1903 Springfield. Its receiver and bolt, safety and extractor, mirrored a Mauser 98's. The ejector, after a Newton design, scotched the need for a slotted lug. The barrel, of nickel steel, lay in a slender walnut stock with schnabel fore-end, sharp comb, and "shotgun" (not crescent) butt-plate. The 7¾-pound Model 54 cocked on opening and was strong enough for .30-06 pressures. While the safety proved awkward under a scope, few shooters then owned scopes.

The new Winchester rifle sold well, thanks in part to a new cartridge announced for it. The .270 was essentially a .30-06 necked to launch 130-grain bullets at 3,100 fps—lightning speed, in 1925! But celebration at the New Haven plant died in October 1929. Winchester Repeating Arms was savaged by the stock market crash; in 1931 it faced receivership. On December 22 of that year, it sold to Western Cartridge Company. Chief executive John Olin considered the Model 54 a profitable venture, so T.C. Johnson and his staff refined the rifle they had engineered, equipping it with a beefier "NRA" stock.

Initially offered only in .270 and .30-06, the 54 soon added eight other chamberings. These were, in order of increasing rarity, the .22 Hornet, .30-30, .250 Savage, 7mm Maus-

er, .257 Roberts, .220 Swift, 7.65mm Mauser, and 9mm Mauser. Sporter versions of the 54 are most common; nine others included Target and Sniper models with Marksman-style stocks, leather slings, and scope blocks. Prices, in 1936, ranged from $59.75 (Sporter) to $111.00 (Sniper's Match). The Model 54's signal failing was its trigger, which also served as a bolt stop and thus fared poorly in competition. While hunters seemed to accept the mushy trigger, they balked at the top-swing safety, which precluded low installation of Bill Weaver's 330 scope. Also, the 54's Speed Lock (added in 1932) didn't work as predicted, and misfires ensued.

Winchester's Model 54 was cataloged and available through 1941, though production slowed to a trickle during the last five years. Of 52,029 Model 54s shipped, 49,009 were boxed by the end of 1936.

Work on a new bolt-action Winchester was authorized December 29, 1934. But it commenced slowly. In the mid-'30s, men eating from soup kitchens had little money for rifles. The Model 54 was still quite popular, and the Marksman stock designed for the Model 70 target rifle had yet to prove itself on 54s. As the economy got to its feet and the target stock helped win matches, Winchester started building Model 70s. The first receivers got serial numbers January 20, 1936. On January 1, 1937, when the M70 was officially released, 2,238 rifles were boxed and ready to ship. List price: $61.25.

Winchester's Model 70 was chambered in cartridges ranging from .22 Hornet to .375 H&H in size, including some special-order numbers. Most pre-'64s were in .270 and .30-06.

The new rifle resembled a 54, but its trigger had a separate sear, permitting adjustment in take-up, weight, and over-travel. The bolt stop, pivoting on the trigger pin, was also separate and worked through a slot in the lower rear section of the left lug race. For long-action rounds, the bolt stop arrested the left lug. One of three bolt stop extensions (to fit the .220 Swift, .250 Savage, and .22 Hornet), were mounted on the extractor collar to limit bolt throw for shorter cartridges. Firing pin travel on the Model 70 was increased $^{1}/_{16}$-inch to eliminate the 54's misfires. The change boosted lock time by 20 percent, to 3.5 milliseconds or so. To augment the 54's bolt-head gas ports, Winchester added a hole in the right side of the receiver ring.

The first Model 70 safety was a tab atop the bolt shroud. It swung horizontally and cleared most scopes. Four years later it was moved to the side. The safety had a middle detent, which prevented firing but freed the bolt to cycle. The bolt handle, lowered to 45 degrees, swept rakishly to the rear. Its receiver notch acted as a safety abutment, should the lugs fail. The square bolt shoulder on the first 70s precluded low scope mounting and was later eliminated. Like the 54, the 70 had three guard screws, but a machined floorplate hinged in front and latched by a spring-loaded plunger in the guard supplanted the 54's fixed magazine cover and guard.

For 2012, Winchester produced a Jack O'Connor Tribute Rifle patterned on the Al Biesen custom M70 Featherweight Jack favored afield.

THE MAKING OF A CLASSIC

Model 70 receivers were machined from solid bar stock, each beginning as a 7½-pound chrome-moly billet. After 75 machinings, a receiver weighed 19.3 ounces. It measured 8.77 inches long and 1.357 inches through the receiver ring. After hand filing to finish, receivers were roll-marked with Winchester's logo on the left wall, a wavy matte pattern impressed on the top of ring and bridge. Heat-treating followed spot-hardening of the extraction cam behind the bridge. Receivers were immersed in a 1,200-degree salt bath for 24 hours, then Rockwell-tested to 47C. This test left a dimple in the cocking-piece groove in the tang. Sandblasting, tumbling, polishing, and bluing readied the receivers for assembly.

Early Model 70 barrels had the same contours and threads as M54 barrels; they interchanged. But barrel materials had evolved. Stainless steel appeared in 1925. By 1932, chrome-molybdenum had become standard. M70 barrels were drop-forged, straightened by hand with a 15-pound hammer, then turned true on a lathe. They were deep-hole-drilled and straightened again. Each bore was then reamed to the proper diameter and hook-rifled by a cutter slicing progressively deeper on several passes, one groove at a time. Rifling took 11 minutes per barrel. After lapping with cadmium lead lubricated by carborundum oil, those first barrels were threaded (16 threads per inch on the one-inch shank), and, depending on model, slotted for rear sights and front sight hoods. Ramps, forged with the barrels on early 70s, were hand-stippled. Later they were soldered on and machine-matted. Each barrel was stamped underneath with the caliber designation and the last two digits of the year, plus the inspector's mark.

Chambering came next. The last of four reamers left the chamber undersized for headspacing. The barrel was roll-marked right and left on top, given a caliber stamp, then polished and blued. (During WWII, the right-side roll-mark was eliminated; a single left-side inscription carried the chambering, too.)

Most small parts for the first Model 70s were drop-forged, then machined. The floorplate hinge and bolt sleeve came from bar stock, and the extractor was fashioned from 1095 spring steel. The bolt body, straightened after treating, got an inspector's stamp at the base of the handle before bluing.

Model 70 stocks were roughed by bandsaw from 2x36-inch blanks of black walnut (Marksman, Super-Grade, and special-order stocks were 3.8 inches wide before contour-

Hill Country Rifles stocked and tuned this stainless M70 in .270 WSM. The Mauser-type extractor is now again standard on Model 70s.

ing). Standard stocks went to an eight-spindle duplicator for shaping. Drum-sanding followed. Inletting was finished by hand, and so, too, the final sanding (with 240-grit paper). Minor flaws were repaired with stick shellac, glue, or wood welding. The first M70 stocks got a clear, nitrocellulose lacquer finish over an alcohol-based stain and filler. These lacquers contained carnauba wax, which produced an oil-like sheen. The war made carnauba wax scarce; harder lacquers then appeared. Hand checkering with carbide cutters readied stocks for assembly.

Headspacing followed final chamber polish, trigger adjustment, and a function check. Barrels and receivers got the Winchester Proof (WP) stamp after digesting one "blue pill" cartridge, which generated 70,000 psi. After each bolt body was etched with the serial number, the rifle was fired for a 50-yard zero. Next it was cleaned, inspected, disassembled, reassembled, inspected again. Finally, it was tagged, oiled, greased, wrapped in brown waxed paper, and nested in a corrugated cardboard box.

The Model 70 had much to offer hunters: a comfortable stock and an accurate barrel, a bull-dog Mauser extractor that controlled feeding, plus an adjustable trigger and a low-slung bolt handle that swept by scope bells. The receiver swallowed long belted magnums like the potent .300 and .375 H&H. Besides these heavies, early M70s chambered the .22 Hornet, .220 Swift, .250-3000 Savage, .257 Roberts, .270 WCF, 7mm Mauser, and .30-06. Between 1941 and 1963, nine more cartridges were added; however, only eight appeared in catalogs. (Winchester "Gun Salesman Handbooks" distributed in 1947 included the .300 Savage, chambered until 1954.) More M70 chamberings arrived in the 1950s and early 1960s, Winchester cartridges all: the .243, .264 Magnum, .308, .300 Magnum, .338 Magnum, .358, and .458 Magnum. Most have enjoyed great success, though their introductions came shortly before the Model 70 suffered what has become the most infamous re-design in all rifledom. Of the 581,471 M70s built before its 1963 overhaul, 208,218 were .30-06s, 122,323 were .270s. Rifles in .35 Remington and .300 Savage totaled 404 and 362.

PRECIPICE—AND A LONG CLIMB BACK

By the early 1960s, Model 70s had come in 29 styles and 48 sub-configurations. Featherweights with 22-inch barrels appeared after the War to replace the heavier M70 carbines with 20-inch barrels. The .308 and .358 chamberings were listed only for Featherweight rifles. Super Grade 70s had special stocks and a floorplate stamp, but no distinctive metalwork. The 70's tang changed during the 1940s, following the move to a side-swing safety. Safety tab shape changed, too. The bridge, initially matted, was later left smooth and drilled for scope bases. Bolt knobs, solid at first, were

The Model 70 has spawned copies. This, from the Montana Rifleman, features an investment-cast receiver. Wayne has used it extensively, with uncannily good results!

hollowed in the 1950s. Changes in bolt sleeve, bolt stop, striker spring retainer, and other components were largely phased in unannounced. Late Model 70 stocks had higher combs for easy aim with scopes. Checkering patterns remained the same, but checkering quality deteriorated, as 1963 approached.

Sadly, Winchester Model 70s proved less appealing to company accountants than to hunters. In 1960, number-crunchers in New Haven decided to arrest plunging profits by trimming production costs. Two years later, engineers had agreed upon 50 changes. These were implemented in 1963. On October 1 of that year, number 700,000 appeared on the first "new" 70. Its reception shook the house.

Riflemen howled with rage. Vicious denunciations targeted the new stock's pressed checkering and a barrel channel with gaps wide enough to swallow car keys. The recessed bolt face had a tiny hook, not a Mauser claw. The early 70's machined steel guard was supplanted by aluminum, solid action pins by roll pins, the bolt stop's coil spring by music wire. A painted red cocking

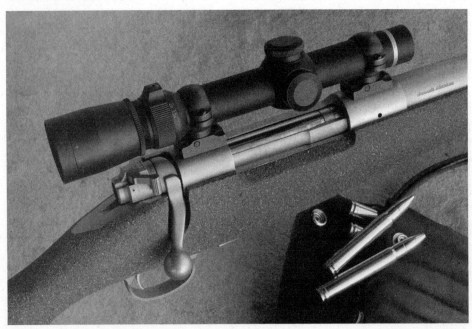

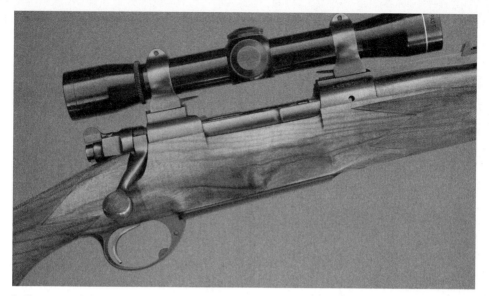

Ace stockmaker Gary Goudy fashioned this Model 70, rebarreled to .35 Griffin & Howe. It's a .375 H&H necked down.

indicator stuck like a tongue from under the bolt shroud; the white stock spacers were no more tasteful.

In the early 1970s, I asked Winchester's management if the early M70 might return. "Never," was the reply. "It'd cost too much." But engineers did refine the new rifle. In 1966, an anti-bind rail smoothed bolt travel. Six years later, an XTR version wore a more attractive stock. Featherweight

rifles got a truly handsome stock, in 1980. A short-action 70 arrived, in 1984. A short run of low-priced, push-feed Model 70 Rangers vanished too soon; they had plain but well-finished hardwood stocks on the same metal used for ordinary 70s. In 1987, the Mauser claw returned on some models. Stainless steel rifles debuted four years later, six years after the first synthetic-stocked 70.

Olin divested itself of Winchester Repeating Arms in 1981, licensing the name to investors who formed the U.S. Repeating Arms Company. But profits stayed out of reach. Beset by rising labor costs in a slow market, USRAC filed for Chapter 11 bankruptcy, in 1984. Five investors purchased the company, in 1987. One was the Belgian firm of Fabrique Nationale (FN), which came away with a 44-percent share. In 1991, the French conglomerate Giat bought FN. When Giat's Jack Mattan arrived from Belgium to take the reins at USRAC, he told me that, "Win-

Wayne killed this Namibian buffalo with his Montana rifle in .375, a Model 70 clone. It wears a 1.5-5X20 Leupold.

A current Model 70 Featherweight took this buck with one shot. The rubber grommet on the barrel is an aftermarket device of debatable value in improving accuracy.

chester is the greatest name in the gun world. But it has focused too long on production. Shooters don't need a new rifle every year. We must recruit new customers."

Though Winchester's flagship bolt rifle had grown more fetching since the dark days of 1963, sales couldn't cover production costs. The factory in which 20,000 workers had toiled during the second World War was doomed. Even on my first visit, when it struggled on under Olin's umbrella, the great New Haven plant harbored mostly ghosts. Oil-soaked hardwood creaked hollowly in rooms with neither people nor machinery. Lonely cells still functioned, workers in soiled aprons feeding an aged lathe or inspecting, with sepulchral stares, modest stacks of completed rifles. The factory that had undergirded the Allied war machine and served generations of sportsmen now gasped with the echoes of solitary footfalls. In March 2006, the New Haven plant closed. Union contracts had driven annual losses "into seven figures." Alas, Winchester's Model 70 died 70 years after its debut, behind bricks stained by decades of industrial soot, under skylights still blackened to foil the Luftwaffe.

No rifleman expected the Model 70 to be left for dead. It had, in fact, already been cloned. The Dakota 76 was a refined M70. The Kimber 84 carried its primary features.

The Montana Rifleman had replicated it with investment castings. In 2000, FNH USA, the U.S. subsidiary of FN Herstal, had taken the last of New Haven's production for its Special Police Rifle, built in FN's modern Columbia, South Carolina, plant.

Winchester manufactures the Model 70 there now. In many respects, it's a better rifle than ever. CNC machines hold tolerances tighter. All eight versions, in two action lengths, wear Mauser-style claws and blade ejectors. One-piece bottom metal trumps the separate guard and magazine tab of early M70s. Stainless and chrome-moly barrels are hammer-forged in 16 chamberings. Wood-stocked rifles feature nicely checkered walnut. Synthetic stocks by Bell & Carlson are the best of their kind, with alloy bedding blocks for enhanced strength and accuracy. Pachmayr Decelerator pads make shooting more comfortable. The MOA three-lever trigger is not as simple as the original, nor to some aficionados as good. It works.

With list prices starting a penny below $800, the Rifleman's Rifle is less affordable now—though, when it came to market at $61, you could buy a house for less than $10,000. In 1963, when $154 bought you any M70 hunting rifle save the .458 African, gasoline sold for 28 cents a gallon, and Ford's Mustang was about to debut at $2,700.

CHAPTER 9

THE REMINGTON 700: AMERICA'S RIFLE

You'll find it everywhere. Shooters are quick to recognize a classic—and loath to leave it!

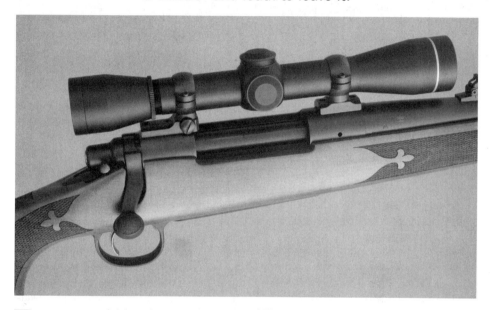

In many game fields and on many shooting lines, Remington's Model 700 shows up more often than even Winchester's 70, which had a 25-year head start. Remington is still America's oldest gunmaker, but its most celebrated rifle just turned 75.

In 1888, Marcellus Hartley, of Hartley and Graham (which then owned Union Metallic Cartridge Company), joined with other investors to buy E. Remington & Sons. The first military contract after its acquisition was for the bolt-action Remington-Lee Model 1885 Navy Box Magazine Rifle, invented by James Lee. The Model 1899 sporting version didn't reach market until Winchester's controlling interest in Remington ended, in 1896. The

A 50-year commemorative rifle came off the line in 2012. It faithfully reproduced the look and feel of the 1962 BDL rifle—and, of course, chambered the 7mm Remington Magnum.

New Haven manufacturer may have perceived the Lee as a threat to its lever-actions. Remington-Lee sporters chambered the 7x57 and 7.35mm Mauser, .236 Remington, .30-30 Winchester, and .30-40 Krag.

Twelve years after these rifles were dropped, in 1909, Remington announced a new bolt-action for hunters. The 30S derived from the 1917 Enfield, which Remington had produced on contract during the Great War. Heavy and expensive, the 30S sold poorly. In 1926, it was replaced by the Model 30 Ex-

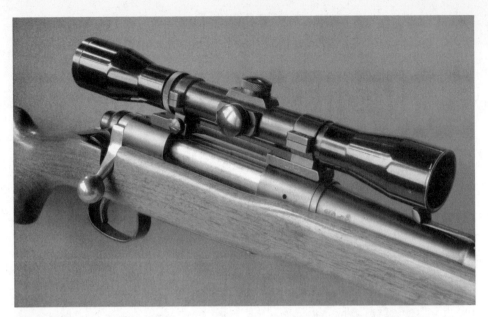

The Model 700 Remington had its genesis in the 721, introduced in 1948. Following in 1962, the 700 had refinements but essentially the same action.

press, offered not only in .30-06, but in .25, .30, .32, and .35 Remington (all developed for pump guns!). The 30 Express cocked on opening, had a shorter (22-inch) barrel than its predecessor, and a lighter trigger pull. A slim stock helped chop overall weight to 7¼ pounds. Priced at $45.75, the 30 Express became reasonably popular, and deluxe and carbine versions followed. In 1931, the 7x57 made the list of chamberings, five years later the .257 Remington-Roberts. The last 30 Express came off the line in 1940.

The Model 720 High Power Rifle, developed by Oliver Loomis and A.H. Lowe to replace the 30 Express, appeared, in 1941, in .30-06, .270, and .257 Roberts. After building only 4,000 rifles, Remington shifted its production to military hardware. The Navy acquired many of the first 720s. Those not issued during the second World War were presented, beginning in 1964, as marksmanship trophies by the Navy and Marine Corps. Remington shipped thousands of 1903 and, beginning in 1942, 1903A3 Springfields in a war effort that all but cancelled sporting rifle manufacture at the Ilion, New York, plant. The company delivered 28,365 Model 1903A4s—the first mass-produced run of U.S. sniper rifles.

Rather than build more 720s at war's end, Remington adopted a low-cost bolt-action designed by engineers Merle "Mike" Walker and Homer Young. A benchrest competitor, Walker insisted on features that enhanced accuracy. The Model 721 and short-action 722 appeared early in 1948, with receivers cut from cylindrical tubing. The 721s measured 8.75 inches, the 722s 7.87 inches. Recoil lugs were thick steel washers sandwiched between the receiver face and barrel shoulder. A clip-ring extractor, self-contained trigger assembly, and stamped bottom metal pared costs. The bolt head with twin locking lugs was brazed to the bolt body (as was the bolt handle), which was a machined steel cylinder. A bolt shroud supported the case head and added security in the event of case rupture. A plunger-style ejector enabled Remington to keep "three rings of steel" around the case head. In the March 1948 *American Rifleman*, the 721 was introduced by Julian S. Hatcher as the strongest, safest, bolt rifle around. He described torture tests it survived after 1903 Springfield, 1917 Enfield, and 1898 Mauser rifles failed.

The 721 in .270 and .30-06 originally listed for $79.95. The 722 in .257 Roberts and .300 Savage cost $5 less. All had 24-inch barrels. Beginning in 1949 the 721 chambered the .300 H&H Magnum. At 8½ pounds with a 26-inch barrel, it weighed considerably more than the standard 721 (7¼ pounds) and 722 (seven pounds). It sold for $89.95. In 1960, Remington offered the .280 in the 721, a year later the .264 Winchester Magnum. The 722 brought the .222 and .244 Remington to American shooters. The .308 made the roster in 1956, the .222 Remington Magnum and .243 in 1958 and 1959. High-grade "A" and "B" versions of both rifles were replaced, in 1955, with the ADL and BDL designations familiar to Model 700 owners. In December 1961, the 721/722 series was dropped, after production of 173,124 Model 721s and 117,751 Model 722s. But so sound was the

mechanism that benchrest shooters continued to build rifles on 722 metal.

A NEW LOOK FOR PLAIN JANE

The only flaw in the 721/722 design was, arguably, cosmetic. Stamped metal parts complemented plain, uncheckered walnut. To my eye, there's a Spartan elegance to these rifles, preferable to the angular lines and ill-crafted detailing on modern rifles. A comely follow-up from Remington designers Wayne Leek and Charlie Campbell was the Model 725, introduced in 1958. It featured 721/722 receivers but with hinged floorplate, checkered walnut, and hooded front and adjustable open rear sights. A 22-inch barrel came standard on initial offerings in .270, .280, and .30-06, and also on the .244 (1959) and .243 (1960) rifles. A 24-inch tube for the .222 arrived, in 1959. During 1961 and 1962, Remington's Custom Shop built a Kodiak Model 725. Chambered in .375 and .458 Magnum, it had a 26-inch barrel with an integral brake. Just 52 of these nine-pound rifles left the factory. In 1961,

Wayne fires a new 700. Strong, reliable, accurate, and available in myriad chamberings, it has become one of the most popular hunting rifles ever.

when the 725 was discontinued, output for all chamberings totaled fewer than 16,700.

Three years before the 725's debut, Remington had introduced the Model 40-X, a fine .22 target rifle. A centerfire version, with features from the 721/722, came in 1959, in .308. Remington later added the .222, .222 Magnum, .30-06, and .300 H&H Magnum. Free Rifle variations followed. Initially priced at $361.05, centerfire 40X Free Rifles soon jumped to $544.40.

In 1962, Remington fielded a brand-new rifle. The Model 700 borrowed heavily from the 721/722—in fact, the mechanism is the same. Early advertising focused on those three rings of steel—bolt shroud, chamber, and receiver ring—supporting the cartridge

The Remington 721/722 bolt face was recessed, with a plunger ejector and clip extractor. Three rings of steel —bolt, barrel and receiver—surrounded the case head. The 700 retained this design.

head. A trim tang, a swept bolt with checkered knob, and cast (not stamped) bottom metal distinguished the 700 from its forebears. So did a more appealing stock. Chasing accuracy, Mike Walker gave the 700 very fast lock time (3.2 milliseconds), tight bore and chamber tolerances, and a short leade. The barrel had just two points of contact with the fore-end, up front.

Initially, the Model 700 came in two action lengths and two grades. Barrels wore iron sights. The ADL in .222, .222 Magnum, .243, 6mm, .270, .280, .308, and .30-06 retailed for $114.95. It had a blind magazine and pressed, point-pattern "checkering." The BDL featured white-line spacers at buttplate, grip cap, and fore-end tip, *fleur-de-lis* checkering, and a price of $139.95. Remington also listed magnum versions of the new rifle: $129.95 for the ADL, $154.95 for the BDL. (Incidentally, Winchester's Model 70 Mag-

The 700 action is a top pick for custom rifles. Rick Freudenberg (www.freudscustomrifles.com) installed a Krieger barrel in .338 Norma on this one. Dave Kiff at Pacific Tool (www.pacifictoolandgauge.com) furnished a custom bolt for the big case based on the .416 Rigby. GreyBull Precision provided the stock.

nums of the day were cataloged at $154.50.) A special-order, safari-style 700, with braked 26-inch barrel in .375 H&H or .458 Winchester Magnum, commanded $310, same as the M70 African in those chamberings; in truth, the 700s were from left-over 725 Kodiak stock and identically priced.

The 700 got a big lift from the concurrent introduction of Remington's 7mm Magnum cartridge. Wyoming outfitter Les Bowman had a hand in developing and promoting it as a versatile big-game round having the reach and smash of a .300 H&H Magnum, but less recoil. The only other magnum slated for first-year production was Winchester's similar but less ably presented .264. Both and the .300 Winchester Magnum that soon followed wore 24-inch barrels, as did the .222 and .222 Magnum. Remington's John Fink tells me early magnum barrels actually taped 23½ inches; by 1965, they were truly 24. The 20-inch barrels standard for the .243, 6mm, .270, .280, .308, and .30-06 were replaced by 22-inch tubes, in 1964. Rifle weight ranged from 6¾ to 7¾ pounds. Magazine capacity: four for standard rounds, three for magnums.

In 1969, the 700 got its first facelift. Remington installed a longer rear bolt shroud and jeweled the bolt. A restyled stock had a butt-plate of black plastic, supplanting anodized alloy. Machine-cut checkering succeeded pressed panels. By the mid 1970s, Remington had replaced the satin stock finish on 700s with tough RKW gloss. Sales remained strong, as Winchester endured the wrath of shooters dismayed by the 1964 cost-cutting redesign of its Model 70. But, in 1968, the fledgling Sturm, Ruger announced fresh competition in its Model 77 rifle, and while the Savage 110E still undersold all, that company offered left-hand rifles.

Remington first listed a left-bolt, left-stock 700 in 1973, in .270, .30-06, and 7mm Magnum. It got a warm reception. By then the Varmint Special had arrived, with heavy barrel *sans* sights. Chamberings included the .22-250 and, later, the .25-06, both wildcat cartridges adopted by Remington in 1965 and 1969, respectively.

A long, difficult stalk in heavy Namibian thorn gave this lady her shot. She hit the fine red hartebeest just right with a bullet from her Remington 700.

Introduced with the Model 700, the 7mm Remington Magnum cartridge proved a huge hit. It combines flat flight with elk-busting power, but with less recoil than those in the .30 magnum-class.

Beginning in 1966, Remington manufactured 700s for military and police forces. Paul Gogol, design engineer and Custom Shop foreman, came up with a sniper rifle on a 40X action. It won a contract from the Marine Corps. Substituting the 700 mechanism, Remington built 995 of these M-40 Sniper rifles over the next six years. Many were fitted with Redfield 3-9X scopes. Chambered to 7.62 NATO (.308), the M-40 saw service in Vietnam. In 1986, the U.S. Army approved a Model 700 SWS (Sniper Weapon System) with long-action receiver, synthetic, Kevlar-reinforced stock, and free-floating, 24-inch stainless barrel. These rifles (2,510 for U.S. forces, 1,000 for Egypt), shipped with a range-finding Leupold M3A 10X scope that housed a range-finding reticle. Accuracy standard: groups of 1.3-inch AMR (average mean radius) at 200 yards. Demand for tactical-style rifles in the civilian market continues to shape the 700 stable.

Remington has added many versions of the 700 since my early hunts with the rifle. The endearing include the 5½-pound 700ti with titanium receiver, introduced in 2001. My .30-06 punches cherry-size groups. The 24-inch barrel belies this rifle's feathery heft; the synthetic stock is beautifully proportioned. The 700 Classic had arrived 23 years earlier. Its satin-finished walnut stock with conservative lines and full-wrap front checkering distinguish it. The Classic came in several chamberings until 1985. In 1981, Remington began limited runs of the rifle, listing one cartridge per year. That program expired in 2005.

THE ICON HAS MANY FACES!

During the past 30 years, tactical and sporting rifles have shed their walnut and donned synthetic stocks. From cheap, injection-molded models to hand-laid composite stocks that weigh less and cost more, they're more durable than wood. Moisture won't warp them. They are affected by temperature extremes, which can affect bedding. As figured walnut has become scarce, synthetic stocks have improved. Still, many shooters prefer wood. The Model 700 SPS, or Special Purpose Synthetic, replaced the 700 ADL in 2005, but the BDL continues to sell briskly in walnut. "We expected the 2002 introduction of our wood-stocked CDL to cripple the BDL," says John Fink. "But a decade later, both versions are hugely popular."

Another successful 700, the Sendero, arrived in 1994 with a 26-inch barrel bored to hot rod rounds like, later, the 7mm Remington Ultra Mag. Less popular was the 700 EtronX, introduced in 1999. It fired electronically primed rounds. Impulses from a 9-volt battery in the buttstock energized a ceramic-coated firing pin. Because no parts moved when you triggered this rifle, lock time was near zero. Chambered in .22-250, .220 Swift and .243, the EtronX never caught on. Remington dropped it, in 2003.

Like synthetic stocks, detachable box magazines (DBMs) have made their mark on the 700. Rifles can be loaded and emptied quickly. There's no nose damage to bullets, no searching for spilled rounds. Flush-mounted DBMs eliminate ungainly protrusions. Still, the floorplate survives, even in the entry-level SPS.

Model 721s and 722s and early 700 rifles featured a side-switch thumb safety that, in its rearward position, arrested bolt and trigger. For hunters pushing through cover, a secured bolt handle is an asset. But a handful of accidental discharges as shooters unloaded rifles by cycling the bolt caused concern at Remington. In March 1982, it issued a recall to owners of Model 700, 721, 722, 600, 660, 40-X, and XP-100 firearms. For $20, Remington gunsmiths would clean and inspect trigger and safety, then remove the bolt-locking device. The customer would get the product back with a $20 gift certificate. No 700s built after the recall have a bolt-locking safety; all can be unloaded with the trigger blocked.

For most of its life, the 700 trigger could be adjusted for weight of pull (lower front screw), sear engagement (rear screw), and over-travel (upper front screw). Remington saw fit to add drops of sealant to prevent accidental screw movement and discourage the incompetent from fiddling with the adjustments. But shooters used them to good effect. In 2005, the company replaced that trigger with a new X Mark Pro. It had a fixed pull of 3½ pounds, no adjustments. Four years later, it was overhauled so shooters could set the pull from 2½ to 4½ pounds. The adjustable X Mark Pro is now standard on 700s.

While some hunters have criticized the 700's moon-shaped beryllium clip extractor, its longevity speaks volumes. Unlike the bully Mauser claw, it requires no cut in the receiver or barrel. Result: fully closed breeching. Gunsmiths have replaced it with a Sako-style hook, but the Remington clip has won in shear tests, and it contacts more of the case rim. In 40 years, I've never had a Model 700 extractor fail. No, it does not allow controlled-round feed, and controlled feed is good. You can't have everything.

Initially, Remington used stainless steel in its magnum 700s. Stainless can't be blued, but because blued metal was then thought proper, these barrels were plated with copper, then tin, and then blued! Not all these barrels were marked "stainless." In 1967, Remington changed to chrome-moly steel for every 700 barrel. Stainless steel later returned, but not blued. Ceramic and other coatings added color and protection. Remington's TriNyte

Wayne approaches a Texas nilgai he downed with a Remington 700 in .30-06. It is still a hugely popular chambering.

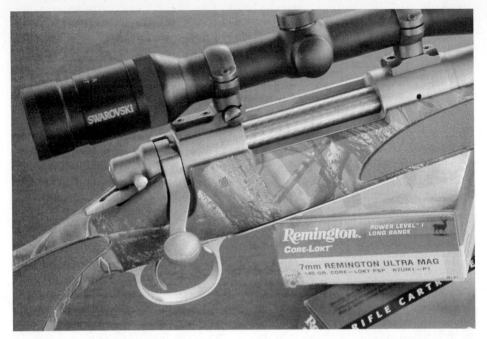

Remington has introduced many variations of the 700. The long action easily takes full-length magnums like the 7mm Remington Ultra Mag.

coating was introduced, in 2005, with the 700 XCR (Extreme Conditions Rifle).

"Even stainless steel can rust," John Fink points out. "The 416 stainless commonly used in rifles contains about .25-percent carbon. Put that metal in a humidity box and it comes out red."

Nickel plating seals off underlying metal, but plating can wear or flake off. TriNyte lays a PVD coating on a nickel base. PVD—physical vapor deposition—is really the process. It happens in a vacuum chamber under heat. The resulting surface is microscopically fine mesh on metal, the outer layer shielding the nickel plate with a super-hard surface.

"At over 80," says John, "it's off the Rockwell scale, double the hardness of 416!"

Rifling in M700 barrels was initially hot-hammer-forged. About a decade ago, the firm switched to cold hammer forging for Ilion-built centerfire rifles (excepting the button-rifled 40-X).

The Model 700's cartridge list? It's long! The 700 has been bored to nearly every centerfire round practical in a bolt-action. Classic rifles added some, like the .250 Savage, 7x57, and .300 H&H Magnum, that might

otherwise have missed out. Indeed, it would be easier to list chamberings *not* offered in 700s! The two action lengths handle the dainty .17 Remington (1971) to the mighty .338 Lapua Magnum (2011). High-performance rounds include the 8mm Remington Magnum (1978), the 7mm STW (Shooting Times Westerner, 1996) and, farther up the Richter scale, Remington's Ultra Mag series: 7mm, .300, .338, and .375 (introduced 1999 to 2002). The 7mm and .300 Remington Short Action Ultra Mags (2001 and 2002) appeal to me. I believe I shot the first elk taken with the .300 SAUM—in a Remington rifle, of course! Best-sellers are still the .30-06 and .270. The 7mm Remington and .300 Winchester top the magnum list.

In several surveys I've taken of hundreds of elk hunters, the 700 and Winchester's 70 run neck-and-neck in popularity, though the 70 had a 25-year head start! As bolt guns proliferate, they can but chip at the market share owned by Remington's 700. None can trump the sales records and field achievements.

CHAPTER 10

RUGER'S ELEGANT NO. 1

A century-old blackpowder rifle seemed an odd choice. But Bill Ruger wasn't ordinary.

The Ruger No. 1 has many elements of the Farquharson action developed by John Farquharson, in 1872. Strong and smooth, it handled big cartridges.

R uger announced its single-shot dropping-block No. 1, in 1967. But the inspiration came from a rifle mechanism patented by John Farquharson in 1872, nearly a century earlier. A resident of Daldhu, Scotland, Farquharson sold part interest in the rifle to George Gibbs, a Bristol gunmaker who built rifles on the action until the patent expired, in 1889. Evidently, fewer than 1,000 of these single-shot rifles left Gibbs' shop before the last was delivered, in 1910. But the Farquharson mechanism didn't die. British maker W.J. Jeffery & Co. copied it as early as 1895. In 1904, Jeffery built an oversize version for the .600 Nitro Express cartridge. Rifles with Farquharson's distinctive underlever also popped up in Herstal,

Belgium, assembled by Auguste Francotte. A "PD" stamp on Farquharsons built after the Gibbs period show the design had become "public domain."

These days, a Gibbs-Farquharson in fine shape will make you dig very, very deep in your pocket. Ruger's No. 1 rifle, however, remains within reach of ordinary shooters.

Like the first Mustang trotted out by Ford just a couple years earlier, Ruger's No. 1 had clean, taut lines. It emerged a compelling combination of grace and predatory panache. A stock by Len Brownell made the most of

Wayne finds the No. 1A Light Sporter both attractive and fast in the hand.

the well-figured walnut common on early No. 1s. The action borrowed heavily from the Farquharson, but it had a leaner look, with a more open guard encircling an adjustable trigger. The tang safety didn't detract from the receiver's clean profile. With and without sights, the No. 1 wore an artfully sculpted quarter-rib notched for Ruger's scope rings.

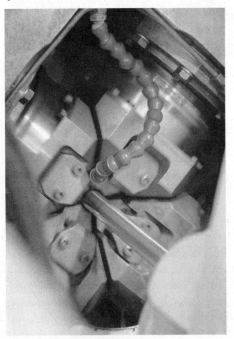

Banded front sight and swivel appeared on rifles designated "A" and "S," later known as Light and Medium Sporters, and on the "H" or Tropical Rifle for big-bore cartridges. These were also distinguished by an "Alex Henry" fore-end with a scalloped schnabel tip. Standard Sporter and Varmint ("B" and "V") rifles had a conventional fore-end with swivel stud, no iron sights.

Despite its fetching lines, fine fit and finish, a broad range of chamberings, and obvious appeal to wildcatters, the new Ruger listed for just $265. I considered a second mortgage to fill my pantry with No. 1s and, regrettably, let the thought slide. At the time, Ruger produced some rifles on special order, others for limited runs to distributors. I snared a No. 1B in 7x57 and should be flogged for letting it go. A .458 that wore the most flamboyant walnut I've ever seen on a No. 1 went to a friend. Shortly after selling it, I declined a No. 1A made for a pal of Bill

Ruger's barrels are hammer-forged. You can see the hammers vibrate here, pounding a short, thick tube around a hard mandrel with the rifling in reverse. The barrel comes out longer.

Ruger's. The .270 barrel was 24 inches long, not the standard 22.

In those days, I hunted mostly with Model 70 Winchesters. For all its elegance, the No. 1 had no magazine. No follow-up shots. Also, reports on the No. 1's accuracy ran the gamut. My first rifle, a 7x57, didn't shoot better than three inches; I was then using half-minute prone rifles in competition. When a fellow shooter asked about throat length, I seated a 175-grain bullet as far out as possible and chambered it. The bullet came back out with no rifling marks. Later, I learned that 7x57 No. 1s of that vintage were afflicted with long throats. A more recent No. 1 in that chambering has treated me to one-inch groups.

The No. 1's fore-end hanger can't ensure a "free-float" condition or consistent barrel contact when you snug a sling or press the rifle hard onto a bipod. Shooters quickly came up with modifications. One was an externally adjustable set screw. Not wishing to make a permanent change in my No. 1B in .300 Winchester, I knew *something* had to be done. This rifle shot well enough (1¼ inches with 180-grain Nosler Partitions backed by 75 grains of H4831). But 200-yard groups fired prone with a sling printed *nine inches to seven o'clock* of groups shot from sandbags! I installed a rubber hose washer near the rear of the hanger, a brass shim at the fore-end tip. The compressible washer would, I hoped, deliver more predictable contact up front, with mild pressure on the hanger. This solution worked! Group differences at 200 yards shrank to four inches, about what I commonly get from bolt-action rifles with one-piece stocks.

Among the liabilities of the No. 1 "A" and "S" models, though an endearing feature cosmetically, is the barrel-mounted front swivel stud shared with Tropical "H" rifles. While few hunters rely on a shooting sling, I do. A taut sling affects barrel vibrations during bullet passage, so seven-o'clock displacement is even greater than with a sling pulling on a stock-mounted swivel.

The No. 1's massive breech block slides vertically for a strong lock-up. You can adjust the mechanism to extract or eject.

A technician tests chambering and extraction in a No. 1. The rifle is chambered for a wide range of cartridges, from the .204 Ruger to .450/400 Nitro Express.

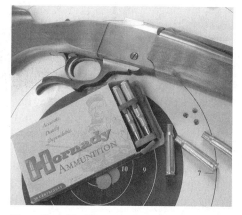

Wayne fired this 100-yard group with a No. 1's open sights. He admits luck was with him, but this 7x57 does shoot well!

With practice, a No. 1 can be loaded very fast. Second shots can come almost as quickly as with a bolt rifle, given recoil recovery. This No. 1 is chambered to .303 British.

EVERY CARTRIDGE A PERFECT FIT!

A short breech makes the No. 1 an efficient launching pad for magnum cartridges. Compared to bolt-actions, the dropping-block design gives you about four inches more barrel for a given overall length. That means better ballistic performance in a rifle still nimble in thickets. Handloaded 180-grain Partitions that clock 3,040 fps from the 26-inch barrel of my No. 1 in .300 Winchester register 2,985 in a 24-inch-barreled M70. Don't need all that barrel? A No. 1A or full-stocked International hangs very low on your shoulder and points like a wand. Recent No. 1 chamberings like the 6.5 Creedmoor, the .303 British, and the Ruger Compact Magnums all perform well in 22-inch barrels. I carried an International in .303 British last year, and it quickly became a favorite. I also ordered one of the first No. 1As in 6.5 Creedmoor. It, too, is nimble in hand and has a nose for the target. The concentration of weight between the hands steadies these short rifles quickly. Hornady loads the 6.5 Creedmoor, and its 129-grain SST and 140-grain A-Max bullets register 2,910 and 2,603 fps, respectively, from my No. 1A. That ammo from the 24-inch barrel of my T/C Icon shows 2,939 and 2,647.

While the dropping-block mechanism is ideal for rimmed cases, Ruger engineered the extractor to nab rimless hulls with equal de-termination. Powerful and positive, it engages the groove at five o'clock. You can adjust spring tension to kick cases smartly into the bushes—or nudge the brass gently just clear of the chamber. I've yet to see a No. 1 extractor fail, even with ambitious handloads.

The single-shot's insistence that you make the first bullet count is tallied as a liability by shooters who favor magazine rifles, but it appeals to No. 1 enthusiasts. "Purists," some call themselves. There's little cause for quarrel, though, as in practiced hands a dropping-block rifle can be reloaded quite quickly.

Ruger's association with ace stockmaker Len Brownell blessed the No. 1. Proportioned for easy handling, the handsome butt-

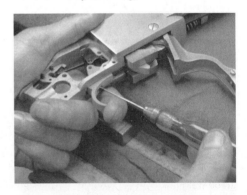

Fitting and tuning a No. 1 in final assembly is not for amateurs! Knowing the skills and materials required, you might think the 1965 $265 introductory price too modest.

Ruger No. 1 Chamberings

My first Ruger No. 1 was a 7x57, an "A" model. I should have bought a rifle in each of the other chamberings, but sustaining that habit throughout the next decades would have been a challenge! The No. 1 has been offered in dozens, from .22 Hornet to .416 Rigby and .458 Lott. Not all have been cataloged. Here's the list:

.204 Ruger
.22 Hornet
.218 Bee
.222 Remington
.223 Remington
.22 PPC
.22-250 Remington
.220 Swift
.243 Winchester
6mm Remington
.257 Roberts
.25-06 Remington
.257 Weatherby Magnum
6.5 Creedmoor
6.5 Remington Magnum
.264 Winchester Magnum
.270 Winchester
.270 Weatherby Magnum
7x57 Mauser
7mm-08 Remington
.280 Remington
7mm Remington Magnum
7mm STW
.30-30 Winchester
.30-40 Krag
.308 Winchester
.30-06 Springfield
.300 H&H Magnum
.300 Winchester Magnum
.300 Ruger Compact Magnum
.300 Weatherby Magnum
.303 British

Ken Nagel had this No. 1 barreled to the wildcat 6.5 WSM. It shoots well, though the wide range of No. 1 chamberings hardly encourages wildcatting!

.338 Winchester Magnum	.416 Ruger
.338 Ruger Compact Magnum	.45-70
9.3x74R	.450/400 Nitro Express
.375 H&H Magnum	.450 3¼-inch Nitro Express
.375 Ruger	.458 Winchester Magnum
.404 Jeffery	.458 Lott
.405 Winchester	.460 Smith & Wesson
.416 Rigby	.475 Turnbull
.416 Remington Magnum	.475 Linebaugh

stock is agile in hand. The comb puts your eye in natural line with the iron sights or a low-mounted scope. The stock's austere lines, the conservatively capped grip, and the thin rubber pad hew to English tradition without compromising utility. The checkering pattern on No. 1s changed a few years following its introduction, after a "130" prefix appeared with the serial number. Early on, grip panels were concave at the rear, an easy difference to spot. Some current upscale versions have full-wrap fore-end checkering and high-grade walnut.

The No. 1 looks so good, you're excused if you question its utility. This is, however, one of those delightful firearms that delivers more than you have a right to ask of it. Strong, well balanced, and lively, it delivers good to excellent accuracy and comes in myriad chamberings. There's no bolt knob to hang up in scabbard or rifle case. The breech block slides like greased glass in its race.

Recently, I visited Ruger's factory and spoke with people building No. 1s.

"They're not as easy to assemble as bolt rifles," said one. "Each requires hand fitting." He was timing the close of No. 1 levers, while his colleague carefully mated buttstocks to tangs. I came away wondering how Ruger could once have sold such a rifle, stocked in fancy walnut, for $265—and wondering why I hadn't taken out that second mortgage.

CHAPTER 11

KIMBER: A PERFECT UNION?

The best bolt-action hunting rifles ever had a firm grip on the market. How to upstage them ... .

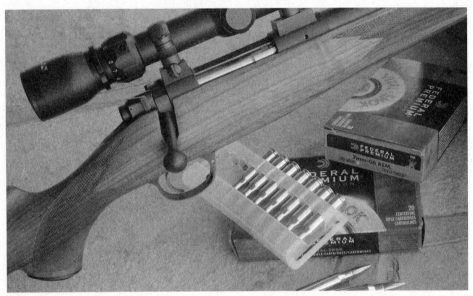

Kimber's first successful centerfire: Under six pounds, the 84M has a walnut stock, three-position safety, controlled feed, and adjustable trigger. The 84L is the long-action version.

"We started with the best mechanical designs around," Kimber's rifle manager told me. "Mauser, Springfield, Winchester's Model 70." That was back in 1998, just before the 84M. The "M" is for medium, though, by some standards, an action for .308-size cartridges is short. The "M" distinguished this rifle from earlier Kimbers built in Oregon, when Greg Warne owned the company.

If you're a rimfire enthusiast, you recall the first Kimber, the Model 82, developed by Jack Warne, an Australian. Jack and son Gregg built the .22 bolt rifle in western Oregon, and, with help from other talented people, came up with the Model 84 for the .17s, .222, and .223. Kimber's Model 89 chambered big-game cartridges like the .30-06 and looked, in profile, like the Winchester M70.

In 1989, Chapter 7 bankruptcy clouded Kimber's future. Jack and Gregg emerged with use of the Australian Kimber name. Les Edelman came away as majority stakeholder in a new company that would later move firearms manufacturing from Clackamas, Oregon, to Yonkers, New York. Beginning in 1992, Gregg put the Kimber label on rebarreled M96 and M98 Mausers after refitting them with Ramline and Butler Creek stocks and converting safeties for scope use. The rifles retained their military triggers and sold for as little as $299. Meanwhile, a new .22 rifle, the Kimber 82C, appeared.

During the mid-'90s, tighter handgun regulations collided with a burgeoning interest in handgun sports. Les Edelman recognized opportunity and tooled up to produce a new, high-quality 1911 pistol. His factory in Yonkers launched a run of 5,000 pistols—and was buried with orders for more! Now, Kimber ships more than 40,000 finely accoutered 1911-style pistols annually.

The company fielded another high-quality .22, in 1998. Designed by Nehemiah Sirkis and labeled simply the Kimber 22, this rifle looked like the Model 82, but featured a side-swing safety. It became the inspiration for a new centerfire, the Model 84M, also designed by Sirkis.

The short-action 84M, with Mauser-style claw extractor, was fitted with slender 22-inch barrels bored to .22-250, .243, .260, 7mm-08, and .308. A trim, classic stock from renowned stockmaker Darwin Hensley kept overall weight to 5¾ pounds. The 84M has since appeared in other configurations. Steel bottom metal comprises a floorplate (with release button in the trigger guard), and complements a steel grip cap. (The synthetic-stocked Montana version has a blind magazine.) A two-position wing safety was later modified for three detents: safe and locked, safe but unlocked for cycling, and fire.

In 2003, if memory serves, a magnum sibling joined the 84M. Half a pound heavier and with a larger receiver ring, the 8400 had a 24-inch barrel bored for the Winchester Short Magnum rounds, then surging in popularity. A long-action 8400 arrived in 2006, chambered for the .25-06, .270, .30-06, and .300 and .338 Winchester Magnums. Standard chamberings got 24-inch barrels, magnums 26-inch, bringing rifle weights to seven and 7¼ pounds. Like its predecessors, 8400s wore adjustable triggers.

About five years later, Kimber got into the tactical market, with a trio of rifles in .308 Winchester. Mil-Spec Picatinny rails were secured with 8-40 screws to glass-bedded receivers. Kimber used its own barrels, button-rifled one turn in 12 inches. All rifles featured oversize conical bolt knobs and five-round magazines. The 8½-pound 84M LPT, or Light Police Tactical, had a stout, 24-inch fluted barrel and a laminated wood stock with black finish. The 8400 Tactical mated a heavier 24-inch barrel with Kimber's 8400 action and McMillan's A-5 stock. A Picatinny rail incorporated 20 minutes of elevation for zero at long range (so shooters didn't push adjustments to their limits or crank the erector tube far off the scope's mechanical axis). The 8400 Tactical weighed 9¼ pounds.

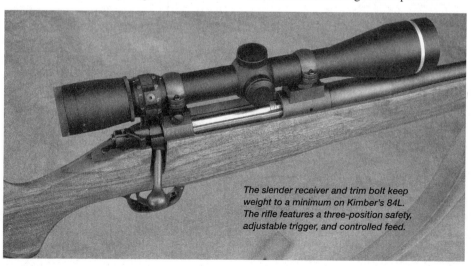

The slender receiver and trim bolt keep weight to a minimum on Kimber's 84L. The rifle features a three-position safety, adjustable trigger, and controlled feed.

Kimber evoked images of Middle East combat with its 8400 Advanced Tactical. Bottom metal and bolt featured a matte-black finish; barrel and receiver wore KimPro II Dark Earth, a self-lubricating material the hue of wet sand. The McMillan A-5 stock in desert camo pattern had an adjustable comb and butt spacers to change length. The Kimber 8400 Advanced Tactical weighed 9¾ pounds and could be ordered in kit form, with Leupold LRT scope and accoutrements.

THE WAY "LONG" SHOULD BE

At this writing, the latest Kimber rifle is the 84L, a hunting rifle barreled for the likes of the .30-06. "Wait," you say. "Kimber makes the 8400 for the .30-06?" Well, yes.

Kimber's big-bore, the Caprivi, features the elegant, Spartan look of the 84L, but with crossbolts, sights, a heavier fore-end and barrel.

In timber, the 84L points fast. This Montana buck gave Wayne a second to fire. An accurate barrel and a crisp, predictable trigger give you the edge for that tough shot at long range.

But the 8400 series, long and short, has a bigger receiver ring.

"How about we build a long action as slim as the 84M's?" Some folks at Kimber had that notion early on.

"Uh-uh," said Nehemiah Sirkus, the wizard behind the 84M. And everyone bowed to the wizard.

But a decade later, that slender rifle did appear. The .308 and .30-06 share .473-inch diameter heads, significantly smaller than the .532-inch heads of belted rounds and the .535s on WSMs. "No need for more metal in the receiver ring if the case heads are the same diameter" goes the thinking now. The 84L looks and feels livelier than the 8400. It is as perfectly suited to the .30-06 and .270 as the 84M is to cartridges based on the .308. In fact, confide Kimber insiders, the 8400 may soon be barreled to magnums only, in short (WSM) and long (traditional belted magnum) versions.

Wrap your hand around the 84L's midsection, slim as a maiden's wrist, and you won't guess the magazine holds five—unless you own an 84M. To better serve the capacity of .30-06-length hulls, Kimber fitted a 24-inch barrel to the 84L—a longer burn chamber. The fore-end is a tad longer to match, but stock and barrel maintain a crisp, linear profile, with perfect tapers and an economy of mass that makes the front end look sculpted, not whippy. The 84L scales six pounds, sometimes less, depending on bore diameter and wood density. Kimber's 84L comes in .25-06, .270, .280 Improved, .30-06, and .35 Whelen.

How about accuracy? Paring a 44-inch rifle to scale under six pounds, engineers must be careful to retain the metal that counts; a rifle that carries easily but doesn't shoot well has limited utility. But a long afternoon's shooting with two 84Ls in .30-06 convinced me these rifles have more than enough precision for hunting in open places. I drilled several sub-minute clusters. A one-holer miked .3-inch. I won't pull your leg and tell you

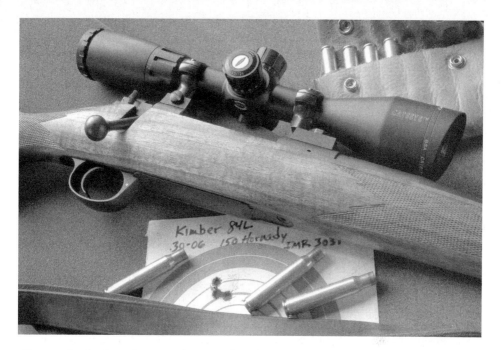

all seven loads that afternoon shot equally well. But they all punched good groups. As for ammo preferences, those 84Ls stayed in lock-step. Black Hills loads with 168-grain boat-tail hollowpoint Match and A-Max bullets delivered tight knots. So did Federal cartridges with 165-grain Trophy Bonded and 180-grain Barnes Triple Shocks.

The 84M and 84L are about as good as lightweight rifles come. You get controlled feed, a crisp, consistent trigger pull, a three-detent safety, and nicely checkered walnut. The svelte receivers carry not an ounce of fat. A traditional two-lug bolt features a Mauser-style claw that grabs cartridges early, then herds them smoothly forward. A fixed ejector kicks cases away smartly. The trim steel trigger and bottom metal complement Kimber's slender button-rifled barrel. The stock is just shy of Spartan in form; call it classic. A straight comb puts your eye smack behind a low-mounted scope. Crisp, point-pattern, 20 lines-per-inch checkering is not quite so generous as to seem showy. Wood clings to metal like skin to a peach. The slim profile of the 84M and 84L promise—and deliver—feathery heft. Still, these rifles are carefully bal-

This Kimber 84L in .30-06 weighs a feathery six pounds but shoots very well. Wayne's handload produced this cluster; factory ammunition also stayed under an inch.

anced. They fly to your shoulder, but swing as if on rails and hang breathlessly while you catch yours.

Kimber 84M and 84L rifles come in Classic, Classic Select (with upgraded walnut and fore-end tip), and Montana (stainless/synthetic), configurations.

While the 8400 remains a fine pick if you're looking for a classy bolt rifle, the slimmer profile of the "M" and "L" hues more closely to Kimber's "less is more" thinking in rifle design. This company didn't shoulder its way into the bolt-gun market building rifles of ordinary bulk and heft. Kimbers, like Audrey Hepburn, Italian motorcycles, and the F-16, are noted for economy of line. They're lightweight without looking thin or frail, elegant in the way they marry necessary mechanics with trim, clean cosmetics. You get that in Kimbers bored for the cartridges most of us like to shoot. The 84M and 84L include features of the most successful bolt rifles in history. And, thankfully, little else.

CHAPTER 12

COOPER, A MONTANA ORIGINAL

Walking through Canada gave him lots of time to think. Rifle design had to come up.

Toward the Missoula end of Montana's Bitterroot Valley you'll find the Cooper plant. Or not. It's an unprepossessing site. Easy to miss. But, in the belly of this flat-roofed shed, marvelous things happen with steel and walnut.

Dan Cooper came to the gun industry late, after Purdue and a stint in law school.

"Thought about a career in foreign affairs."

Disillusioned, he left academics and started walking. He walked from Mexico to the Bering Strait.

"That took longer than I thought it would."

During most of 1980 and '81, Dan and a pal trudged north. Dan stopped in Deese Lake, British Columbia, where he built cabins "until work ran out." He retreated to western Oregon, where he got a job mowing Jack Warne's lawn. Jack, an Australian entrepreneur, had started a gun company in Clackamas. He called it Kimber, from the Aboriginal *kimba*, or "bush fire."

Soon, Dan was working at the Kimber factory.

"I couldn't do much with heavy tools, because I'd hurt myself logging. I inspected rifles."

Because he had committed to reaching Alaska on his hike, Dan left the firm, in 1983, and took up walking again.

"That northern section was tough. Bad weather. No trails. Lots of lonely. Big, *big* bears."

Not until 1985 did Dan see the Bering Strait.

His perseverance impressed people at the Institute of Arctic Biology. Dan worked for them at a remote University of Alaska field station, until 1988, when he returned to manage Kimber's Government .22 project.

"We were proud of that rifle. But sales lagged."

The company sputtered and stalled. Jack Warne sold it. Dan found work delivering for a construction firm.

"My *real* wilderness year."

Hardly one to sit still, he hitched his dreams to another star. In 1990, he sold a '49 Lincoln and a motorcycle to build a new rifle.

"We incorporated in Mollala, Oregon, late that year," He recalls. "Then I drove to South Dakota, to visit Tom Houghton at H-S Precision. Tom had a great shop and built fine rifles. But he had a lot more money than me."

On his way back west, Dan slept under his truck near Helena, Montana, where a friend, also the state's assistant Attorney General, found him and then sent him to the Department of Economic Development.

"When they smelled funding, my partners liked Montana, too."

The group moved the business of Cooper Arms to Stevensville.

The first Cooper rifle came from a garage near Bell Crossing, south of town. The action borrowed from the work of Dan's favorite gunmakers, Len Brownell, Pete Grisel, P.O. Ackley, and Darwin Hensley. The single-shot, three-lug Model 36 rimfires had accurate barrels and figured walnut stocks.

"Each cost $2,000 to build." Dan grins. "We sold 'em for $600. We made 75 before deciding high volume wouldn't reverse that margin."

In a promotional blitz, Dan visited the state capital.

"Stan Stevens was ready to accept one of our .22s at a ceremony," Dan remembers. "I asked my pals at Economic Development if a rifle on the capitol steps would cause a problem. 'Of course not,' they said. 'This is Montana!' Before I got to the door I was in cuffs, an officer on each arm."

Cooper Firearms would occupy four sites in the Bitterroot Valley. In 1994, Dan and his partners bought property just north of Stevensville. The original building grew. Reorganization of Cooper Arms during the mid-'90s interrupted production of the Model 36 rifle. But Dan was hard at work on another.

The Cooper big-game rifle owes much to Dan Cooper's work at Kimber in Oregon. He established the new firm in Montana's Bitterroot Valley. It's still there, though Dan has retired.

The Model 38 single-shot was chambered for 12 rounds, .17 Squirrel to .221 Fireball; think Hornet, Bee, and dwarf wildcats. The subsequent Model 21 in .204 Ruger, along with the .20 Tactical and .223 added reach. Cooper Model 22s, introduced 1994, come in 19 chamberings, .22-250 to .25-06. Like the 38 and 21, the 22 is a single-shot. "You shouldn't need a second bullet," declares Dan.

In 2001, the 57M combined "the best features of the Kimber 82, Winchester 52, and Anschütz 54 actions." A box-fed repeater, it featured a bolt with three rear lugs, a crisp trigger, hand-checkered walnut. The throw was long enough for the .22 WMR and Hornady's .17 HMR. Sales of the 57 spiked. I snared a .17 HMR for tests. The rifle, beautifully fitted, punched half-inch groups at 100 yards. I bought it.

"Single-shot rifles are easy," Dan told me, when I stopped to chat him up about a new high-power rifle. "Magazines make life complicated." He showed me a prototype box.

Fine fit and finish are hallmarks of Cooper rifles. The handwork boosts the cost a little, but also sets the Models 52, 54, and 56 apart from standard bolt rifles.

Receivers for Cooper big-game rifles are machined from bar stock. Note the three-lug action design. A single-stack box keeps the magazine cut small, the receiver rigid.

Cooper big-game rifles have three-lug bolts and plunger ejectors. The extractor is mounted on the side, not the face. Feeding is smooth, but not truly controlled.

Straight up. Detachable. "We want the action to stay stiff, the feeding reliable. This is how to do it." I didn't dare mention Mauser.

Some months later, when Cooper's center-fire Model 52 appeared, the shop was quickly buried in backorders. I drove five hours to the Bitterroot to nab one. Dan apologized. He had no uncommitted 52s. Like the Models 36, 38, 21, and 22, the 52 "is finished by hand. We don't turn them out like cookies. And if I lock the doors after six, the crew threatens to take weekends off!" Then he caught himself. "Hey, we just shipped a .270 Classic to the Midwest. We'll call it back!"

To my astonishment, he did. While I paced, UPS trucked the rifle back to Stevensville. I threw it in my Suzuki, sped home, and installed a Swarovski variable. My first three 130-grain factory Core-Lokts funneled into a ⅝-inch group. Who says pretty can't perform?

Barreled to .30-06-class cartridges, the 52 is an elegant rifle with taut lines; a clean, purposeful presence. I like the sweep of the slender trigger and open, steel-capped grip, the vertical fall of the bolt handle, the smooth knob that's the right size in just the right place. I like the 52's deep-fluted comb. The action and Remington-style (but thicker) recoil lug are glass-bedded, but inletting is so snug you won't suspect that. The air-gauged Wilson barrel kisses a single glass pad in the channel.

The 52's three-lug bolt wears a Sako-style extractor. The original blade ejector on my .270 has since been replaced by the ubiquitous plunger. Dan designed the trigger. My .270's was factory set at 3½ pounds, but adjusts down to 1½. The two-position thumb safety rocks silently forward. Unobtrusive, it is placed for intuitive use. It does not lock the bolt. The almost-flush magazine doesn't rattle. True to Dan's word, cartridges march with fluid predictability from its single stack. The box is held by the bottom metal, so it doesn't affect accuracy. It robs little steel from the receiver. A forward latch puts the box obediently into your hand. You must load it outside the rifle, but you can single-feed through the port.

A PLEASANT SURPRISE FROM NEWTON'S .25

Cooper Arms uses mostly Claro in its stocks. It substitutes English and French walnut, myrtle and maple, and other woods to order. The oil-based finish yields a warm, classic look. I must say it has often failed to fill open-pored wood.

In the metal shop, hand-lapped, button-rifled Wilson barrels are fitted to tubular receivers. Matte-finished steel gets bead-blasted with 220-, then 400-grit abrasives. A 500-grit buffing preps high-gloss rifles. Randy Craft, who started with Cooper at age 19, was hand-stoning the extraction surface on a bolt when he told me all Cooper bolts are hand-finished.

"Once upon a time," Dan confided later, "Randy and my nephew Jason claimed they could sell an accurate .223 single-shot. I replied they were full of prunes. Heck, they were just out of high school! But they built one and brought me a target with three shots in a knot. I sent that rifle to Ronan Sports. We promptly got an order for five rifles a week until told to stop."

In 2008, Dan relinquished Cooper's reins to Hugo Vivero, who owns the Wilson barrel company. Ian, Hugo's son, is an engineer deep in rifle design. Impressed by the 52, the Viveros were quick to build on its success. First came the inevitable, a short-action centerfire. Sized for the .308 family of cartridges, the Model 54's maw is long enough for the 6mm Remington and .257 Roberts (on the 2.235-inch 7x57 case). The Model 56 arrived in 2011, a proper magnum action that accepts not only the 7mm Remington and kin, but belted rounds with the 2.85-inch measure of their ancestor, the .375 H&H.

As the Models 54 and 56 Coopers appeared, the bolt was modified slightly. Besides replacing the mechanical ejector with a plunger, the company added a taper to the lug faces. I snared one of the early Model 54s for

Dan Cooper says the magazine is among the most difficult rifle component to design. He chose a single-stack box for smoother feeding, a smaller action slot.

Cooper's 52, for .30-06-length cartridges, was its first big-game rifle. Here Wayne fires his .270, an accurate, well-balanced rifle with clean lines.

a review, one built to my specs for the .250 Savage. A long-neglected but delightful deer cartridge, this 1912 brainchild of Charles Newton is one of 15 rounds listed for the short action. I fought the urge to sift through Cooper's racks of walnut. "Best use what customers expect in a Classic," I told him.

The Cooper crew had my .250 ready in three months. Visiting to pick it up, I managed a peek at—okay, a couple of hours rifling through—the company's walnut racks. Then I got a tour through the wood shop, where figured blanks were turned to shape on CNC machines, then rasped and sanded to

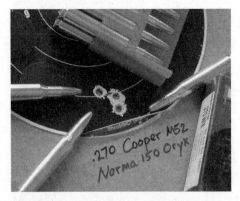

Scoped with a Swarovski 1.7-10X, the Cooper 52 in .270 punched many groups like this during Wayne's range tests.

finished profile. Steel in place, careful handwork with fine sandpaper ensured seamless fit of grip cap, butt pad, and fore-end tip. In the checkering room, brilliant bulbs beamed on cutters furrowing fresh walnut.

"You must get the master lines right," said one of the women.

As I'd never seen a Cooper panel even slightly skewed, I concluded they got the master lines right all the time.

Model 54 receivers start as bar stock. Each is machined to tight tolerances, then polished until the bolt slides like a race car piston. The thick-walled steel magazine box slips in as smoothly.

Every Cooper centerfire comes with Talley or Leupold scope bases. I like both, specified Leupold for the 54; I'd already set aside 30mm Leupold rings and a 2.5-10x42mm Zeiss Varipoint scope.

The trigger break, snappy and just under three pounds, needed no change. I installed the Zeiss, bore-sighted, and fired a volley of commercial ammo. Alas, a golf ball would have slipped between the holes. But .250 Savage loads have received little attention since, well, the second World War. A handload of 34 grains IMR 4895 pushing 87-grain Sierras shrank groups dramatically—*to .35-inch*, then even less. Handloads with 100-grain Speers driven by 36 grains H414 punched a vertical column .6-inch tall. Subsequent shooting showed the factory loads unredeemable. With handloads, the 54 was unerring.

Both the 52 and 54 scale 7½ pounds or so. But near-perfect balance makes them lively in hand. The Cooper 56 (magnum) scales 8¼ pounds, thanks to a 26-inch barrel and its longer receiver. When the 56 appeared, the full-length action lured me to the elegant, powerful, .340 Weatherby. But Cooper's list of short belted chamberings included the more versatile (and civil) .308 Norma. (This .30 Magnum performs like the .300 Winchester, but it's of more efficient shape. A truly fine cartridge!) A 56 in .308 Norma eventually arrived, distinguished by crossbolts either end of the magazine well. The honey-colored walnut is plain, but, like its smaller siblings, the rifle cheeks quickly and steadies easily. Hurling 180-grain soft-points at 3,000 fps, I appreciate its ample stock, intelligently shaped to keep my eyeballs in their sockets and to pamper my clavicle. The thick Decelerator pad helps a great deal at the bench. Accuracy of the .308 Norma almost matches that of the .270 and the .250, hovering at an even minute of angle.

Cooper's trio of big-game rifles shows thoughtful design and careful fit. Cooper offers myriad options, including full-length stocks and case-colored metal. Stainless barreled actions are also available. Barrels of any reasonable length come at no extra charge. I specified a 23-inch barrel on the .250, because to me it looks and balances better than the standard 22-inch. Cooper's stock is well proportioned for the 24-inch barrel on my .270, and for the 26-inch tube that tames my Model 56.

Price? My 52 listed for about $1,600 in its day. The .250 commanded more. The last I looked, the Model 56 started at $2,795. Handcheckered walnut and closely fitted metal,

Wayne fired this snug knot with Safari Arms ammo, Barnes bullets. He requested the Model 56 in .308 Norma, because it has long been one of his favorite elk cartridges.

While factory loads didn't distinguish themselves in the Cooper 54, the rifle shot extremely well with Wayne's handloads.

a fine trigger, and nickel-size groups, don't come cheap. But the market is full of lesser rifles priced higher. Coopers represent value. In my view, they rank among the best rifles built between Mexico and the Bering Sea.

CHAPTER 13

PRECISION IS IN THE NAME

To build rifles, not just assemble them, you must
make all the parts. "Superior parts," says H-S.

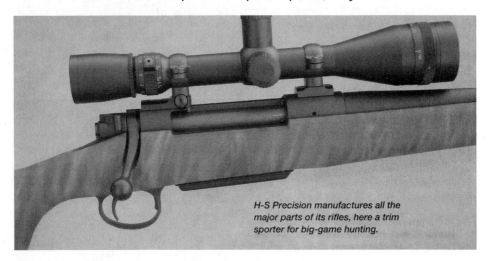

H-S Precision manufactures all the
major parts of its rifles, here a trim
sporter for big-game hunting.

In 1978, Tom Houghton could have donned a lab coat and trudged toward retirement in a company like DuPont. His chemistry degree certainly didn't point toward rifle manufacture. But Tom liked firearms.

"I called my company H-S Precision, because I planned to focus on accuracy. That was only logical. The big companies would have killed us off in the competitive deer rifle market, and we had no desire to make pretty rifles for people who couldn't afford custom work. So we started building lean hunting guns that shot well."

But how many hunters care enough about accuracy to pay double for a rifle that drills incrementally tighter groups? Tom found plenty of them. Like Carolina rifle wizard Kenny Jarrett, Houghton tapped a latent craving for longer reach and greater, well, precision. But, while Jarrett specializes in long-range hunting rifles, Houghton actively plumbed military and police markets, too.

H-S Precision now supplies drop-in gun stocks, bipods, and other accouterments to complement rifle sales.

"Actually, only a quarter of our sales derives from complete rifles," explains Josh Cluff, Director of Sales and Marketing. A former golf pro with a degree in business from Arizona State University, he met Tom on a Scottsdale golf course after the entrepreneur had moved back to the Sunbelt. "Sales are split about evenly between sporters and tactical models." Sixty percent of H-S business is direct. The remainder of H-S hardware sells through wholesalers and retailers. The Pro-Series 2000 rifle comes in standard configurations, "but we chamber rifles to any SAAMI cartridge." Josh tells me the company builds almost as many tactical rifles as sporters, but 60 percent of all rifles are sold on the commercial market.

Tom's ability to discern and quickly accommodate needs in the marketplace was largely responsible for the company's fast growth early on. Born in Prescott, Arizona, H-S Precision came to Rapid City, South Dakota, in 1990, because it needed more room. A year later, it moved into a 15,000-square-foot plant designed for its varied operations. I visited that facility more than a decade ago, when it was staffed by 37 people and when you could buy a basic H-S rifle for $1,400. Now the factory and the workforce are bigger. Rifles start at $2,680. Bullet penetration tests once conducted for law enforcement and military groups have gone away.

Houghton, now in his mid-60s, has turned daily operations over to his son, Tom II. Chief Executive Officer since 2002, the younger Houghton shares his father's optimism about the future, stressing the company's commitment to high technology and high quality in H-S products. He sees shrinking markets for traditional hardware-store hunting arms, but thinks bold new ideas and an emphasis on superior performance will ensure growth at H-S Precision.

"We also believe we should use the products we make," grins Tom. "I need more time afield!"

H-S ships 1,100 to 1,200 rifles a year, "and the orders pile in faster than we can fill them," says Josh. Still, waits are not long by custom rifle standards. "And when you place an H-S Precision order, it *is* a custom project." Tailoring each rifle is possible at the Rapid City plant, because "we make every part right here, lock, stock, and barrel. We design and build the triggers, even machine guard screws." Josh concedes that swivel studs and butt-pads come from Uncle Mike's. "And we outsource screw stock."

Controlling every aspect of manufacture is a rare luxury for a gun firm the size of H-S Precision. But it allows H-S to offer what you can't get from big-name companies.

"We make our rifles of stainless steel," Josh points out. "Barrel and action, trigger, and even the magazine. Extended boxes wear

Josh Cluff wrings out a heavy-barreled H-S rifle. Note the adjustable comb. H-S produces its own stocks, too!

H-S machines its own receivers from tube stock. They're rigid and trued with the barrel.

H-S Precision manufactures its own actions with twin-lug bolts. The enclosed face contains a plunger ejector. Close tolerances distinguish H-S mechanisms.

a polymer boot. We bead-blast the stainless to finish, or coat it with, black Teflon."

H-S is famous for its cut-rifled barrels, which were once available as components but now sell only in completed rifles.

"All barrels .30-caliber and smaller are guaranteed to shoot half-minute groups," Josh says. "We guarantee minute-of-angle accuracy from rifles with bores bigger than .308." You can specify your gun's barrel length, weight, contour, fluting, even add a muzzle brake. H-S is the nation's leading producer of test barrels for ammunition companies. Hornady, Remington, Federal, Olin, and Black Hills all use barrels from H-S to run pressure and accuracy trials.

Hand-laid stocks of Kevlar, fiberglass, and carbon fiber come from custom molds at the H-S plant in Rapid City, South Dakota.

The hand-laid synthetic stock of this H-S sporter keeps rifle weight low. Its straight comb mitigates recoil.

LOCK, STOCK, AND BARREL

All H-S Precision stocks are hand-laid: they consist of woven Kevlar, fiberglass cloth and a uni-directional carbon fiber bonded by laminating resin and an epoxy-based coat. An alloy reinforcing rib (bedding block) runs from the grip around the action and through the center of the fore-end to the front swivel stud. Lightweight stocks feature a half-length rib. H-S was the first riflemaker to offer an aluminum bedding block, back in 1981. The company now offers 113 stock configurations, for both its own rifles and OEM (original equipment manufacturer) sales. It supplies Remington and Savage with synthetic stocks. You can most likely buy a drop-in H-S Precision stock for your bolt rifle, and the warranty is good for as long as you own the stock. Repair or replacement cost no more than one-way shipping. "We don't get many stocks back. In fact, of the 8,000 we built for the U.S. Army's M24 sniper rifle, we've yet to see one returned," Josh told me.

As I write this, a drop-in stock for a Remington 700 retails for about $350. Most stocks for sporting rifles are painted in attractive two-tone spiderweb or camouflage patterns. Choose from tactical stocks with adjustable butts and combs, thumbhole and silhouette and traditional varmint models. I like the long, open grip of the H-S hunting stock, its straight comb and understated cheekpiece. The company makes stocks for in-line muzzleloaders, too, and even lists a handgun stock!

"It's for our pistol," Josh explains. The Pro-Series 2000 is a single-shot bolt-action handgun with the heart of an H-S Precision rifle. It comes in 4½-pound Silhouette and 5½-pound Varmint versions.

Another special H-S Precision product is its take-down rifle. The two-piece stock comes apart just in front of the receiver, so barrel and fore-end stay together. To assemble, you turn the barrel and fore-end 90 degrees, insert the barrel in the receiver, then twist to seat interrupted threads and align a camming device on the stock's underside. When you press the cam lever into its groove, everything is lined up and locked up. A knurled ring adjustable to take up thread wear ensures return to zero after many re-assemblies.

"It is more accurate than most rifles that don't come apart."

Tom Houghton, Sr., tested the rifle by firing five-shot groups one shot at a time, removing the barrel after each. Groups stayed under half an inch! Says Josh, "We give customers the same accuracy guarantee as our fixed-breech rifles." H-S commonly supplies extra barrels in different chamberings, and bolts for different case heads.

The flagship of the H-S Precision line is a hunting rifle (really a series), that looks ordinary but is not. The tubular receiver is of 17-4PH stainless steel, drilled for 8-40 scope base screws. A washer-style recoil lug abuts its face. The bolt, machined from 4142 steel, employs a recessed, semi-coned head with front-mounted extractor and plunger ejector. The bolt stop is a rear-mounted tab with a nose that bears against the left-hand lug. A Model 70-style three-position safety swings behind a bolt shank silver-soldered to the body. Stainless bottom metal brackets a detachable staggered magazine box (also stainless) with center-feed lips. The trigger adjusts from two to five pounds. H-S Pro-Series 2000 rifles come with right- or left-hand bolt. Finished weights run from 5½ pounds for the short-action PHL (Professional Hunter Lightweight) to just over eight for the Varmint and PHR long-action Big Game rifles. The PHR includes a built-in recoil reducer and adjustable open sights.

Late last spring, I re-acquainted myself with the Pro-Series 2000, snatching a 6.5/.284 SPR Sporter from the firm's limited inventory. Contemporary by virtue of its synthetic stock and detachable magazine, it has a clean, linear profile. The grip, a bit thick, is long enough for my hand without seeming

A straight-line detachable magazine feeds H-S rifles, available in several configurations.

pendulous. The fore-end is meaty enough for sure control, but slim enough to feel lively. Cycling the bolt, you feel top-quality machine work. Feeding, too, is smooth, sure— *clickety-clack*. The trigger breaks without preamble.

On paper, the SPR corralled 140-grain Nosler Partitions from Norma factory loads inside ¾-inch. The half-minute guarantee? Hey, I can't always *hold* inside half an inch. A big-game rifle that puts all bullets into a three-inch circle at 400 yards is more accurate than necessary.

As importantly, I like how the SPR handles. It gets high marks for its straight-up feeding, the run of its bolt, the way its stock dissipates recoil and readies me for a follow-up shot. All the parts work as they're supposed to, and the rifle has a solid, gunny feel, with an unspoken promise to wear gracefully, getting smoother, but not looser, with time, like an early Model 70 or a Sako. It's a rifle that affirms Tom Houghton's decision to jettison that chemistry degree.

CHAPTER 14

THOMPSON/CENTER: BEYOND THE HINGE

Accuracy guarantees generally put me into a cold sweat. With these bolt guns, 1 MOA is *no* sweat.

Wayne fires T/C's Icon, the company's first bolt-action big-game rifle and still its top-of-the-line model. The square-bottomed receiver mates to a bedding block.

For Kenneth Thompson, a New York toolmaker, the end of World War II marked the birth of his own firm. From his Long Island garage, he shipped molds and tooling for the investment casting industry. His products proved as good as his business sense, and soon he was hiring. In 1963, after a brutal winter but a sales year that had grossed an encouraging $180,000, Thompson and his crew moved to Rochester, New Hampshire. The community's woolen mills and shoe factories were struggling at that time, so Thompson was able to get good workers at reasonable wages. But seasonal swings in demand for investment casting tools interrupted production. Thompson decided to sell a consumer product. A firearm came to mind.

In 1965, gun designer Warren Center joined the firm. Like Thompson, he'd worked as a machinist and die maker. He'd also built firearms for Iver Johnson and Harrington & Richardson. In his basement shop, Center had designed a single-shot pistol he called the "Contender." He'd applied for patents and was looking for someone to manufacture the pistol, when he met Thompson. Teaming up on the pistol project meant doubling the size of Thompson's plant. In 1967, the first Contender came off the line.

The odd-looking handgun could easily have failed. A single-shot, it targeted a narrow market and was by no measure aesthetically pleasing. Nor was it cheap. But it had interchangeable barrels, and potent chamberings like the .30-30 and .35 Remington gave it the punch to take any North American game.

By 1970, Ken Thompson and Warren Center had established Thompson/Center Arms and were at work on new gun designs. The Hawken muzzleloading rifle appeared first. State wildlife agencies were authorizing special seasons for "primitive weapons." Hunters eager for more time afield would ensure the Hawken's success. Other blackpowder guns followed, including, in 1974, a Hawken kit. Adding 6,000, then 7,600, then 20,000 square feet of manufacturing space, T/C could barely stay abreast of orders. In 1982, the firm bought 15 acres for future plant expansion. The following year a centerfire rifle appeared, the TCR 83 single-shot. It and the subsequent TCR 87 had interchangeable barrels like the Contender.

Another 20 years brought more growth and new renditions of hinged-breech rifles and handguns. Then T/C announced its first bolt-action centerfire rifle, the Icon. I visited the plant to view and fire the prototype.

Wayne killed this fine eland with a T/C Icon in 6.5 Creedmoor. The rifle wears a Bushnell scope.

"Our goal was a truly new design, comprising the best elements of several rifles," explained then company president Greg Ritz, conceding that the closure of Winchester's New Haven plant, in March 2006, "encouraged us. Not that we like to watch worthy competition go under. But we did see an opening there and knew someone would fill it. We decided it would be us."

"We" included Greg and designer Mark Laney, with engineering manager Carl Ricker.

"We're planning to keep the price south of $800," Greg declared. "With high-quality checkered walnut." T/C then had some 600 blanks in stock from its old days in the wood trade.

The rifle I took to the range wore a smooth, well-figured piece of walnut with a red stain and oil finish. Generous panels on grip and fore-end featured borderless, 20 lines-per-inch checkering, neatly cut. A black pad capped the butt. No fore-end tip, grip cap, or Wundhammer swell. The comb was straight, *sans* cheekpiece; length of pull, 14 inches. The stock had clean, classic lines, a relatively open grip, and a fore-end that felt like a pre-war Model 70. The rifle shouldered and pointed easily.

Greg and Mark explained the Icon to me in detail. The full-diameter bolt has three front locking lugs and a sloping rear shroud. The bolt comes apart easily with a plastic "donut" tool provided with each rifle. The beefy spoon-style bolt handle is not integral.

"We'll offer a round knob and an oversize tactical knob as alternatives. You can switch handles in seconds. But assembled, the handle is one with the bolt."

The forged receiver is a single piece of 4140, pre-heat treated, then machined to tight tolerances in one trip through a seven-axis CNC machine.

"We complete one in 40 minutes," Greg told me.

The long tang on this rifle minimizes bolt wiggle at full extension. The wide, flat receiver bottom has three lugs that mate with a quarter-inch alloy plate glass-bedded and double-pinned into the stock. Scalloped edges ensure the plate will not shift. There's more than enough steel to arrest even the most violent setback during recoil. The stock is secured to the action by three stout guard screws, one into each lug, torqued to 65 inch-pounds.

PICATINNY ON TOP, NEW ROUND UP THE SPOUT

A detachable, sheet-steel box magazine tapers to feed rounds from six o'clock.

"Besides keeping the slot small, straight-up feed is smooth and reliable," explained Mark.

The box's front catch is designed for one-hand manipulation. The rifle has a lug-mounted extractor and plunger ejector. Icon's bolt stop is a slender lever at the traditional spot on the left receiver wall. It pivots from the front. The stop is undercut 15 degrees and designed so the force of a bolt flung rearward bears on the radiused rear of the stop in the receiver wall, not on the pivot pin.

The receiver top wears an integral Picatinny rail on front ring and bridge. The rail will, of course, accept Weaver scope rings, as well as those with beefier bases. The stock comb of the Icon is just the right height for instant aim through a scope mounted in low or medium T/C rings on the rail.

The trigger, designed by T/C expressly for this rifle, is adjustable from 2½ to six pounds

Dave Emary uses sticks to steady his Icon in 6.5 Creedmoor. Rifle and cartridge gave good account of themselves in South Africa.

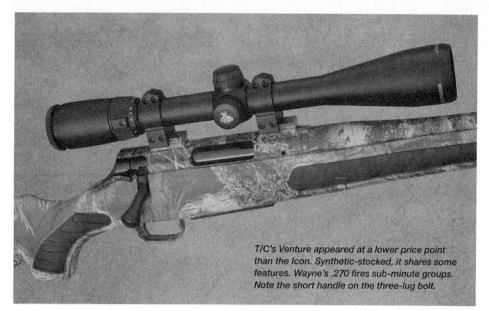

T/C's Venture appeared at a lower price point than the Icon. Synthetic-stocked, it shares some features. Wayne's .270 fires sub-minute groups. Note the short handle on the three-lug bolt.

without disassembly. You just reach through the tang with a supplied Allen wrench. The trigger's coil spring also loads the sear. Access to sear engagement and overtravel screws requires stock removal. Both have lock nuts. Dry-firing and at the range, I found the trigger delightful, a crisp, consistent 2¾ pounds. A two-position thumb safety works smoothly, crisply and quietly. It disengages the sear from trigger. You can manipulate the bolt with the safety on.

T/C's own 24-inch barrel is button rifled. Chamberings in 2007 included the .30 T/C, developed in Hornady's lab. It's similar to the .308 Marlin Express—in fact, it has the same case length, 1.920 inches, compared to 2.015 for the .308 Winchester. The .30 T/C round is rimless, though, and operates at higher pressures than its Marlin counterpart.

Most of a decade later, a couple of Icons have permanent spots in my rack. One in 6.5 Creedmoor recently went with me to the mountains of South Africa, with Crusader Safaris. The Stormberg's ragged purple rim could as well cap Wyoming. Andrew and I left the Cruiser at road's end and trudged up to a high meadow. A rocky fringe on its western edge rimmed a great cleft in the earth. It gaped hundreds of feet deep, hundreds

of yards wide, falling a mile before gentler slopes arrested it. We slid into a shaded crevice, sun to our backs, and dug out the binoculars. Presently, Andrew spied three vaal rhebok. We tried a sneak and failed. Keen-eyed as bighorn sheep, the animals spotted us far off. We heard the whistle.

"Both sexes whistle when alarmed," said Andrew. The pika-like sound carries far in the clear air.

Long minutes and a climb later, we crawled onto a ledge 250 yards from the ram, still alert. I snugged the sling, shaded a hand's width into the gusty wind, against vitals the diameter of a coffee saucer.

The ram vaulted from his perch at the shot, then crumpled. We made our way through the rocks. "Big eyes," said Andrew. "Feel the hair; it's as soft as rabbit fur."

Southern Africa's steeps also harbor the mountain reedbuck, stockier, but about the same size as the vaal rhebok. You needn't be an athlete to hunt either of these antelopes. On the other hand, loose rock and mid-elevation thorn slow your step. Wind and vertical stone meet you at the crest. Endurance counts.

Late one afternoon, Andrew and I spied a fine mountain reedbuck ram. The wind favored us, so I bellied forward. Atop the ridge

Though the Dimension weighs just over six pounds, the well-designed stock keeps recoil at bay when shooting from the bench.

shadowing the small herd, I eased beside a bush and leveled the Icon. The ram soon fed into my shot alley, dainty in his step, orange sunlight fringing his horns. Recoil obscured the impact. "A good day," observed Andrew, coming up from behind.

ACCURATE, AFFORDABLE, AND NOW SWITCHABLE

Thompson/Center followed the Icon with the Venture. Mark Laney had stepped up to become the firm's Director of Research and Development.

"The Venture is a modestly priced rifle with some of the Icon's features" he told me, "but a lighter, round receiver and an injection-molded stock. A washer-type lug handles the recoil. There's no bottom metal; the guard is part of the stock. We've kept the 5R rifling, five grooves with angled groove-land junctures. It delivers tight groups, resists fouling, and cleans easily."

The adjustable trigger on the Venture sent to me for testing (a .270) was factory set at 3¼ pounds. It gave consistent pulls with very little creep. The three-lug bolt ran smoothly in its race, thanks in part to a groove cut in the full-diameter body. (The bolt release engages the cut and serves much as might a guide rail.)

Because the test rifle arrived as I was packing for travel, I relented when my friend Rich McClure whined about .270 components crowding his loading bench. During my absence, he fired 150 rounds and turned in some groups that impressed both of us. Back on my range, I had the same good fortune. This rifle wanted to shoot! It was not at all fussy, lobbing 110-grain Sierras ahead of 25 grains of RL-7 at just shy of 2,000 fps into sub-¾-inch groups—then did the same with full-house 130-grain loads. Handloads of 53 grains of IMR 4064 behind 100-grain Hornadys clocked a sizzling 3,465 and printed inside .4-inch. A charge of 61 grains

*Not many bolt rifles shoot better than this! T/C's lightweight, switch-barrel Dimension nipped this knot for Wayne **without** its rear guard screw engaged!*

of RL-22 drove 130-grain Speers at 3,200 fps into .6-inch. Federal Premium ammo with 130-grain Barnes TSX bullets nipped into a minute of angle. So did Hornady 140-grain InterLocks. No ammunition shot poorly, though Rich and I tried 15 loads. T/C's minute-of-angle guarantee was apparently quite reasonable.

My only criticism, a hard bolt lift. Primary extraction with a three-lug bolt is more difficult than with the traditional Mauser dual-lug design, because it must occur in a shorter 60-degree rotation. T/C could assist by giving the Venture a longer bolt handle. "That's easy to fix," smiled Mark.

Since the Venture's debut, T/C has moved to Springfield, Massachussetts, home to parent firm Smith & Wesson. And it has introduced a bolt rifle with interchangeable barrels. The synthetic-stocked Dimension, introduced in 2011, is surprisingly affordable. At $649, it lists for less than a barrel alone for switch-barrel rifles from the likes of Mauser and Dakota.

There's no figured Turkish walnut or fitted case. What you get with a Dimension is a 7075 alloy receiver that's really a shell for the bolt, magazine, and trigger group. Weight savings here bring overall weight to just 6¼ pounds. The fluted bolt mates directly to a barrel extension. Barrels (10 to start), are of chrome-molybdenum steel, 22 and 24 inches long, with 5-R rifling. Two guard screws in alloy sleeves secure an injection-molded stock to barrel and tang. Torque them with a supplied wrench. An alloy block up front and a pillar in the rear ensure consistent bedding. Barrels stay zeroed if you leave each scope in the cantilever mount (optional). The mount is stabilized at the bridge by a wedge and a set screw.

The Dimension adjustable trigger has a range of 3½ to five pounds. The safety, a two-detent side-mounted lever, does not lock the bolt. The stock wears Armorsoft coating and includes colored spacers to change length. There's a ventilated recoil pad. A wide barrel channel accepts all barrel diameters.

The Dimension is T/C's latest bolt rifle at this writing. Its receiver is a lightweight shell for interchangeable barrels and bolts. Lightweight, it's also inexpensive, as switch-barrels go.

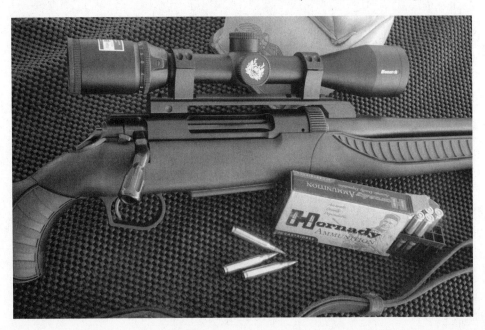

The Dimension's barrel holds a cantilever scope mount. A geared ring connects it to the receiver shell (tool provided). In Wayne's test, barrels maintained zero through changes.

T/C designed the Dimension for four cartridge families: .223-length, short (.308), long (.30-06), and magnum. Because the Dimension receiver is a housing that need not hold pressure, there's just one for all chamberings! Magazine groups are specific to cartridge families; each barrel assembly includes the proper magazine group. Assemblies and bolts for different cartridge head diameters are modestly priced. There's no danger of miss-matching bolt and barrel; if you do, the bolt won't close. The three-lug bolt is much like the Venture's, with face-mounted extractor and plunger ejector.

Each Dimension comes with two simple tools. One has a gear wheel that engages a knurled ring on the barrel. The other serves as an anchor to torque the ring. I found the process simple and quick after a couple practice runs. After a few drills switching barrels on one receiver, I benched a Dimension rifle and fired groups. Later I attached a Brownell's Latigo sling to fire from field positions at ranges to 700 yards. Throughout the day's shooting, the stock absorbed recoil well. Offhand, I found the rifle's balance and handling qualities pleasing, no matter the barrel.

The forward guard screw is the one that matters. It slips through the receiver and threads into the barrel itself. When I left the rear guard screw out of the receiver tang for a series of shots, three 150-grain Hornadys from the .308 chopped a .3-inch knot!

To see how switching barrels affected zero, I changed out a .223 barrel three times. Groups fired after each swap printed less than an inch apart. T/C won't guarantee such repeatability; however, it does set a 1-minute accuracy standard. In my shooting with .223, .308, and .300 Winchester barrels, the average group size came in at about .9-inch.

The Dimension's bolt cycles as it should; the follower dutifully lifts cartridges. I had no feeding failures or misfires, no hitches in extraction or ejection. The trigger tripped obediently at four pounds. As on the Venture (which uses the same magazines), the bolt handle is short and primary extraction stiff. The barrel-change design is clever indeed, with few components quickly and easily fitted. Tools provided are foolproof and sufficient, no need to raid the junk drawer. The stock's barrel channel is capacious enough for varmint-weight barrels, so you'll have to live with big gaps either side of lighter profiles. But to keep costs down, T/C could hardly afford hand-checkered French wood snugged by irascible old men with scrapers. You can't have everything.

CHAPTER 15

FIFTY YEARS INSIDE WEATHERBY

The High Priest of High Velocity founded an institution. Think you know Weatherby? Read on!

The .300 Weatherby Magnum, a blown-out .300 H&H Roy developed, in 1945, has a huge following. David Miller so chambers his elegant rifles for long shooting at game like Coues deer.

"Weatherby is a great place to work. It's an American story!" An unassuming, soft-spoken man, Dean Rumbaugh has worked for the gunmaker for 50 yearsand at this writing, he has no plans to retire. His hair has whitened over time, but his eyes smile as he shows me around Weatherby headquarters in Paso Robles. Close by the central California coast, it became the company's home in 2007, following a 12-year tenure in Atascadero, a few miles to the south.

"We moved to Atascadero in late 1994, early 1995," Dean recalls. "We were all ready to leave Los Angeles."

That's where Roy Weatherby had opened his first retail store in 1945, "under a big neon sign on Long Beach Boulevard," says Dean. "Roy moved to a better facility five years later." That shop, on Firestone Boulevard in Southgate, was Weatherby headquarters for more than four decades. Southgate handed Weatherby its corporate image. Big, glossy, full-color catalogs pictured Roy in his office there, nattily dressed, courting war heroes, business tycoons, and entertainment celebrities with gleaming rifles. His enormous mural of the East African plain became a trademark Weatherby background.

Weatherby eventually outgrew the Firestone/Southgate digs.

"In 1964, not long after I joined the company, we added 10,000 square feet," says Dean. It wasn't enough. Two years later, the firm leased a skating rink and converted it. In 1971, Roy bought it.

But Los Angeles was changing. When Roy's son, Ed, moved up the coast to find a rural homesite, and Brad Ruddell came aboard as Vice President of Sales and Marketing, commuting from his home even farther north, Dean figured a relocation was imminent.

"Judy and I had moved out of the city to Orange County, in 1973. When Ed took the headquarters to Atascadero, we followed. Still, we all felt a bit hollow. Roy had died, in 1988. The Firestone Boulevard store represented a great pioneering effort. Roy came up with many of the sales strategies used by successful gun stores today. He was far ahead of his time."

Born in 1910 to a Kansas sharecropper, Roy Weatherby spent most of his childhood working in the fields. He earned his first BB gun peddling garden seed on foot to neighboring farms. College was just a

Roy Weatherby, an insurance salesman from the Midwest, started his rifle business in Los Angeles, wildcatting cartridges in the early 1940s.

dream for most country boys in the 1930s, but Roy worked to make it come true. While employed at Southwestern Bell, he took night classes at the University of Wichita. As restless as he was ambitious, Roy left the Midwest, in 1937. He and his wife, Camilla, headed for California, and its fabled fortunes. Roy started an insurance business and prospered. Equipping his basement shop with a lathe and a drill press from Sears, he wildcatted cartridges and built rifles on surplus military actions.

By 1945, Roy had developed several of the cartridges that would later bring him fame. Based on the .300 Holland & Holland Magnum, they had minimal body taper and radiused shoulders. Eventually, Roy dropped his insurance job and began hiring people to help him build and promote his semi-custom rifles.

Cash was scarce; he had to borrow from friends to stay afloat. In 1946, he sold half his business to Bill Wittman, his attorney and friend, to get $10,000 in additional venture capital. About then, Camilla inherited $21,000 from the sale of her family's 160-acre Kansas farm. Roy used that money to buy back the stake he'd sold. Still, the company struggled. An auto accident just before Christmas in 1946 put Roy on crutches for three months. He took comfort in the image of the Weatherby rifle on the cover of *American Rifleman* that month.

Roy showed a talent for hobnobbing with people of high station, and he knew how valuable they could be in promoting his business. Sheldon Coleman became a customer, and Gary Cooper. He courted Elmer Keith and Jack O'Connor, Jimmy Doolittle and Joe Foss. Photos of Hollywood stars, from Roy Rogers to John Wayne and Robert Stack, appeared in photos with Weatherby rifles. Roy didn't neglect the gurus of the shooting press. Phil Sharpe gave Weatherby rifles and cartridges prominent exposure in his 1948 revised edition of *Complete Guide To Handloading.*

Despite a growing inventory in the Long Beach store and the reflected glow of Hollywood, Roy craved faster growth. To raise more money, he decided to offer stock. Weatherby's (later Weatherby), Inc., was formed in May 1949. It drew $70,000 from investors, among them Herb Klein, a wealthy Texas oil man. Klein committed $10,000 for stock in the company and, with Phil Sharpe, became a vice-president.

Dean Rumbaugh says Herb was crucial to Roy's survival in those early years. "But those two did not always see eye to eye, especially with regard to business." When Herb's young nephew Lloyd Klein was brought into the company as Roy's legal assistant, the union faltered. By this time, Klein owned half interest. To resolve problems with his long-time associate and benefactor, Roy proposed a buyout. Herb agreed, with conditions. He and Roy remained friends until Herb's death, in 1974.

BIRTH OF THE HIGH-VELOCITY MAGNUM

Roy's first rifles were built on 1898 Mauser, 1903 Springfield, and 1917 Enfield ac-

The .30-378, a necked-down .378 (circa 1953), dwarfs even the .300 Winchester Magnum. It has topped Mark V sales charts for more than a decade.

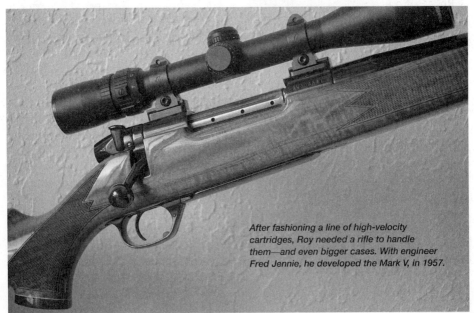

After fashioning a line of high-velocity cartridges, Roy needed a rifle to handle them—and even bigger cases. With engineer Fred Jennie, he developed the Mark V, in 1957.

The Mark V has a full-diameter bolt, three sets of three locking lugs, a 54-degree bolt lift. A strong action, it has been built in Germany, Japan, and the U.S.

tions. He also used Model 70 Winchesters and other metal supplied by customers.

"The first *commercial* Weatherbys, those not custom-built, were on FN Mauser actions."

They're still sharp in Dean's mind.

"Roy imported these, beginning in 1949." Charter chamberings included the .220 Rocket, a blown-out .220 Swift. It did not become a commercial offering. Neither did the .228 Weatherby Magnum. But the .270 Magnum that followed took root. It became a favorite of Roy's and, later, his son, Ed. The .270, with the .257 and 7mm Weatherby Magnums that appeared about the same time, set the stage for a spate of short belted rounds from other makers. The .300 Weatherby, with its 2.85-inch case, arrived in 1945. It drove a bullet nearly 300 fps faster than the .300 H&H Magnum from which it was formed. Roy hawked his .300 in print and demonstrated its power in films, severing a thick tree branch with a single shot and a straight face.

"Sako also provided Mauser actions to our specifications," Dean says. "Roy deep-hole-drilled his own barrels and contoured them. He shaped his own stocks. He installed Jaeger triggers, Buehler safeties and scope mounts. Roy and Maynard Buehler were close friends."

In 1954, Weatherby had Hertel and Reuse make a Weatherby Imperial scope with two

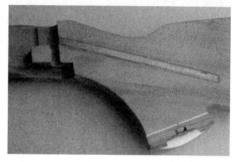

To prevent wrist splits—a real possibility, given the Weatherby's stock profile and recoil from heavy magnum loads—a reinforcing through-bolt became standard.

adjustments on top of the tube. One was for focusing. The other incorporated both windage and elevation dials.

In 1957, Roy and company engineer Fred Jennie developed a rifle action of their own. The Mark V rifle came to define "Weatherby Magnum." It replaced the Danish Shultz & Larsen action, one of only a few then big enough for Weatherby's .378 Magnum round. Introduced in 1953, the .378 was not only longer than the .300 H&H Magnum (case lengths 2.908 and 2.850 inches, respectively), it was also larger in diameter (.603- and .532-inch at the belt). The subsequent .460 and .416 Weatherby Magnums, announced in 1958 and 1989, are based on the .378's hull—essentially a belted .416 Rigby. The

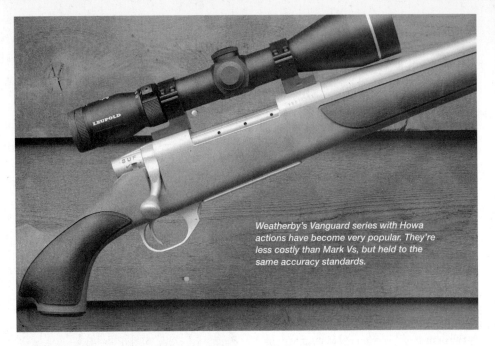

Weatherby's Vanguard series with Howa actions have become very popular. They're less costly than Mark Vs, but held to the same accuracy standards.

Claro walnut that distinguished Weatherby rifles would sometimes yield to the pounding of these potent rounds. Roy substituted dense-grained European walnut and tough, heavy mesquite.

According to Dean, the first Weatherby Mark V receivers were manufactured from sand castings by Pacific Foundry International, in California.

"The high failure rate quickly sent Roy to J.P. Sauer, where receivers were forged. That was in 1959, just before I started at Weath-

A hunter shoulders a Weatherby Vanguard in Montana elk cover. Weatherby rifles have an international reputation for reach and power.

erby. German Weatherbys, and the Japanese- and U.S.-made rifles since, are of very high quality and incredibly stout. By the way, you won't find any Mark Vs with single-digit serial numbers. If memory serves, the PFI rifles were numbered from 15,000 into the 16,000s. Sauer-built actions began at 20,000."

Roy had a hard-charging work ethic.

"He was always looking for new ways to sell rifles," Dean says. "In 1950, he got a van for travel to dealers. The side-panel advertising Weatherby rifles would hardly make sense in urban L.A. now, but Roy insisted on it. He took delivery of a Chrysler coupe outfitted with zebra seat covers, and a Buick wagon with a built-in walnut gun vault. Pull-out drawers held scoped rifles for display. He believed in a mobile and active sales force. Looking back, it's easy to see why. He was a super salesman. Personal contacts earned him a lot of business. For years long after postage costs made it a questionable business practice, Roy sent Christmas cards to everyone who bought a Weatherby rifle."

A hunter and shooter, Roy enjoyed taking his rifles afield, but always with an eye to business. His safaris, in 1948 and 1952, helped sell his products. So did the colorful figuring in Weatherby's distinctive, gloss-finished rifle-stocks. By the late 1970s, Weatherby had a close working relationship with Calico, a California walnut supplier.

"Calico still furnishes most of our wood," says Dean.

By the time the Mark V had been in production 20 years, Weatherby had introduced most of its current line of cartridges.

"In 1962, we brought out the .340, a necked-up .300," Dean recounts. "In 1968, we announced the .240. It's essentially a 6mm on a .30-06-size hull. Very pleasant to shoot. The .30-378 came in 1998. That powerhouse still tops our popularity chart."

Dean explains that the .30-378 resulted from a request from Alabama's Redstone Arsenal for a round that would launch a bullet at over 6,000 fps—in 1959! "We actually clocked a very light bullet at over 5,000."

In 1977, Mark V production was moved from Germany to Japan, a cost-saving measure that didn't affect rifle quality. Weatherby brought the Mark V Stateside, in 1996, contracting with Saco Defense in Saco, Maine, to build the nine-lug magnum version. Assembly of six-lug rifles for the likes of the .30-06 and other rounds then on the list went to Acrometal, in Brainerd, Minnesota.

"Acrometal's plant is among the cleanest, most modern you'll find," Dean tells me.

The Criterion division of John Krieger's company provided button-rifled barrels. Bell & Carlson got the stock contract. Adjustable triggers on the six-lug action yielded consistent sear engagement of .012 to .015. Excellent products from the Brainerd facility and an ownership change at Saco shifted all Mark V rifle production to Acrometal, in 2001. By this time, Buehler scope mounts had been replaced on Weatherby rifles by those from Talley, currently run by Dave Talley's son Gary Turner.

Weatherby's Custom Shop has been Dean's first love.

"Building rifles one at a time gave Roy

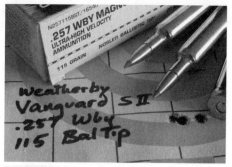

Wayne fired this group with a Vanguard rifle in .257 Weatherby. Norma has loaded all Weatherby-boxed ammunition since early in the company's history.

his start," he reminds me. Custom work, suspended for a time but revived in 1998, now produces 10 percent of Weatherby revenues. That segment includes "banquet rifles" marked for conservation groups like the Wild Turkey Federation and the Rocky Mountain Elk Foundation.

Dean and Roy shared another passion: antique cars.

"Roy owned a 1930 Franklin, when I came to work in 1961," Dean recalls. "He dreamed of picking up a Deusenberg. That didn't happen. But Roy had Lincolns and Packards. He owned a Patrician, namesake of our company's first pump shotgun."

Early on, Roy Weatherby groomed son Ed to take the corporate reins.

"Surely, Ed has contributed a great deal during his tenure," says Dean.

With Brad Ruddell, who joined the company in 1991 and only recently gone to pursue his own business in the shooting industry, Ed has brought positive changes.

"Under their leadership, Weatherby grew its rifle line to include the profitable Vanguard series with Howa actions."

Legendary for its fast-stepping magnum cartridges and the glitzy rifle with the smooth-shucking actions and distinctive stock profiles, Weatherby now builds its Mark Vs back home.

"We've brought all assembly to Paso Robles," says Dean Rumbaugh. He expects it to stay in-house. "Like me," he grins.

CHAPTER 16

FASTEST BOLT RIFLES EVER

Strength, not speed, distinguished the Mauser.
But these bolt guns can out-cycle lever-actions!

Wayne killed this fine ram on a European hunt, with a quick shot from his Steyr, a 9.3x62.

*B*ang!-Bang!
You'd have thought, by hearing, that the rifle was an autoloader. In fact, it wore a bolt handle. It snapped back and forward eye-blink fast, before the bounce of recoil had left the barrel.

Not all bolt rifles are that fast.

The Mauser 98 runs loosely, most often with lots of wobble at the end of its throw. But it is easy to manipulate and dead certain to extract and chamber. You can cycle it as fast as you like without fear of a malfunction. The bottom rim of the 98 Mauser's bolt face is milled flush with the center of the face, so case heads can ride smoothly up into the extractor claw. This "controlled round feed" matters to soldiers. Early snaring of a case precludes double loading and a jam. The

same is true of Dakota, Winchester, and other rifles with the Mauser claw. Honestly, push-feed rifles like the Remington 700 and Savage 110 have been refined to the point that any limit to cycling speed is human. Most are as reliable as Mausers.

Faster than the Mauser is the Mannlicher-Schoenauer. M-S rifles were actually made by Steyr. All of them. Mannlicher and Schoenauer were rifle *designers*, not manufacturing or corporate magnates! Named for a thirteenth-century Austrian town at the confluence of the Steyr and Enns Rivers, Steyr got its start during the 1860s, when young Josef Werndl returned from a stint in the

U.S. working for Colt's. He applied his fresh knowledge of gun manufacture in his father's shop. In church one day, Josef thought up a new rifle design. Given its genesis, the mechanism was called a "tabernacle breech." Austria's army bought it. By the end of the nineteenth century, Steyr had 10,000 workers on its payroll! Josef Werndl provided housing for many. In 1883, he brought hydro power to the city, making it the first in Europe with electric lights.

Steyr's first rifles were built for blackpowder cartridges re-engineered for smokeless fuel. New models appeared at roughly two-year intervals, until 1910. Steyr also built rifles for other nations on their patterns—the Norwegian Krag and the 98K Mauser, for instance. The original factory lay just above the Steyr River's meeting with the Enns, which flows another 30 kilometers to the Danube. In 1912, the gunmaking shop moved a few miles away, to a new facility. In 1918, Steyr started making automobiles, then lorries, tractors and bicycles. Josef Werndl passed away that year, at age 58, of pneumonia contracted while he battled one of the town's periodic floods. Between World Wars, new cartridges outnumbered changes in Steyr rifle design. In 1934, a merger formed Steyr-Daimler-Puch. That union dissolved in 1996, leaving firearms production alone under Steyr's name.

Steyr's Mannlicher-Schoenauer Model 1903 had a signature split bridge and butterknife bolt handle. Chambered initially in 6.5x54mm, this rifle cycled so effortlessly that, with the bolt drawn back, a downward flip of the muzzle could bring it forward and *rotate it into battery*! A spool magazine fed cartridges fluidly.

From the 1903 came a long series of M-S rifles, the last built four decades ago. But the Steyrs that replaced them are almost as slick in operation and have several advantages. A three-position tang safety serves as the bolt release behind a Mauser-style bridge. The twin lug lock-up is so stout it endures test-

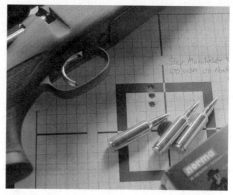

The slick Mannlicher-Schoenauer rifles of yesteryear were built by Steyr (not all had full-length stocks). This modern Steyr delivers speed and accuracy in the same package.

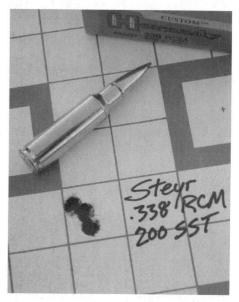

Wayne fired this tight group with a current, synthetic-stocked Steyr rifle in .338 RCM.

firing with a full-power load *behind a bullet deliberately lodged halfway up the barrel*!

My experience with modern Steyrs bears out the claim of improved accuracy. A Classic version in .270 WSM kept bench groups under .8-inch. One in .338 RCM put three shots into half an inch. A full-stocked Classic in my rack prints sub-minute knots with a lightweight 19-inch barrel in 9.3x62mm. I used that rifle, in Austria, to nail three driven boars in quick succession.

Wayne's first deer rifle, a surplus SMLE bought for $30, fed as fast as a lever-action deer rifle. The stamped steel magazine was uncannily reliable; the cock-on-closing bolt ran like lightning.

A big bolt handle, such as on this Kimber, can speed bolt operation significantly. You needn't sacrifice accuracy to get a rifle you can cycle fast!

CHEERS TO THE SMLE AND '03!

My first bolt gun was not built by Steyr or Mauser. At $30, the war-surplus Short Magazine Lee Enfield cost $10 less than a 98, and much less than a Mannlicher-Schoenauer. The SMLE's stamped steel box looked cheap, but fed its 10 rounds so smoothly I could cycle *empties*! After restocking the rifle and replacing its military blade and notch with Williams open sights, I killed deer with it. My friend Ron had a lever-action 94 Winchester he insisted was faster. Neither of us could afford to waste rounds in speed-shooting contests, so we stuffed our magazines with hulls and shucked furiously on signal until we'd spilled seven. The .303 with its cock-on-closing action proved as fast as the 94 every time!

The 1903 Springfield isn't that fast as issued, though tuned rifles acquit themselves well in rapid-fire stages of the National Match course. I recall '03s and 03A3s for $29.95, back when you could have them delivered by the postman. I still covet Springfields. One in my rack is a military '03 graced with a simple stick of new walnut and a Redfield receiver sight. I took it to Alaska, climbed a mountain, and shot a Dall's ram. On the flats below, it garnered a moose. Two Springfields wear synthetic stocks and svelte barrels in .30-06 Improved. A fourth is a target rifle with a thick barrel and iron sights, a classic bull gun.

On a hunt, a lethal first hit makes cycling speed irrelevant—but not all bullets land where intended or behave as they ought.

"If you can get the strength, reliability, and accuracy of a bolt-action with double the speed, why wouldn't you?"

Bernard Knobel knows about speed. An accomplished skeet shooter, he thrashed me soundly during an impromptu event at a gun club somewhere in the patchwork of forest and farmland quilting rural Germany. That's where he directs operations for Blaser, a firm that builds truly innovative rifles and shotguns.

Relatively young by industry standards, Blaser (that's BLAH-zer, not BLAE-zer), appeared in 1957. Its R93 straight-pull bolt rifle, introduced in 1993, has defined the company with sportsmen worldwide. It offers a broad selection of chamberings on a trim, unconventional switch-barrel action. I've carried it in Africa, where I quickly learned to like it. The 93's successor, the R8, is named for the year Blaser refined the R93. Bernard insists that neither rifle fits the German stereotype.

"They're *not* over-engineered and underdesigned!" he blusters. After using these rifles, I heartily agree!

Blaser's North American operation is headquartered in San Antonio. There, Norbert Hausmann introduced me to the R8. He assured me the features that distinguished the R93 were all there: hammer-forged barrel, radial-head bolt, single-stack magazine tucked into a compact unit with the target-quality trigger. That magazine/trigger assembly, with a telescoping bolt, trims overall length. An R93 with a 24-inch barrel is shorter than a Remington 700 with a 22-inch tube!

The 93 and R8, don't operate like ordinary bolt rifles. No rotation. You run the bolt with a flick of your hand, back and forth. From the shoulder. The thumb-piece that cocks the R8

Blaser straight-pull bolt rifles lock with an expanding collet. Feeding is very smooth. The bolt handle swivels slightly to the rear as you unlock and eject, snaps forward on closure.

is its safety. Shove it up and forward. You're ready to fire. To de-cock, push ahead again, but down slightly, and let it return to the rear.

"The R93 and R8 are the only bolt rifles you can carry safely with a chambered round," Norbert points out. "They're not cocked until you're ready to fire."

NO LUGS, NO PROBLEM!

Like its predecessor, the R8 bolt head locks with a collett forced into a circumferential groove in the barrel shank.

"But the R8 is stronger," says Norbert, a master gunsmith. "Its locking angle is steeper than the 45 degrees on the R93. Also, a bushing slides into the collett's center for added support. We've tested this mechanism to pressures of 120,000 psi, damaging gauges before the rifles failed."

The Blaser R8's hand-detachable trigger group includes the magazine, a cleverly designed, lightweight polymer box that feeds without fault.

The Blaser R8's compact mechanism accommodates cartridges as big as the .500 Jeffery. Options on the big-bores include an internal recoil reducer.

Blaser barrels come in various lengths, weights, and contours, fluted and not. Most chambers are hammer-forged. Plasma-nitriding on barrels increases surface hardness.

"Scope rings and base clamps are softer than the barrel," said Bernhard. "They don't slip. Our saddle rings fit so well, you can remove the scope and replace it without losing zero."

I went to the range not believing that last claim. Scope removal always means some shift in zero.

"Hand it over." A bear of a man with a ready grin, Blaser's Tom Mack snatches the R8 before I could say no. He frees the Zeiss scope with a couple of tugs on the thumb latches and holds it up like a prize. Hoo boy. I've been flailing at a five-gallon bucket filled with Texas chalk at 600 yards. Now I'll have to re-zero.

"Have atit," Tom insists, cinching the 6-24x56mm back in place.

Bellied into prone, I favor for a nine-o'clock breeze and press the trigger. White dust bursts from the bucket.

"Bingo!" Tom cackles. "Again."

I run the Blaser's bolt—a flick of the wrist. Another Federal load rockets downrange.

"Got it." He's smug. "One more."

I cycle the R8, fire and hit.

"No need to re-adjust, huh?" drawls Tom. "Even at 600 yards."

You can switch Blaser barrels with equal confidence. I'd confirmed that with the R93, in Namibia, replacing one barrel with another previously zeroed. My Norma loads drilled bull's-eyes at 300 steps. You need but a single tool, a T-handled Allen wrench, to change barrels or remove the buttstock. (The wrench supplied with the R8 is 5mm, the R93 4mm.)

Like the R93, the R8 has a single-stack polymer magazine. But the R8 magazine/trigger group is hand-detachable as a unit. Just pinch those tabs in front of the guard. You can top-load without removing the box, or recharge the rifle with pre-loaded maga-

The Blaser R8 chambers cartridges as powerful as you'll want for elephant. This hunter tries his hand at a swing-out target at the FTW Ranch, in Texas.

zines from your pocket. Should you wish to lock the magazine in place, there's a sliding tab inside the box. One box accepts all cartridges for which the R8 is chambered (more than two dozen, .223 to .416 Remington Magnum). Inner parts, a snap to change by hand, work for *families* of cartridges. When you remove the magazine/trigger group, the rifle de-cocks automatically. It remains non-functional until the assembly is replaced. To protect that assembly while it's out of the R8, Blaser supplies a snug polymer jacket. There's also a polymer insert for the receiver.

In Europe, R8s come standard with a trigger pull of 1.6 pounds. U.S. hunters get an equally crisp break at 2.5 pounds. You can special-order a lighter trigger; however, parts must be installed by Blaser, as weight adjustment happens in the *receiver*. Like the R93, the R8 has very fast lock time.

The R8's stock has a straight comb, which, admit Blaser folks, is for most applications better than the hump-back comb traditional in central Europe. It has cast-off at toe and heel, and even 3.5 millimeters in the grip, to make sight alignment quick and easy. As on the R93, the Turkish walnut comes in several grades.

Sub-minute groups at 300 yard have repeatedly shown me the R8 is accurate. Beyond that, its compact design and excellent balance make it ideal for quick shooting in timber—and that straight-pull bolt is without

peer for running boar targets. The .308 I used most often wore a Zeiss Vari-Point (red dot) scope. The hapless pig got very ragged as it raced back and forth on the rail, brass piling up beside me. No cycling hitches.

Available with synthetic stocks or walnut, the R93 and R8 have been beautifully fitted and finished. The profile is European, with a steep, substantial grip. I prefer a more slender wrist with an open radius. It seems to me rifles handle most nimbly and surely when the grip doesn't *fill* the hand, but rather gives it something easy to grasp. Both hands must be allowed to shift slightly if you swing on a running animal. If you pick up a broomstick, you'll find it quick in your hands, a snap to point. A stock that's a bit short speeds the rifle to your cheek, because you needn't push the rifle forward to clear your coat. A short stock also better accommodates the odd shooting positions you must sometimes adopt quickly.

Whether you shoot with a conventional bolt rifle or a Blaser straight-pull, the thing that gives you the greatest edge in speed is practice. Cheeking the rifle then cycling the action from hunting positions helps a great deal. Cycle often enough *while firing* to trim your recoil recovery time; and ditch the habit of slowly sliding the bolt back to pick out the hull. You'll eventually send repeat shots so fast, bystanders will think they're hearing a self-loader!

CHAPTER 17

FROM THE OLD COUNTRY

Soviet shadows followed the bombs. Names changed. CZ emerged. Riflemen hail the result!

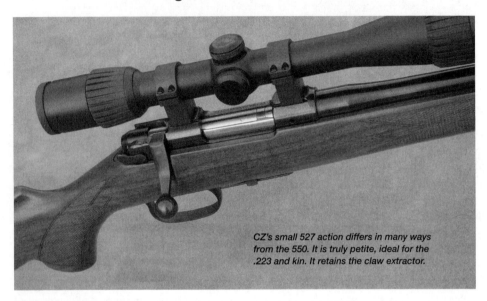

CZ's small 527 action differs in many ways from the 550. It is truly petite, ideal for the .223 and kin. It retains the claw extractor.

Nobody can call CZ's 550 willowy. Best described as a modified Mauser, the action has a brawny profile and substantial heft. The double square-bridge receiver has no top holes; you fasten a scope with mounts that clamp 19mm dovetails front and rear. The big, flat footprint of the action makes for plenty of bedding area. Epoxy ensures full recoil lug contact on rifles chambered to powerful cartridges. Magnum 550s feature a second recoil lug under the barrel that mates with a steel stock insert. The fore-end screw on these rifles is absent on 550s for less potent rounds (from .22-250), ditto the double cross-bolts, standard fore and aft of magazine wells on Magnums.

The 550's bolt is of traditional two-lug design, with a Mauser extractor. The bolt face is partially enclosed, allowing for controlled feed. A fixed extractor emerges from a slot just below the left locking lug as the bolt reaches the end of its throw. A Winchester 70-style bolt stop bears against the left lug. The two-position thumb safety locks the striker (three-stop safeties are available on some models). The trigger is CZ's own, an adjustable, single set mechanism you can pull as you would any trigger, or push ahead to engage it for a lighter pull. Bottom metal, all steel, includes a one-piece guard and magazine housing, and a hinged floorplate secured by an M70-type button in front of the guard.

Most CZ 550s are stocked in plain American walnut, either in the Czech Republic with imported wood or Stateside after the barreled action arrives at the Kansas City headquarters of CZ-USA.

Uhersky Brod lies just 25 kilometers from Slovakia, 240 northeast of Vienna. As far as practical from Germany, it seemed a good place, in 1936, for the Czech government to move its arms factory.

"The original CZ plant was in Strakonice, far to the west."

When I spoke with him, Milan Kubelen had retired after 30 years at CZ. "Hitler's intentions were clear in eastern Europe, long before they took root beyond the Channel." Milan said Zbrojovka Brno produced rifles for the government in the central Czech town of Brno, before World War I. In 1921,

Wayne found the Czech-built CZ 527 sporter the equal of much heavier varmint rifles, with regards to accuracy. This load performed very well, as so did others.

it became Ceska Zbrojovka, or "Czech armsmaker." To augment post-war rifle output at the Brno facility, CZ took root in Strakonice, where it produced CZ pistols. In the late 1930s, the Uhersky Brod facility was a subsidiary of CZ Prague. But, after Neville Chamberlain gave in to the Nazis in Munich, Hitler promptly snatched Sudetenland. To no one's surprise east of Berlin, he soon occupied the rest of the country, too.

After the war, Germany relinquished the land it had seized. Czechoslovakia became, briefly, self-governing. In 1948, Communists took control. Seven years later, the Uhersky Brod facility separated from Strakonice. In 1964, the government further throttled firearms manufacture at Brno, but because the Brno name had so much traction, retained it on the ZKK, ZKM, and 527 rifles of the 1960s. These rifles came from the Uhersky Brod plant, which had undergone marked expansion in 1960.

"The new buildings have flat roofs," said Milan. "Original structures still wear peaked tile roofs, designed so the factory would look like houses when viewed through a bomb sight."

During the 1970s and '80s, CZ Uhersky Brod focused on military arms. In 1989, a revolution led by poet Vaclav Havel overthrew Communist rule. Two years later,

The CZ 550's bolt head shows its Mauser heritage. The ejector slot is located off the lug, though, per the Winchester Model 70's.

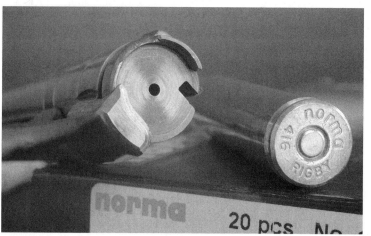

A modified Mauser, the CZ 550 chambers a wide range of cartridges. Wayne killed this Canada moose with a 9.3x62mm.

IRON TO BOTTLE THE .505

An upscale 550 is the Safari Classic, a subset of the 550 Magnum with fancy walnut and old-time chamberings with lots of horsepower.

"We wanted to offer a rifle of custom-shop quality at reasonable cost." At this writing, Alice Poluchova is president of CZ-USA. "We chose to chamber it for classic safari cartridges—the .404 Jeffery, .450 Rigby, .500 Jeffery, and .505 Gibbs."

The biggest of these rounds would not slip into most magnum bolt actions, but the CZ 550 Magnum accommodates them. Weighing in at 11 pounds, the .500 and

Czech industry was privatized. In 1993, the nation split to form autonomous governments. The Czech and Slovak Republics remain independent.

In 2004, Zbrojovka Brno went bankrupt, because of internal improprieties. Two years later, a new Brno began building shotguns and single-shot rifles to be marketed by an expanding CZ! Now, CZ makes all the major parts for its firearms. Barrels are all rifled by hammer-forging under 40 tons of pressure. The 1,300 people employed at Uhersky Brod work with both traditional and CNC machines.

"Rifles make up about 35 percent of sales now," Milan told me. "Handguns account for the rest. We've pushed to increase sales of the 550 and smaller Model 527 bolt rifles in North America." Safari rifles, he added, have been particularly popular. "Americans." He smiled. "Always they want the biggest."

.505 incorporate a mercury recoil reducer in the stock. Other Safari Classics scale 10 pounds, including the .300 H&H, recently added. You also can pick a .338 Lapua (with recoil reducer), .338 Winchester, .375 H&H, or .416 Remington. The Safari Classics line offers many extra-cost options, including muzzle brake, rust blue, ebony fore-end tip and special-order chamberings like .458 Win-

Two lines of CZ safari-style rifles feature open sights and crossbolt-reinforced stocks. They offer haymaker punch (to .505 Gibbs!) at reasonable prices.

chester and .458 Lott. Glass bedding is standard, and so, too, a barrel band front swivel and a trued and lapped action. To date, Safari Classics have been priced under $2,300.

For hunters who'd rather spend their money on air tickets to Zambia, there's the American Safari Magnum in .375, .458 Winchester, .458 Lott, and even .505 Gibbs. It lists for half as much as the Safari Classic. You can also get a European-style Safari Magnum in .375, .458, and .458 Lott. In my humble view, the .375 is all you need in Africa, unless you sell ivory by the boatload. A professional hunter who culled elephants with a .375 told me his head would start ringing after hurling 500-grain .458 solids. "I get as much penetration with the .375," he said. "Sometimes more."

Not long ago, Jason Morton, a friend who works for CZ, sent me a American Safari Magnum in .375. The stock was beefy enough to use as a corner post. A handful of .375 cartridges (five!) vanished in the maw of that big action, the same one used for the .505 Gibbs. But CZ took care to balance this 10 pounds of steel and walnut. The 25-inch barrel of medium contour hangs easily on target and swings readily (the Safari Classic .375 also comes with a 20-inch barrel). The heft assists with offhand aim, when you're out of breath shadowing an Endebele tracker who'd qualify for the Boston Marathon running backwards. A barrel-band front sight complements three rear leafs, two folding. Their shallow "V" notches all have white center lines for quick aim.

"We offer 15 heights and sizes of front sights," Jason pointed out. "So the rifle is pretty much guaranteed to shoot to the sights, no matter the load."

The CZ's substantial weight made bench shooting comfortable and probably contributed to this rifle's fine accuracy. My handloads, 300-grain Herter soft-nose bullets pushed to 2,420 fps by 81 grains of H4831, printed inside 1¼ inches.

Wayne shot this Nebraska buck with a CZ 550 in .30-06, with Leupold scope, Federal ammo.

The trigger came from the box at a manageable 2¾ pounds by my Timney scale. Set, it broke at just one pound. The bolt cycles more smoothly than a Mauser's, with the same subtle bumps. Cartridges slide dutifully from box to chamber with nary a hiccup save, occasionally, with the last round on the lift. The beefy stock and broad butt-pad help mitigate recoil. Its straight comb babies my cheek at the shot, then puts my eye quickly in the sights for a follow-up, and it's as well suited to a scope in medium rings like vertically split Talleys. Incidentally, Gary Turner, who runs the Talley shop, offers QD levers with CZ rings, so you can remove a scope for travel or iron sight use then replace it, no change in zero.

Sure, I'd prefer 22 lines-per-inch checkering instead of 18. And CZ Safari Classics wear fancier wood. But the American Safari Magnum is an *affordable* .375. Rugged, reliable, and accurate, it is a *hunter's* rifle, a suitable mate to the 550 in 9.3x62mm I carried to British Columbia for moose and goat. When you're many miles from another rifle, a CZ in hand is great comfort!

CHAPTER 18

A CENTURY OF SAKO

You needn't pronounce the real name.
These rifles from Scandinavia speak for themselves.

Sako's Model 85 comes in several forms.
One of the most appealing this .375 Kodiak,
with laminated stock, stainless steel, and
excellent open sights.

The moose stood patiently. *Bang!* The bolt snicked shut, the reticle danced. *Bang!* I crushed the last ounce from the third shot with only a second to spare. *Bang!*

The electronic scoreboard gave me a nine and two 10s. The moose moved off. He would have his revenge.

I thumbed three rounds into the Sako. From behind the block wall galloped the moose. Smooth as if on rails (because he was!), he sped ahead of my crosswire. I swung too fast, shot in front. Left to right, I managed to peg the wire behind his dewlap. Another right-to-left, and the rifle fired passing his shoulder. Two 10s and a zero.

"You must hit every shot." The stone-faced Finn said it matter-of-factly. Missing a moose at 80 steps is not allowed. "And before the buzzer."

I stepped once more to the line. The next six shots were ragged, but all landed in scoring rings, a hiccup ahead of deadline. The Finn regarded the board as if marking a record in charity. "We pass you."

Hardly an enthusiastic endorsement. Perhaps I'd fare better on real moose.

Compared to the sport in the U.S., Finland's hunting is highly regulated. I'm told that all game is managed by 300 state-sanctioned hunting associations that comprise, at this writing, about 2,370 clubs and 140,000 members. A Central Association of Hunters administers 15 game conservation districts. You needn't be a club member to hunt, but membership affords access to good spots. You'll appreciate access restrictions; 300,000 riflemen are looking for a moose with you, more per capita than in any other European country. Moose hunters spend a lot of money in Finland, and moose meat sold at market adds to the total. Roughly 84 percent of the 10 million kilograms of game—22 million pounds—marketed in Finland is moose.

Of course, the favorite moose rifle is a Sako.

Oddly enough, the first important Sako rifle was fashioned for hunting small game. The Vixen came out around the end of World War II, chambered for the .22 Hornet and .218 Bee. It was later offered in .222, .222 Magnum, and .223. Stoeger imported the Vixen to the States, beginning in 1946. A year later, Sako added a heavy-barrel version and a full-stocked carbine. In 1957, Sako expanded its rifle line with the L-57 Forester. Its action was sized for the then-new .308 and .243 Winchester. L-57s were chambered in .22-250 as well and, like the Vixen, came in Sporter, Carbine, and Heavy Barrel configurations. The L-61 Finnbear followed three years later, a longer action for the popular .30-06. Sako also offered Finnbear rifles in .25-06, .270, .264 Winchester, and 7mm Remington Magnum, and in .300 and .338 Winchester Magnum and .375 H&H. No heavy barrels, but the L-61 did appear in Carbine form.

In 1961, Sako introduced the Finnwolf, a hammerless lever-action rifle with a one-piece stock and front-locking bolt. Available in .243 and .308 with a four-shot detachable magazine, it lasted just a decade and was succeeded by the similar Model 73. This rifle left the line around 1975. Then, eight years under new owners, Sako was also redesigning its bolt guns. A new Model 74 replaced the Vixen, Forester, and Finnbear. Sako built three action lengths from 1974 until 1978, when the 74 gave way to the "A series"—the A1, A11, and A111 with short, medium, and long receivers. In the mid-1980s, Sako replaced them with the Hunter, again in three action lengths and now with a left-handed option. By this time, Sako was also producing the Model 78 rimfire, a refined bolt-action repeater in .22 Hornet.

Finnish-built Sako rifles are popular in Scandinavia, and also abroad, where the name is known for high quality, dependability, and accuracy.

Early Sakos were characterized by hand-checkered walnut stocks that, from the late 1950s, wore a glossy finish. Metal finish was uniformly excellent, the wood-to-metal fit showed care. Never inexpensive, Sako rifles earned a reputation for fine accuracy. Adjustable triggers and buttery bolt operation helped sell them to discriminating riflemen, dovetail receiver rails that required the purchase of costly Sako rings did not. The extractor was much smaller than the 98 Mauser's, but apparently matched its reliability.

In 1993, Sako's TRG rifle appeared. Designed for target and tactical shooters, it became available in a sporting configuration, too. The long, three-lug action incorporates a detachable straight-stack magazine. The TRG is best known as a .338 Lapua. Four years after its debut, Sako announced the Model 75 in four receiver lengths. Its three locking lugs are a departure from early sporters, reducing bolt lift to 70 degrees.

The Sako 85 Kodiak is equipped with a detachable box that's easy to load when it's in the rifle. You must be able to "top off" a dangerous-game rifle without dropping the magazine.

A two-position thumb safety is traditional. Barrels are hammer-forged, though automation has changed the process. One notable feature of the 75—its lockable bolt. A twist of the supplied key in the bolt shroud renders the rifle inoperable, or "safe," if you prefer that euphemism.

Various versions of the 75 are available in 18 chamberings, including .17 Remington and .22 and 6mm PPC. Order it in .340 Weatherby or .338 Lapua, or in 6.5x55mm, 7x64mm, or 9.3x62mm. Hunter, Hunter Stainless, and Deluxe versions wear walnut stocks and 22-, 24-, and 26-inch barrels. The walnut-stocked Battue has a quarter-rib and 19-inch barrel, the synthetic-stocked Finnlight a 20- or 22-inch stainless fluted barrel. Like the TRG, the 75 has integral top rails. Dovetail cuts, angled 3.7 degrees, accept Sako's Optilock mounts.

MUSCLE-BOUND, WITH GRACE

Sako followed the 75 with the 85. Not long ago, I chanced upon a Model 85 Kodiak, a handsome rifle in .375. It has the bearing of a dangerous-game rifle, with a muscular 21-inch barrel that wears useful iron sights, and a barrel-band swivel stud intelligently located just ahead of the fore-end, so you can indeed use a shooting sling. The hooded front bead is big and white and concave. It won't reflect light off-center, but it's quickly vis-

ible even to tired eyes like mine. It sits atop a graceful ramp screwed to the barrel. A tidy screw in front of the bead enables you to adjust elevation. The shallow "V"-notch rear sight is windage adjustable. It's perched on a contoured block. The sights are properly high enough to match the sight line established by the stock's comb, built to align your eye with low-mounted scopes.

The Model 85 action features a bolt with three lugs at three, nine, and 12 o'clock. A mechanical ejector at six o'clock operates through a slot in the bolt face. The extractor is a short, side-mounted claw that has survived decades with little change. The bolt body is round, with no anti-bind device. It runs with some rattle, but easily and without any ten-

This young lady found a Sako .270 just the ticket for a fine impala. This rifle was equipped with a suppressor, a noise- and recoil-reducing device accepted in Europe and Africa.

dency to hang up. There's no gas port in bolt or receiver, but a tapered shroud shields you in the unlikely event of a gas leak. A cocking indicator projects below the shroud.

The spring-loaded bolt release on the receiver's left side ducks smoothly beneath the bridge. Sako has retained the tapered dovetails for scope mounting. The left-hand receiver wall is flattened outside and angled. Flush-fitting crossbolts strengthen the stock either end of the sheet-steel magazine box. A forward magazine release drops the box conveniently into your hand, but the magazine must be pressed upward a bit to release the tab. This clever feature was engineered to prevent accidental magazine drops in the field. The magazine, by the way, fits flush, so you can tote this rifle comfortably by the belly. Still, it holds four rounds, even in .338 Winchester or .375 H&H Magnum. And it can be loaded easily while in the rifle!

The 85's sliding thumb safety has only two detents, but a tab in front of it lets you cycle the bolt with the safety on. Just press the tab and lift the handle. A long, gently curved trigger and generous guard accommodate gloves. Fresh from the box, the trigger on my Kodiak broke cleanly at three pounds, so I saw no need to adjust it.

Stocks also have much to do with field accuracy. The conservative profile of the Kodiak's stock enhances both its looks and handling, while affording the control you need to make center shots. Of gray-stained laminates, the stock has a comfortable cheekrest on a straight comb. The buttstock, capped by a half-inch black pad, has a long grip and deep flutes at the comb nose. The fore-end is comfortably tapered, slender enough for quick pointing, but with enough beef for control during recoil. Checkering panels have cleanly cut diamonds. There's a plug where the front swivel would be, so you can install one there if you prefer it to a barrel-band stud. The barrel floats, but does not wallow; this rifle is fitted with care. It

Wayne killed this eland with a Sako in .30-06, a rifle he has used repeatedly in Africa. The dovetail scope mounts don't give way.

also has what seems to me perfect balance. Weight falls right between my hands, a tad forward. Cheeking the Kodiak, I find the sights instantly. And they hold remarkably steady, the mark of fine balance.

All metal parts on the Kodiak are of stainless steel, claims Sako. I always assume that means the *major* metal parts, as there's always some little contracted component that isn't stainless. Regardless, it is by all measures a stainless rifle, ideally suited to foul-weather hunting.

Of course, accuracy matters, even in rifles for use on game the size of commercial refrigerators. When I benched the 85 Kodiak, I thought for a moment I'd picked up a varmint rifle. One series of shots left me staring at a single hole that looked so round I had to believe the other bullets had strayed. Not so. An anomaly? Perhaps. I can't shoot *that* tight. But any .2-inch group certainly speaks well of the rifle and load (260-grain Nosler AccuBonds, by Federal).

CHAPTER 19

ENCORE FROM FINLAND

Once it made sewing machines. Now under another roof, Tikka builds rifles—really good ones!

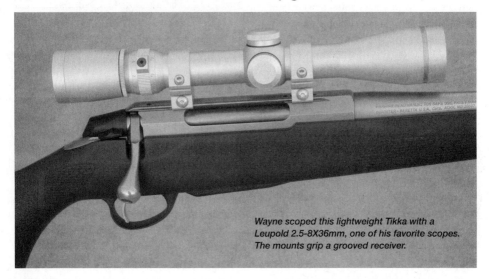

Wayne scoped this lightweight Tikka with a Leupold 2.5-8X36mm, one of his favorite scopes. The mounts grip a grooved receiver.

While the Sako rifle line should satisfy the needs of most shooters, it's not the only hardware that comes from Riihimaki. In 1983, Sako joined with another Finnish firm, Tikka, to produce the Model 555 rifle. A gun parts maker for 80 years, Tikka was older than Sako. During the second World War, it had built sewing machines and submachine guns, later abandoning its own sewing machines to design, produce, and market its Models 55 and 65 rifles and 17 shotgun. The 77 shotgun followed. The 555 venture resulted in Sako's acquisition of Tikka, along with Valmet, a manufacturer since 1925 that specialized in over/under shotguns. By 1989, Tikka's production at its Tikkakoski Works had moved to the Riihimaki plant. About then, Sako-Valmet in Tourula evolved to a partnership to manufacture shotguns in Italy.

HERITAGE OF RIFLES WELL BUILT

Sako and Tikka rifles hail from Riihimaki, almost small enough to be rural. The tallest structure in Riihimaki appears to be a church steeple, though apartments stacked high conserve heat during brutal Finnish winters. On my first visit, I ventured a pre-dawn jog down the streets of Riihimaki and passed many people out walking. Some carried ski poles and strode as if any minute snow and skis would appear beneath their feet. They wore the stoic expressions of people used to privation, who spend much of each year shivering, but little time complaining.

Helsinki, the capital, had seemed much the same. Along the docks before dawn, vendors bustled with tea and fish, cloth and trinkets. Boats backed to the thoroughfare served as booths. An aged woman under a canvas awning nursed a cup of coffee, as a cutting wind raked away the steam. At just over half a million, Helsinki's population includes about 10 percent of the country's Finns. Many locals are Swedish.

This rugged land was explored by Swedish missionaries as early as 1155, and Finland remained a Swedish protectorate until 1809, when it was surrendered to Russia. The Czar then proclaimed it a Grand Duchy. Finland didn't become an independent republic until 1919, two years after breaking with Russia.

The Finnish firm of Suojeluskuntain Yliesikunnan Asepaja was established April 1, 1919. It grew between the World Wars to supply rifles to hunters and target shooters. Along the way, someone decided that "Sako" was easier to say. Americans fumbled even that (the correct pronunciation, SOCK-oh).

The twin-lug T3 bolt has a plunger ejector and, predictably, a Sako extractor. The enclosed face adds security. Easily disassembled, the bolt also shows excellent finish.

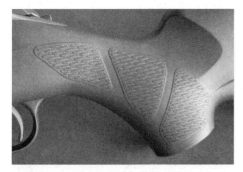

The T3 features intelligent texturing at the grip and fore-end, a help for slippery hands on wet hunts.

An uneasy peace between Finland and the U.S.S.R. ended in the winter of 1939-'40, when the Soviets invaded. Vicious fighting ensued, during what history records as the Winter War. More fighting followed in the Continuation War, while, to the south, the Nazis vanquished Europe. The Finns lost some land to the Soviets, but retained their independence. Hostilities ended in 1944.

The Swedish language is still taught in some schools. The Finnish tongue is closer to Hungarian, as it comes from the Finno-Ugric linguistic family. Sami, spoken in Lapland, is also an official language.

About 80 percent of Finland is timbered, and forest products account for 30 percent of exports. A patchwork of small farms reminiscent of our Upper Midwest supports growing numbers of whitetail deer. In 1934, six whitetails were imported from Minnesota. They escaped from an enclosure, in 1938. A decade later, six more fawns arrived from the States, four surviving until released. By 1960, Finland began hunting deer. Finns now shoot 17,500 annually. Whitetails thrive partly because there are few predators; wolves, a hazard to livestock and children through the late nineteenth century, were trapped and shot aggressively.

Sako's rifles come from a tough and lonely land. You'll find hardy, resourceful people here, and wild creatures ever on the cusp of survival.

THE U.S. FINALLY PAYS ATTENTION

Few U.S. shooters had heard of Tikka before its Whitetail rifle appeared in the early 1990s. But even that pitch to the American market failed to draw much attention. Then Tikka announced its T3, also built in the Sako plant and to the same tolerances as the more expensive Sako 75. It looked better than the Whitetail, sleeker and with a more distinctive profile. Paavo Tammisto, then press relations manager for Sako and Tikka, told me the aim was to reintroduce Tikka to shooters Stateside. Third-generation Tikkas included

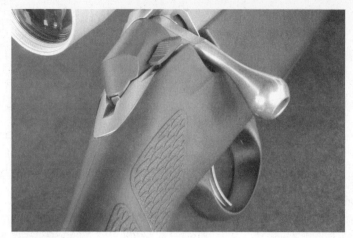

Tikka's T3 is made in the same plant as Sako rifles. Aficionados will note similarities, here in the bolt handle and shroud. In detail they differ from those of the Sako 85.

the two-lug bolt of earlier models, but with the 70-degree lift of the three-lug 75. The recessed bolt face had a plunger ejector and Sako extractor. The T3 receiver, slimmer than the Whitetail's, retained its rigidity, partly because the ejection port was smaller. Receivers were grooved for scope rings, but also drilled and tapped.

The first Tikkas came in two action lengths. There's only one T3, with two bolt stops for different cartridge lengths. Single-stack three-shot magazines are of quiet, lightweight polymer. You can buy deep boxes that hold five or six rounds, depending on the cartridge. The flush magazine latch is out of the way in front of the well. The stock (walnut or synthetic), has a long grip and correct pitch. Spacers supplied to lengthen the butt are a nice touch. Shadow ridges on the fore-end secure your fingertips, and raised, rubber-like panels on grip and fore-end keep your palms from slipping. Deep fluting at the comb nose opens to the heel of your hand. The polypropylene stock has detailing that makes it look streamlined.

T3 triggers adjust from two to four pounds, courtesy a hex key you insert through the magazine well without removing the stock. The trigger guard is the only alloy part on a T3 action; all other parts are of steel, save the polymer magazine and bolt shroud. The two-position safety locks bolt and trigger. A steel stock insert engages a slot in the receiver to serve as recoil lug. The barrel does not contact the fore-end. Hammer-forged rifling is the same as on Sako 75s. The T3 Lite weighs a feathery 6¼ pounds.

While superlatives are best used sparingly, I've since made exception when asked about the T3. It is technically excellent, with

A lightweight polymer box feeds the T3 with a straight-line stack. It doesn't rattle. Cartridges slide smoothly into the chamber.

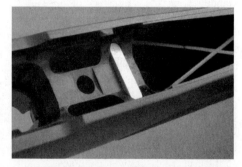

The T3's recoil lug, embedded in the fore-end, fits a slot in the receiver. Note the reinforcing ribs in the fore-end, to add stiffness.

a gunny feel that can't be described, but just as surely can't be faked. You know before you pick it up that, like Sako's 75, it was designed to shoot by people who shoot. The bolt glides. The trigger breaks like an icicle. Cartridges cycle without bumps. No, it's not perfect. I'd like an adjustment for sear engagement. And the safety button is hard to feel or move with a slippery thumb or a thick mitten. But few other refinements come to mind.

The first T3 in my hands wore a 24-inch barrel bored to .300 WSM, one of 13 chamberings from .223 to .338 Winchester Magnum. A 22-inch barrel is for standard rounds. In Finland, I carried this rifle behind a Norwegian elkhound and his handler. Our job was to move moose through the forest, so standers posted on roads and cuts would get shooting. The dog would follow scent, rooting moose from their beds. But our hound was prospecting elsewhere, when suddenly I spied a patch of moose hide. A cow moved across our front and stopped to listen. An alley to her forward ribs barely contained the wobblings of my crosswire. But when the Tikka recoiled, a 180-grain Fail Safe blew billows of steam into the shadows. She sprinted in a tight circle and collapsed.

It was not my last Finnish moose. The next, a young bull, trotted by at 70 yards,

The Tikka T3 comes with both wood and synthetic stocks and in a wide variety of chamberings. The adjustable trigger and accurate barrels get high marks from shooters.

but afforded no open shot. I held my fire. Quartering away, he climbed a hill and, for a moment, came clear of the poplars. Off-hand, I triggered a bullet to the off shoulder. The bull vanished.

Soon, one of the drivers appeared.

"Moose?" he asked. I nodded, but suggested we wait. If I had missed or winged the bull, the others would see him or move him. The posters appeared minutes later, and we climbed the hill. The bull lay dead, my bullet having drilled the lungs high into the far scapula.

When the T3 was introduced, the chrome-moly, synthetic-stocked version listed for just $549. The stainless synthetic rifle and walnut-stocked chrome-moly Hunter cost $618, magnums more. Since then, a weakened dollar has boosted prices. Still, the T3 is good buy, in many ways superior to popular American-made bolt guns. Tikkas in .30-06, 7mm Remington, and .300 Winchester Magnum later gave me one-inch three-shot groups. My best targets came prone, not all that surprising, as some lightweight rifles seem to respond well to sling tension.

CHAPTER 20

RIMFIRE: EVERYONE'S FAVORITE!

Tired of noise and recoil? Rediscover rimfires.
New loads are frisky and accurate—and still cheaper!

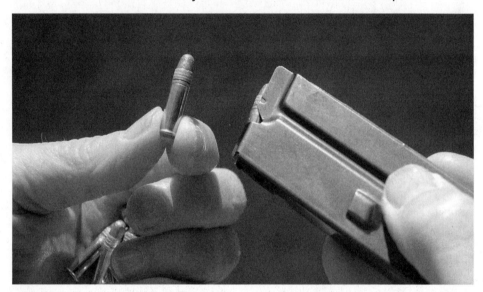

The prairie has a vastness that humbles. A train of Suburbans bearing rifles is, to the Big Empty, no more significant than the canvas-topped schooners that left wheels and pianos and their sickly young along the Oregon Trail. The shooters come, then they're gone. Hawks pluck at the carcasses of rodents unhinged by bullets so fast and fragile they've been known to come apart in the air. The prairie, though, cannot be breached by bullets. Wind yet bends their fragile arcs, and gravity pulls them to earth far short of the horizon.

"We have .223s, .22-250s, a Swift. Oh, yeah. Rimfires, too." What do you call him? Hunt Master? Trail Boss? One signed his correspondence "Dogfather." He was a friend. The

Developed by Horace Smith and Dan Wesson, in 1857, the .22 rimfire is still hugely popular. The .22 Long Rifle appeared in 1887.

ramrod of any prairie dog shoot has more to do than find sod-poodles. He must organize caravan and lodging, bring together enough ammunition to conquer a small republic, and play host to shooters who think they matter a great deal more than the prairie wind will allow.

"I'll take a .22." It's my choice, not a concession to those grabbing at the flossiest centerfires. I do appreciate a crisp trigger, as I do a scope enough to help me distinguish a rodent's eye from a stone at 50 steps. I bring a sling because no one else does. I learned long ago that seasoned prairie dog shooters fire from rests. A towel on the window ledge

While some shooters hit Dogtown with centerfires, the .22 Long Rifle is more fun and a lot cheaper. It also affords stalking and wind-doping practice for big-game hunting.

prairie dogs and, to a lesser extent, rockchucks, are pests. What they eat, cattle can't. Holes in the prairie may not be as lethal as legend has it, but they can twist ankles. Finding a place to shoot rodents is still much easier than getting permission to hunt big deer.

"See you at lunch." I'm not anti-social. I just think the best shooting on the prairie happens away from the masses. A brick of hollowpoints pulls my fanny-pack below belt-line as I trudge toward a green horizon. The sharp crack of Varminters and Swifts kicking polymer-tipped spitzers at 4,000 fps fades. I'm alone with a .22 under a wide blue sky. Hills stretch weeks into the distance. There's nothing electronic here. The land falls away into another swale. It looks the same, I think, as it might have before telephones had buttons instead of dials—heck, before telephones.

The sun is climbing, yellow now in a whitening sky. I feel its heat. It glints on something black in the shadow of sage ahead. Sliding into the sling, I check quickly for

will suffice. Better a swiveling bench bolted to the back of a pickup, with a bench-quality fore-end rest and a parasol for shade. An ice chest big enough to bury a cowboy with his saddle is the mark of professionals. Ditto a U-Haul trailer for the ammunition.

Sunny June days can yield hundreds of rodents to sharp-eyed riflemen taking lunch between shots and cooling barrels with water. Ranchers have learned to charge for the carnage, but some don't charge a lot, because

Weatherby has offered rimfire rifles, too. This beautiful bolt-action was built on an Anschütz action.

rattlesnakes and ease into prone atop a bald mound. The glint becomes an eye. Its skull shattered, the prairie dog cartwheels to the .22's report.

I've liked rimfires since the days I sat on a fence rail and shot barn rats with a Remington 121 and .22 Shorts. Peering through that J4 Weaver was like looking into a farm pond. I bought better glass for an Anschütz 1413, after shooting on a University smallbore team. Eley Match ammunition sped into one hole at 50 meters. A McMillan-barreled Remington 37 snared a second state title. By the time targets got too fuzzy in iron-sight stages, hunting-weight .22s had found their way to my rack. Cooper, Weatherby, and Kimber bolt guns joined the Marlin 39s, an autoloading T/C, and a Remington 121 that's as fetching as the borrowed rat rifle of long ago. A Ruger and a Savage in .22 WMR and a nail-driving Cooper in .17 HMR add reach on the prairie. Some .22s have stayed only a short time. I should have kept them all—surely the

Priming for a .22 rimfire is blown inside the rim, where the hammer or striker crushes it.

Browning BLR and Winchester 9422. I'm obliged to keep the Winchester 75 Sporter, an inheritance on my wife's side. "It's mine," she says. Had she owned them all, we'd still have them all, including the 52A with a 10X Fecker she used to thin ground squirrels near an Oregon farmstead.

CHOICE OF CHAMPIONS

Some centerfire shooters scoff at the .22 Long Rifle, as if it were okay for kids, but short the power and precision demanded by "real"

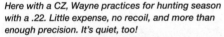

Here with a CZ, Wayne practices for hunting season with a .22. Little expense, no recoil, and more than enough precision. It's quiet, too!

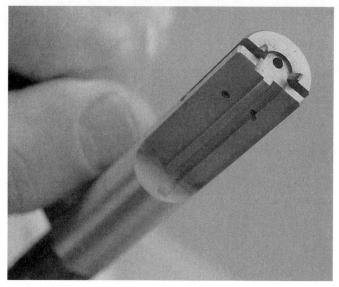

The best .22 bolt rifles feature dual extractors. This bolt is from a Cooper rifle.

riflemen. But the .22 has served the most talented exhibition shooters and competitors. Annie Oakley, Ad Topperwein, Herb Parsons, Tom Frye, and Tom Knapp have awed crowds with their rimfire exploits. Lones Wigger has earned a pile of Olympic medals with the .22, as have many other sharpshooters from the USAMTU (U.S. Army Marksmanship Training Unit), at Fort Benning.

Getting good with any rifle requires a lot of shooting. Few of us have the resources for that much practice with centerfires, or wish to endure for hours the noise and recoil of rifles potent enough for big game. The .22 rimfire is gentle, has been since Horace Smith and Daniel Wesson came up with the first of its kind, in 1857. The .22 Long Rifle arrived, in 1887, courtesy the J. Stevens Arms & Tool Company. A blackpowder cartridge with five grains driving a 40-grain bullet, it evolved to take smokeless in a case with a crimp for the heeled bullet. Remington claimed the first modern high-speed load, in 1930. Current .22 ammo includes friskier offerings, but they're all easy on the cheek and so quiet you can practice indoors. Feeding a .22 costs so much

less than stoking a centerfire, you can pick up a late-model Harley with the difference.

The main reason I pick a .22 over a centerfire for prairie jaunts is that it encourages me to *hunt*. A caravan of Suburbans laggered up as if to repel Zulu hordes has little to do with fair chase. You can't hunt from a bucket seat or a bed-mounted bench under a parasol. So equipped, you're on a *shoot*. Unless you pack a .22.

One of my rimfires is a Remington 504 with Leupold 4X scope. It's an accurate rifle with the feel of a centerfire. Okay, it's a bit lighter than the average '06, but six-pound deer guns have become common, and the 504 doesn't feel at all like the Nylon 66s of my youth that weighed just over four pounds. The

Wayne shot this 100-yard target in prone competition, with a McMillan-barreled Model 37 Remington. Wind-sensitive at this range, the best .22 ammo can also be very accurate!

full-size stock and between-the-hands balance make it, like my Cooper 57 and Ruger 77/22, a useful understudy rifle. The Leupold has been designed for rimfires, but with my eye to the glass, there's no telling whether the game is marmot or moose. The 504 wears the same Brownell's Latigo sling I use on big-game hunts. If I'm in a lever-action mood, I turn to an early Marlin 39 with receiver sight. I paid too much for it at a gun show, because the flint-eyed owner recognized uncontrollable lust. I rue the sale of my BL-22.

With a .22, I walk and stalk, using binoculars to spot prairie dogs or, on the bluffs above streams exiting the mountains, rock-chucks. Rather than take long shots, I crawl or belly in as close as possible. A short-range shot confirms a successful approach. Shooting long means more misses and cripples. Because rodents usually stay near their holes, you can't count on follow-ups to bad hits. And while some shooters tell me they don't care if their hits are quickly fatal because they're "only" prairie dogs, I take a different view. A bull elk may have more economic value and mean a good deal more to you in memory, but those antlers are inert. The elk and the prairie

Browning's ingenious and comely T-Bolt left for a time, then returned refurbished and in .22 WMR. Its detachable magazine is a modification of the spool design most notable in Savage's 99 lever rifle.

dog alive are both sentient and equally impossible to replace. A clean kill seems to me an imperative, no matter the quarry.

Solid .22 bullets work well enough on game the size of prairie dogs and Belding ground squirrels, but you'll find hollowpoints more surely lethal. The fast-stepping hollowpoints that have become flagship rounds for major ammo firms are especially deadly. Don't fret about ballistic coefficient. At .115 for the standard 40-grain solid bullet, the BC is so low that a hollow nose won't make much difference. The .22 bullet was intended for short shooting. From hunting positions, I limit field shots to 75 yards or so. Zeroed at 25, most high-speed .22 bullets land an inch or so high at 50, returning to sight line just shy of 80. As you hike the speed from, say, the old high mark of 1,300 fps to over 1,600, arcs don't get much flatter, but bullet upset with hollowpoints improves. I'm pleased by the terminal performance of new lead-free .22s.

THE MAGNUM GOES .17

If you want more reach, the .22 WMR (Winchester Magnum Rimfire), is a logical step. I recall the round, introduced in 1959, as pushing 2,000 fps with a 40-grain bullet. That claim proved a bit optimistic, and 40s are now listed around 1,900. New rimfire stables include hotter loads that exceed 2,100 fps with 34-grain bullets. The .22 WMR has its fans (I'm one), but many shooters correctly point out that it rarely drills tight groups. Occasionally I'll find a rifle and a load that like each other. The .22 WMR barks more loudly than the .22 LR, but you get twice the bullet energy from that noise, and recoil is still negligible. A 125-yard shot is well within reach of the .22 Magnum. New 30-grain V-Max loads from Federal, Hornady, and Winchester around 2,200 fps can be stretched even farther.

The .17 HMR (Hornady Magnum Rimfire), set rimfire circles abuzz, in 2001. A necked-down .22 WMR case corked by a 17-grain polymer-tipped bullet promised 2,550 fps and chalk-line flight. Maybe Hornady's gnomes knew it would also be supremely accurate—but I didn't, until I scrounged 10 of the first rifles chambered in .17 HMR. Velocity readings from my Oehler were nearly spot on: 2,545 fps from the 21-inch barrel of a Savage rifle. I was truly astonished by a subsequent 10-shot group at 100 yards; the bullets cut one hole less than half an inch wide! That rifle averaged 1.1 inches over five five-shot groups. Averages for Anschütz, Cooper, Marlin, and Ruger .17s each came in at .9-inch. I was stunned. Nothing since has drained my enthusiasm for this fast-stepping round. There's no kick, and the report seems to me less disturbing than that of the .22 WMR. The eye-ball precision of Hornady's tiny spitzers makes brain shots practical—and predictable—on small rodents. New 20-grain bullets buck the breeze better than 17s.

In the weeks following the .17 HMR's debut, Hornady (and Speer/CCI, which loaded Hornady's .17 bullets), logged orders totaling 12 million rounds. The cartridge was such a hit, the engineers in Grand Island followed with the .17 Mach 2, a necked-down

This autoloading Volquartsen in .22 WMR ranks among the finest of "special" .22s. Few autoloaders have successfully cycled the .22 Magnum.

This single-shot .22 on a southern Namibia farm killed a big bull kudu decades ago. "I was foolish to use it on big game," said the farmer. "But I was young. And lucky. I still got a hiding."

.22 Long Rifle. It works fine with a 17-grain bullet at over 2,000 fps. But it lags the HMR at market. Shooters satisfied with the Long Rifle hull evidently see no compelling reason to launch smaller bullets from it.

Prairie dogs and ground squirrels commonly come unhinged when struck with a .17 HMR bullet. I've found the cartridge lethal

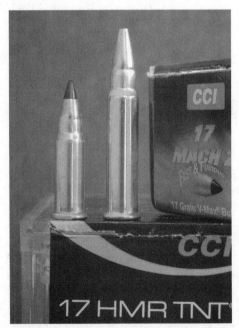

The .17 HMR (right) and .17 Mach 2 derive from the .22 WMR and .22 Long Rifle. Hornady introduced them. Both are fast, accurate. The HMR remains most popular.

on rockchucks, but its effect is not as sudden. In my view, a .22 WMR with 40-grain hollowpoints beats all .17 rimfires, when you're killing rodents big enough to barbecue. Yes, I've heard reports of coyotes dropping instantly to the .17 HMR. And it is, unquestionably, more accurate.

Whichever cartridge you pick, test various types of ammo. In rimfires especially, ammunition can make a big difference in group sizes. Competing in outdoor prone events, I'd get samples of different *lots* of Eley Match and shoot that expensive ammo in tests. Then I'd order half a case of the tightest-shooting lot. Sporting ammunition in sporting rifles might not deliver the consistency you'll need to justify sifting through lots, but still, you can find dramatic differences between *loads*.

Before you pile into that Suburban, make sure your rifle is zeroed! I've often found that rifles for communal use on the prairie are not precisely zeroed, and your pet rifle may need a tweak. If the sight line lands even an inch to the side of your bullet track at 50 yards, how many dogs will you brain at 75?

The true test of your commitment to rimfires comes when someone opens that coffin-size cooler and offers you a chilled can of something you'd like very much to drink. The telling response, as you hike that .22 higher on your shoulder, "No thanks! I'm going hunting!"

Rimfire Roundup

Ammo options for smallbore rimfire shooters have never been more plentiful. Most development has focused on hunting. Hollowpoint and polymer-tipped bullets excel for game bigger than prairie dogs. Standard-velocity solids are often most accurate; they work fine for sod-poodles and ground squirrels. For each manufacturer here, I've omitted loads duplicating the ballistic values of those listed. Units: velocity in feet per second, energy in foot-pounds, drop in inches with a 50-yard zero.

Brand name	load	muzzle vel./ energy	100-yd. vel./ energy	100-yd. drop
Federal .22 LR	31-gr. Game-Shok HP	1430/140	1050/75	7.1
Federal .22 LR	36-gr. Champion HP	1260/125	1000/80	5.6
Federal .22 LR	38-gr. American Eagle HP	1260/135	1010/85	5.5
Federal .22 LR	40-gr. Prem. Gold Medal	1200/130	990/85	6.0
Federal .22 LR	40-gr. Game-Shok HP	1240/135	1010/90	5.6
Federal .22 LR	40-gr. Champion	1240/135	1010/90	5.6
Lapua .22 LR	40-gr. Polar Biathlon	1106/109	914/74	8.0
Remington .22 LR	33-gr. Yellow Jacket T. C.	1500/165	1075/85	4.1
Remington .22 LR	36-gr. Viper Truncated Cone	1410/159	1056/89	4.7
Remington .22 LR	36-gr. Cyclone HP	1280/131	1010/82	5.5
Remington .22 LR	38-gr. Sub-sonic HP	050/93	901/69	7.7
Remington .22 LR	40-gr. Target	1150/117	976/85	6.2
Remington .22 LR	40-gr. Thunderbolt	1255/140	1017/92	5.6
Winchester .22 LR	26-gr. Varmint LF HP	1650/157	1023/60	4.2
Winchester .22 LR	32-gr. Xpediter HP	1640/191	1078/83	4.1
Winchester .22 LR	29-gr. Super-X sub-sonic	770/38	681/30	5.8
Winchester .22 LR	37-gr. Super-X HP	1280/135	1015/85	5.4
Winchester .22 LR	37-gr. Super Speed HP	1330/154	1038/88	5.1
Winchester .22 LR	37-gr. Varmint HE HP	1435/169	1080/96	4.8
Winchester .22 LR	40-gr. Super-X low-report	1065/101	922/76	6.4
Winchester .22 LR	40-gr. Super-X std. vel.	1150/117	976/85	6.2
Winchester .22 LR	40-gr. M22 LRN Black	1255/140	1017/92	5.5
Winchester .22 LR	40-gr. Power-Point HP	1280/145	1001/89	5.4
Winchester .22 LR	40-gr. Super-X	1300/150	1038/96	5.2
Winchester .22 LR	40-gr. Hyper Speed HP	1435/183	1070/102	4.8
Federal .17 HMR	17-gr. Prem. V-Shok TNT JHP	2530/240	1800/125	0.4
Federal .17 HMR	17-gr. Prem. Hornady V-Max	2530/240	1880/135	0.3
Hornady .17 Mach 2	15.5-gr. NTX Lead-Free	2050/149	1450/75	1.1
Hornady .17 Mach 2	17-gr. V-Max	2100/166	1530/88	1.0
Hornady .17 HMR	15.5-gr. NTX Lead-Free	2525/236	1829/119	0.4
Hornady .17 HMR	17-gr. V-Max	2550/245	1901/136	0.3
Hornady .17 HMR	20-gr. XTP	2375/250	1776/140	0.5
Winchester .17 HMR	15.5-gr. Varmint LF NTX	2550/224	1901/124	0.3
Winchester .17 HMR	17-gr. Poly Tip V-Max	2550/245	1915/138	0.2
Winchester .17 HMR	20-gr. Super-X JHP	2375/250	1776/140	0.5
Federal .22 WMR	30-gr. Prem. V-Shok TNT HP	2200/320	1420/135	1.3
Federal .22 WMR	40-gr. American Eagle FMJ	1880/315	1310/155	2.1
Hornady .22 WMR	30-gr. V-Max	2200/322	1421/134	1.3
Remington .22 WMR	40-gr. JHP	1910/324	1350/162	5.7
Remington .22 WMR	40-gr. PSP	1910/324	1340/159	5.8
Winchester .22 WMR	28-gr. Varmint LF JHP	2200/301	1394/121	1.2
Winchester .22 WMR	30-gr. Varmint HV V-Max	2250/337	1490/148	1.3
Winchester .22 WMR	30-gr. Varmint HV JHP	2250/337	1450/140	1.3
Winchester .22 WMR	34-gr. Varmint HE	2120/339	1435/155	1.4
Winchester .22 WMR	40-gr. Super-X JHP	1910/324	1326/156	1.7
Winchester .22 WMR	40-gr. Super-X FMJ	2200/301	1394/121	1.2

CHAPTER 21

THE AR TSUNAMI

Still all knees and elbows, they're shooting more accurately, hitting harder, and reaching farther.

Remington was the first to promote the AR-15 actively as a hunting rifle. Camo finish put it out of the "black gun" category. The rail for a scope became a must.

Just so there's no mistake, I'm sweet on rifles with walnut handles, and mechanisms that don't move until I decide they should. I prefer smooth, slim profiles, like those of a Maserati crouched on a strip of desert asphalt, a beautiful young woman stretched, sunning, on beach sand.

Back to rifles. The lithe, carnivorous lines of best-quality British doubles jack my pulse. They're hard to match in repeaters. Still, there's magic in the smooth musculature of pre-war Mausers, the racy silhouettes of early Mannlichers. Like John Browning's 1886, 1892, and 1894 lever-actions, these rifles trigger a visceral lust. We reach for them without knowing why, instantly seduced.

For shooters brought up on classics, the angular Armalite has as much appeal as a rock band at bedtime. To their credit, AR rifles cost little (my racks now hold four of them, and not one double rifle). They cycle fast and fire cheap ammo. They've become scope-friendly and reliable. Some shoot tighter than I can hold, and some have dared don colors other than black. But they cannot seduce.

"Perhaps you could learn to like electric automobile windows," suggested Alice the other day, out of the blue. Oh, sure. And seat-belt chimes, and doors that lock themselves. Having in another life plied skidder roads double-clutching a '63 Peterbilt with 20 unsynchronized gears and 30 tons of ponderosa on the bunks, I can't warm to a sedan draining its battery to protect me from myself. Makes as much sense as safeties on lever

NRA's Karen Mehall shot this Oklahoma buck with an AR-15 by Smith & Wesson. Deadlier bullets and new cartridges designed expressly for this rifle make it suitable for deer-size game.

guns. "Maybe," pressed my wife, "you could even learn to like ARs."

My pal Brian Schuetz concurred.

"I used to shoot only bolt rifles. But Olympic Arms is all about ARs. Building them, I've come to like them. They're truly versatile. Our Gamestalker has the reach and power of a .30-06. And it's not an AR-10, it's a 7¼-pound AR-15!"

Brian's .300 Olympic, on the .243 WSSM case, launches a 150-grain bullet at 2,975 fps from a 22-inch AR barrel.

"Bolt, carrier and extension are modified," he said. "But the upper fits any AR-15 lower."

Olympic's line includes three WSSM chamberings: .223, .243, and .25. There's a 7mm Olympic.

"We make a .22 Long Rifle upper with a .222 bore, plus recoil-operated ARs in 9mm, .40 S&W, and .45 ACP."

AR factory chamberings include more than 30 entries. From the .22 rimfire to the .50 Beowulf, even the compact AR-15 boasts versatility once attributed only to bolt guns. The 6.5 Grendel, .264 LBC, 6.8 Remington SPC, .30 Remington AR, and .450 Bushmaster hurl bullets legal for deer in all states that allow centerfire rifles. They land with more authority than .223s and function as well. I like all but the .450 Bushmaster,

The LAR-8 from Rock River features an up-sized AR action for .308 cartridges. The bolt release is a shoe behind the magazine. Otherwise, the rifle looks much like an AR-15.

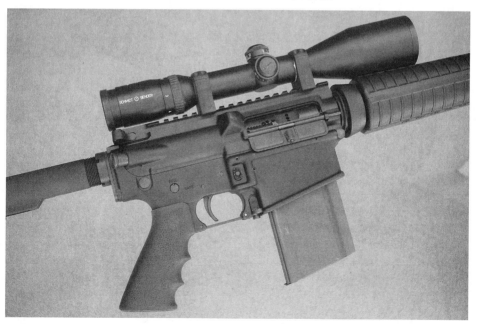

an unruly cartridge as regards blast and recoil. The 6.8 SPC (a short .270 on the old .30 Remington case), deserves more attention than it gets. I've used it to good effect on 400-yard targets, and on deer at 100. The .30 Remington AR is no .30-06, but with a 150-grain pointed Core-Lokt at 2,575 fps, it delivers more energy at 200 yards than the friskiest .223 loads at the muzzle! The .300 Olympic delivers a mix of bullet weight and speed once thought unattainable in a short-action self-loader. I've killed deer with the 6.8 SPC, as gentle and flat-shooting as the .257 Roberts. The 6.5mm Grendel and .264 LBC-AR bring X-ring precision to four-figure yardage.

The longer AR-10 action handles several bona fide big-game rounds. The .308 Winchester and .338 Federal clobber elk, moose, and big bears. I've taken elk with the .260 and 7mm-08, both available in AR rifles. DPMS now offers the 6.5 Creedmoor in its LAR series (AR-10) rifles. Recently, I killed an elk with this Hornady round at very long range.

Rock River is a big player in the AR arena. I've used several of its rifles, most recently the LAR-8 Varmint. It's an AR-10 chambered to the 7.62 NATO (.308). Besides its up-sized receiver (an A4 flat-top), the LAR-8 differs from AR-15 rifles most noticeably in its bolt latch. The release is not on a hinged tab on

Once beaten soundly by the .308 at 600 yards, the .223 with heavy match bullets in fast-pitch barrels can give good account of itself. Mild recoil is a bonus in 200-yard rapid-fire strings.

the left side, but a double-sided shoe forward of the winter (big) trigger-guard.

The heart of any rifle is its barrel. The 26-inch heavy stainless tube on my Rock River LAR-8 has a target crown (as does the 20-inch alternative). It is button-rifled 1:10, air-gauged, and cryogenically treated. The exterior is polished bright, in contrast to the satin black of receiver and handguard.

Rock River lists the two-stage trigger as its own. I found the take-up smooth and

Brand	Velocity (fps)	Standard deviation	100-yd. group (3 shots/inches)
Black Hills 175 BTHP	2669	28.0	1.2
Federal 165 TB High Energy	2857	19.2	1.2
Federal 175MatchKing	2685	8.7	.8
Fiocchi 150 SST	2961	20.5	1.2
Hornady 150 SST Light Mag.	3115	12.3	1.8
Hornady 165 IB (44 gr. Varget)	2720	7.0	1.2
Hornady TAP 168 A-Max	2739	19.0	.7
Lapua 185 SPRN	2597	22.4	1.5
Remington 125 SP Managed Recoil	2645	16.6	2.0
Remington 150 PSP Core-Lokt	2879	22.2	.6
Remington 165 Scirocco	2686	22.2	.9
Winchester 150 E-Tip	2853	27.8	2.0

short enough. At 4½ pounds, the let-off hardly qualifies as light, but it is consistent and clean. The A2 stock has a fixed swivel. A QD stud on the fore-end tube is properly placed for my Brownell's Latigo sling or a Harris bipod.

I scoped the Rock River Arms LAR-8 with Trijicon's fine 30mm 5-20X50mm. It has an amber tritium dot in a Mil-dot reticle, plus the signature fiber optic window, a side-turret parallax/focus dial, and resettable target knobs. At the bench, a Pact chronograph registered velocities at 15 feet. The chart to the left explains it, with group measurements:

My rifle bore out Rock River's 1 minute-of-angle accuracy claim. Remington's 150-grain Core-Lokts shot the tightest group at .6-inch. Scirocco bullets from Remington

cartridges also stayed inside a minute, as did Hornady's A-Max boat-tail hollowpoint and Sierra's MatchKing in a Federal load. I didn't have to discard targets to come up with good ones. Indeed, the LAR-8 Varmint A4 shot eight loads out of 12 into 1¼ inches!

Whether or not you think it a deer rifle, this AR is a champ ringing distant iron. You can hammer gongs to 600 meters with long bullets from a .223; beyond 600 the .308 rules. Want to bang 1,000-yard plates in wind? The advantage of Hornady's 168-grain A-Max or a 175-grain MatchKing over a 75-grain .22 is that of an ocean freighter over a dinghy in high seas. Rattling steel far off can be as much fun as killing big game, and more instructive. You needn't apply for tags, endure rough weather, or limit yourself to one

The .30 Remington AR, like the 6.8 SPC and several other short rounds, was developed for the AR-15. They hurl heavier bullets than the .223, a benefit to deer hunters.

shot per annum. And, if you want a rifle that shoots gently, nips sub-minute clusters, and supports comfortably the powerful scopes needed for distant targets, there's no better pick than this LAR-8 from Rock River!

Remington's R-15, like the fine rifles from Rock River, Stag, Olympic, and other makers, was offered first in .223, but now chambers other compact rounds. An up-sized action handles the .308 family.

Cosmetically, the AR will never charm traditionalists. It can't climb as high on horsepower charts as bolt rifles or, on balance, shoot quite as accurately. But ARs I've used, from DPMS, Remington, Rock River, Stag, and others, have performed better than expected. The AR is still awkward to cradle, and the high line of sight seems a geometric transgression. I'd rather rest my cheek on figured walnut than on a metal pipe, grip the stock *behind* the trigger and pluck empties from a smoking breech.

Then again, I still prefer window cranks in pickups.

THE MOST POPULAR CARTRIDGE IN DECADES

The number of prairie dogs shot with the .223, or 5.56 NATO, is growing faster than our national debt (well, almost). Thank

The huge and growing selection of .223 ammunition helps AR shooters get the most from their rifles and precisely match the load to the application.

the AR-15! But the .223 is also popular in "Moundville," because the ammunition is inexpensive and doesn't crack your molars when you fire it. Sales of .223 rifles have generated a spate of new loads, too: soft-nose, hollow-point, and poly-tip bullets, 35 to 77 grains.

The .223 appeared, in 1957, as an experimental round for Armalite's AR-15 combat rifle. Adopted in 1964 as the 5.56mm Ball cartridge M193, it owed much of its success to Bob Hutton, technical editor of *Guns & Ammo*. With Gene Stoner of Armalite, Hutton paired a 55-grain bullet with a case a tad longer than the .222's to meet the spec for retained velocity: supersonic at 500 yards. With an exit speed of 3,250 fps, the M193 load was issued to U.S. forces in Vietnam, and after the war until 1984. In 1980, it got the blessing of NATO countries, which substituted the FN-designed 62-grain SS109 boat-tail bullet with a mild steel-penetrating component. The SS109 left the muzzle at 3,100 fps and hit harder at long ranges than the 55-grain boat-tail. Faster barrel twist (a change to 1:7), gave it superior accuracy, as

well. The U.S. Army called the new load the "M855."

The AR-15, with its small, high-speed bullets, was designed to shoot people. While exceptions abound, people are relatively fragile creatures. Soldiers firing .30-caliber rifles in jungle environs were, it seemed, over-gunned. Where shots were short, the enemy slight of build and often concealed, rate of fire and magazine capacity could count for more than downrange energy. Weight savings in ammunition had become important, when the bolt-action battle rifle was supplanted by hungry self-loaders. A selective-fire M16 could chatter through a magazine while an infantryman of the old school was cycling the bolt on his Mauser or Springfield. The .308 (7.62 NATO) shaved cartridge length and weight, but didn't appreciably reduce the load in a soldier's pack. The .223's bullet weighed only a third as

The .264 LBC (for Les Baer Custom) is much like the 6.5 Grendel, an accurate, efficient round that gives the AR-15 greater effective reach than the .223 at targets and game.

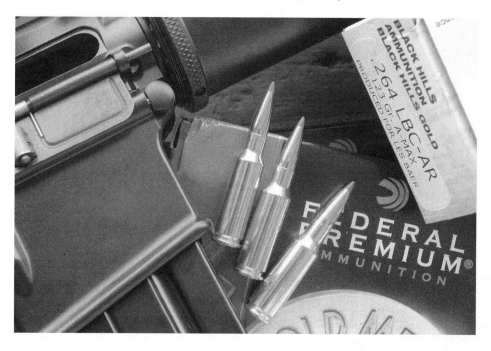

much as the .30-bore spitzers of mid-century, and it laid people low.

Big game is hardier, pound for pound. And big bucks are getting bigger where supplements give them feedlot finish. Conventional wisdom has it that .22 centerfires do not kill deer reliably. Lists of legal hunting cartridges commonly start at .243. Oddly enough, the .38-40 passes muster, as does even the .25-20, and carbines in .44-40 killed a lot of deer.

Wait a minute. The .44-40's 200-grain bullet in a Winchester factory load registers 630 ft-lbs of energy at exit, and 450 at 100 yards. That's substantially more than the .38-40 (540 and 325), a great deal more than the .25-20 (410 and 275). But it falls short of the energy generated by Winchester 55-grain .223 Ballistic Silvertip, 1,280 and 1,005 ft-lbs. You could argue that this bullet was not designed for big game, that the killing power of a 200-grain .44-caliber bullet is underrated in energy tables. Still, Winchester's 64-grain Power Point, started at 3,020 fps instead of 3,240, has about the same muscle as the 55-grain. So does Hornady's 60-grain TAP FPD load. Both are deadly on deer with shots through the forward ribs. So, too, the 62-grain Remington Core-Lokt Ultra Bonded, leaving at 3,100 fps with 1,325 ft-lbs. Federal's 64-grain soft-point at 3,050 fps carries equal authority. A Hornady 75-grain TAP FPD, clocking 2,790, lands a heavier blow at distance than do its brethren that beat it off the blocks.

All .223 hunting ammunition shoots flatter than traditional lever-gun loads. The 117-grain .25-35 bullet, widely considered adequate for whitetails at woods range, just matches the muzzle energy of frisky .223s. At 100 yards, it is 100 ft-lbs weaker. At 200, where 55- and 60-grain .223s retain 780 ft-lbs—the Hornady 75 TAP tops 900—the 117-grain .25-35 yields only 620 ft-lbs. This is not to call the .223 an ideal big-game round. Hardly! But recent .223 ammo includes deadly deer loads, like those from DRT.

Dynamic Research Technologies is based in Grant City, Missouri, but the lead-free, high-performance .223 ammo used by law en-

Some hunters say the .223 isn't suitable for deer in cover. Actually, it's as good there as in the open. The object, when you fire, is to shoot <u>between</u> the branches.

Short barrel or long? Direct impingement or piston gas tube? Fixed stock or adjustable? ARs have proliferated to offer many options. Iron sights matter mostly to match shooters.

A deer hunter steadies his S&W M&P-15 on a BogPod tripod. Precise bullet placement is especially important with cartridges like the .223.

80 yards, the deer facing me. I took a center hold through the Trijicon scope and triggered the S&W M&P15. The deer spun and bolted. Streaking through the oaks, it died at full throttle, piling up against a tree a few yards away.

The use of centerfire .22s on deer didn't start with Stoner's rifle. Hunters prowling Pennsylvania alfalfa with converted Mausers and Lyman Super Targetspots during my youth knew woodchuck loads for the .219 Donaldson Wasp would put the skids under whitetails. These marksmen handloaded the .220 Swift with wind-worthy bullets that carried death in chalk-line arcs. One shooter in the Southwest desert found the Swift upended wild burros. The .22-250 isn't far behind. Jerry Gebby apparently named it the "Varminter," in the 1930s, though Charles Newton, who developed the .250 Savage, in 1912, may have necked it early on to .228. Spitting 64-grain spitzers at 3,500 fps, the .22-250 brings more energy to 100 yards than 170-grain soft-points from the .32 Special! Other fast-stepping .22s, from the .225 Winchester to the .224 Weatherby and .223 WSM, deliver the same package. To leave the .223 Remington out of this club is to dismiss the most popular .22 centerfire ever, and the one that now accounts for more game, big and small, than any other!

forcement agencies is now available to hunters through CorBon, of Sturgis, South Dakota. The DRT bullet is powdered metal in a copper jacket. Upon striking flesh, the jacket ruptures and the core disintegrates. There's nothing left to recover. But the wound channel is broad, and also deep enough to destroy the lungs. DRT literature makes much of hydraulic damage and the bullet's centrifugal force. I can't buy into every claim—such that even marginal hits kill routinely—but I do know the whitetail I downed, and others my colleagues shot with this bullet, died quickly. My chance came at

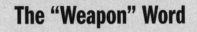

The "Weapon" Word

Firearms have long had identity crises. "Six-shooter," "Single Action Army," "Peacemaker," and "1873 Colt" should bring to mind the same revolver. But "M1" could mean the Garand or the Carbine. "Tommy gun" is a nickname. So, too, "Brown Bess" and "Yellow Boy." Manufacturers try to help out with catchy, descriptive names, "Auto 5," for example. But "BAR" applies to both the original Browning and a lighter, less aggressive hunting rifle. Confusion benefits no one.

So I take exception to the use of "weapon" in describing firearms never intended to be weapons— and even those that were. "Weapon" has nothing to do with a mechanism or a firearm type. It refers only to use. My .22 prone rifle, a Remington 37, can be a weapon, but it was designed expressly to drill holes in paper. A best-quality British 20-bore could be a weapon, but the fellow mortgaging his cottage to buy one probably wants it to shoot grouse or dress up a gun room. A Hammerli target pistol is a concealable weapon—but only in the hands of an assailant who can't, instead, find a Glock.

A steak knife can be a weapon; we call it a utensil. An automobile can be a weapon; we call it a vehicle. A hammer can be a weapon; we call it a tool. The trouble with calling any firearm a weapon is that it unfairly imputes purpose. "Lever-action" denotes function, "carbine" dimensions, "Winchester" manufacture. "Pre-war" dates the rifle, "Model 94" differentiates it. All have to do with the firearm's physical characteristics. All are useful in description, as is the chambering. "Weapon" is the odd word out, because it specifies use. It is misleading, because John Browning didn't design the 94 Winchester as a weapon. Call it a deer rifle or a saddle gun, and you'd be close enough to get a pass from any word maven. Relatively few Model 94s have been used as weapons, that is, have been fired at adversaries.

This Bushmaster Carbon-15 Superlight has the profile and features popular with most AR shooters.

Actually, the same can be said for many modern rifles commonly perceived as weapons. The AR, for instance. Officially the U.S. infantry arm, the M-16 might also answer to "battle rifle," even "assault rifle." It's been called a weapon often enough in military service that soldiers with few other firearms credentials naturally hew to the military jargon. Sadly, in civilian circles, "weapon" can ring as both inappropriate and libelous. It inaccurately describes the AR-15s used for hunting and target shooting. It brands, as well, the riflemen who will *never* wield them as weapons. That's most of us. Even people who keep a loaded AR in the corner to defend life and property will seldom be forced to use it that way. I own more firearms than a lot of people would say I need. I've never used any as a weapon. So I don't describe them that way—not even the Smith & Wesson 66 I carried as a service revolver when working as a state wildlife agent.

Labeling firearms as weapons, you imply to people who know nothing about either that the words are synonyms. Citizens concerned about crime can be led quite easily to support tight government control of weapons. After all, we fear proliferation of nuclear weapons. That same logic begs limiting weapons on the street. If firearms are weapons—as television insists—isn't it reasonable to restrict them?

For every firearm used as a weapon, hundreds of thousands reside in collections (or at bedside) or serve competitors and hunters at the target range and in the field. This isn't to say firearms have no place as weapons in the hands of civilians. The use of weapons by law-abiding citizens can be both justified and desirable. But to impose that application on all firearms is to unfairly diminish their vastly more prominent role as sporting implements.

The focus of the shooting public has taken a militant turn of late, arguably to the detriment of the shooting sports. Not long ago, marketing campaigns featured youngsters, grandpas, and buttoned-down marksmen. Illustrations showed deer and bears, squirrels and crows, knots in black bull's-eyes, and perforated tin cans. You'll still find the old outdoors in catalogs and ads hawking traditional sporting arms—albeit the plaid mackinaw has given way to licensed camouflage patterns, itself a shadow of armed force. The AR rifle is not yet, alas, comfortable in the white wall tent.

A cottage industry in hardware that can be hung on Picatinny rails also plays to Special Forces wannabes. Catalogs of firms that manufacture sights for a wide range of rifles now present police and assault teams in combat dress—one example of an industry that can't resist playing to the "black ops" image. While self-defense is surely a legitimate reason to own a firearm, and soldiers and police officers do merit our support, the advertising emphasis on firearms as *weapons* is chilling—at least to the many shooters who recall magazine ads dominated by red plaid instead of S.W.A.T. uniforms.

In my youth, lever-action air guns like the Daisy Red Ryder trailed TV westerns and sold briskly. The AR has adopted the commando in place of the cowboy. Some of us who have seen both, prefer the cowboy. Like the storm trooper, he was always ready to stand and fight. But he showed more courtesy than hubris. He spoke politely. He even sang.

Before you dismiss such nostalgia as simply that, consider the current alternative—and the future of a firearms culture controlled by people whose only contact with shooting is on screens that show black autoloaders pointed at people. We who grew up playing Cowboys and Indians, before Indians became Native Americans, pointed sticks at each other. But we also admired the classy demeanor of our heroes, and their humility. We didn't use make-believe Winchesters and Colt's to exterminate vermin, but to bring justice to the neighborhood. We didn't wear dark glasses or grimaces; we wore colorful bandannas and we smiled a lot.

People who watched us smiled, too.

CHAPTER 22

RIFLES THAT SHOOT FAR

Riflemen crave more hits at greater distance.
This hardware surely marches to that beat.

H is group measured 14 inches by 36, less than a vertical minute of angle at 1,760 yards—a mile! But even 300-grain .338 match bullets drift in wind.

"Three feet. And it was a still day."

Preston Pritchett began building rifles on his own actions five years ago, in his machine shop near Prague, Oklahoma. Disarmingly modest, he talks with a drawl, engages you with a boyish grin. Pritchett's specialty is heavy rifles that shoot exceedingly well at long range. Testimonials abound, like this one from a Montana hunter:

I've been running 155 [-grain] Scenars at 2,980 fps ... with a 5-25X Schmidt & Bender PM2 ... . I've taken 96 coyotes [16 at] over 500

For really long shots, the .50 BMG is hard to beat. Here a class of shooters practices with their Barrett .50s at the NRA Whittington Center near Raton, New Mexico. Yes, they rattle the windows.

meters. The longest shot [was] 1,120 meters.

That hunter also claimed a "five-shot group at 750 meters that went just under 2½ inches."

These days, high-velocity ammo and powerful optics encourage even casual riflemen to shoot far. F-Class competition for amateurs has joined traditional long-range events like the Palma Match. But what features enable rifles to hit reliably beyond normal hunting ranges? Say, 1,000 yards?

Pritchett shrugs. "A good barrel and a rigid action. We like Krieger barrels cut-rifled 1:11

for .308s, 1:9.35 for the .338 Lapua. We're particular about crowns." Short and long actions for Pritchett's Surgeon rifles are built on site, with CNC tooling and an electrical discharge machine that holds tolerances to half a tenth. That's half a *ten-thousandth* of an inch. Eight-inch receivers vary less than three-tenths, end to end.

A magnum receiver weighs 19½ pounds before milling.

"We cut all our actions from bar stock. We thread the barrel shank and mill the action face and lug abutments with the receiver secured in one fixture," says Pritchett. "Surfaces stay square and true."

Final machining follows heat-treating to 40 C Rockwell, to eliminate heat warp. Each bolt is machined from 4140 bar stock and tapers slightly to the front to limit play. Nitride treatment of bearing surfaces prevents galling. An Picatinny rail adds 20 minutes of elevation to the short-action, 30 minutes to the long-action. You can zero a Surgeon rifle at distance without running out of clicks or moving the erector tube far from the sight's optical axis.

Short-action rifles wear the Remington extractor, long-action bolts a claw fitted inside the right-hand lug. "It throws the case out in a low arc to target knobs on scopes," Pritchett uses Jewell and Remington triggers and McMillan stocks, pillar bedded. Charles Cowden of the Oklahoma Highway Patrol chose a Surgeon rifle with a Schmidt & Bender 5.5-20X Tactical scope on the agency's sniper course. His groups measured ".2 minute at 400 yards, .4 minute at 500 yards, .3 minute at 600."

ACCURACY FROM ALIGNMENT

All Preston Pritchett likes in a long-range rifle shows up in the long-action, 16-pound Remedy he loaned me. Equipped with a two-pound Jewell trigger and a 4.5-14X Leupold LRT scope, this .338 Lapua put my first three factory loaded Hornadys into a .2-inch hole.

"It's just 100 yards," shrugged Pritchett.

Springfield Armory built this rifle, a .308 that delivers tight groups at distance. The "tactical" rifle is gaining popularity, though for long shots the bolt-action still rules.

Wayne handloaded for the .338 Norma (a shortened .338 Lapua) and a rifle on a Remington 700 action with Krieger barrel, Pacific Tool bolt, and gunsmithing by Freudenberg. It's a solid long-range outfit.

Indeed. But not all long-range rifles shoot that well up close. "Groups can improve as bullets go to sleep," says D'Arcy Echols, who builds the most consistently accurate magnum hunting rifles I've seen. In 1996, Echols was turning out four exquisite, walnut-stocked sporters a year from his Utah shop. To produce more affordable rifles, he committed to a mold for a high-end synthetic stock with classic lines. His Legend is a Winchester Model 70 with many refinements: re-machined receiver

belly, bolt face, receiver face, recoil lug seats and lugs; lapped locking lugs; new pins in the trigger, ejector, and bolt stop to remove play; reconfigured ramp and rails; stainless five-round magazine box and follower engineered to the cartridge; custom bottom metal; steel scope rings machined to receiver contours and secured with five 8x40 screws.

Echols attributes the performance of his rifles to tight tolerances. "I surface-grind receivers on a mandrel between centers, so each is within half a thousandth of parallel with the bore." A special gauge ensures perfect bore/chamber alignment. Most Legend rifles weigh around nine pounds with mid-weight, 26-inch Krieger barrels in .300 Weatherby, "though we've built some .300 Winchesters."

Echols lets bullets coast just .125-inch before engaging the lands, a third of the start they'd get in Weatherby rifles. "The throat—that unrifled section of bore in front of the chamber—can be short or long, parallel or funnel-shaped," he explains. "It allows the bullet shank to protrude from the case with-

A bullet may have to travel far across Alberta stubble. This hunter took care with his shot and made it good. Cartridges like the .270 and .280 and the 7mm magnums excel here.

out engaging the rifling, and it gives the bullet a running start. Funnel-shaped throats, from blackpowder days, allow more bullet waggle than do parallel throats .0005-inch over bullet diameter." The funnel throat for the .300 Winchester Magnum is .3-inch at the rear of full-depth rifling, .315 at the case mouth. A parallel throat that allows the bullet to slide like a piston offers more guidance than does a tapered throat. But because bullet diameters vary, parallel throats must not be too tight.

The closer a bullet's fit in the throat, the less critical is throat length.

"A long-throated rifle is said to have freebore, but there's no dimension that defines that, so the term is really meaningless," D'Arcy says. "Besides, the most critical factor in accurate shooting at long range is the shooter."

Texas gunmaker Charlie Sisk agrees.

"Most rifles shoot better than most shooters," Sisk observes. "You can't flinch. Also, *the rifle must be held exactly the same every time*. The striker sets up vibrations as it falls, before the bullet exits. Pressure from the rest and your hands affect those vibrations, as well as barrel alignment as *it* vibrates during bullet passage!"

Among rifle components, Sisk says the barrel matters most. He told me, "I use Kriegers and Liljas. Others are good, too. It's as important to have all components—barrel, receiver, mount, rings, scope—pointed at the same spot. That's not as easy to achieve as it sounds. Few factory rifles have trued actions and perfectly aligned barrels with concentric chambers. Scopes and mounts lack the stress-free fit you need for accurate shooting at extreme range. Minor flaws in hardware that don't show up at 100 yards become visible at 300, astounding at 1,000. Distance magnifies problems."

Chamber dimensions affect accuracy. To accept all factory ammo, whose dimensions vary, and to allow easy loading under field conditions, chambers in hunting rifles are generous. Their dimensions also hinge on the reamer's condition.

"A well-used reamer may produce a chamber .012-inch smaller in diameter than one cut with a new reamer," says Charlie.

Because brass stretches, loose fit doesn't

The GreyBull/Leupold scope dial is machined to your specific load, so you can turn it to a known distance, hold center, and plant a bullet right there. It has ¹/₃-minute clicks for increased range.

Prone in prairie grass, Wayne steadies a heavy-barreled .33 wildcat on a Remington action. The 4.5-14X Leupold is standard GreyBull fare. It has given him saucer-sized groups at 780 yards.

matter to hunters. But, for tight groups at long range, you'll want a snug chamber fit.

Ammo matters, too.

"I spin bullets to sift out those with variations in jacket thickness," says Sisk. "Once, after spinning, I measured groups from the best and worst lots. The most uniform bullets printed groups a third as big as the others." He favors Berger bullets and Sierra MatchKings. "Concentric bullets at uniform velocities deliver the best accuracy. High ballistic coefficients minimize drift."

Sisk emphasizes that stiff barrels and actions deliver the best accuracy.

"Long barrels have more flex than short ones of the same diameter. That's why some very accurate rifles have stubby barrels. I also like relatively sharp rifling twists. Heavy bullets spun fast may give mediocre performance at 100 or 200 yards; they take awhile to stabilize. But, at long range, they shoot flatter and with less wind deflection than light, quick-stepping bullets; groups, measured in minutes of angle, actually improve."

I met Rick Freudenberg years ago on the Seattle waterfront, near where he builds target rifles that drill tiny groups. His own hunting-weight .30/284 shoots into half a minute.

"I like it because it delivers .30-06 velocity from a more efficient case."

He's built .308 rifles for Palma matches, using three-groove Lilja barrels with a 1:13 twist and a 155-grain Palma bullet in front of Varget powder. He also favors the 6.5-284 with Sierra's 142-grain MatchKing.

"At 3,000 fps, both these loads shoot flat, with tolerable recoil."

Freudenberg has also used muscle rounds like the .330 Dakota and .338 Lapua. A .300 Dakota on a Kelby action with a McMillan stock is "competitive at 600 to 1,000 yards with 190-grain MatchKings."

For matches like the Palma, with its iron-sight stages, Freudenberg boosts sight radius with a 31-inch barrel.

"Irons or a scope," he says, "you need a mirage band (an elastic strap from receiver to muzzle to keep heat waves from distorting the sight picture), for extended fire. I've also used a tube from a roll of Christmas wrap on my scope's objective."

Freudenberg says many shooters don't get the reticles square with the action.

"Tilt the scope a bit or cant the rifle, and you won't see much effect at 100 or 200 yards. But at 1,000, adjustments will move point of impact off-axis, and you won't be able to shade reliably for wind."

One thing these accomplished riflesmiths agree on: disciplined practice from field positions is the only way to ensure hits at distance. Holding the rifle still and releasing each shot cleanly will improve results more dramatically than can a rush to new hardware.

CHAPTER 23

STOPPING RIFLES

You want the beast to hit a brick wall. Now. Or you pay dearly. These rifles bring the bricks.

African PH Don Heath wisely blends with an anthill as he steadies his double rifle against it. Even when it gives you little protection from huge beasts, such cover can delay their finding you!

I t is the middle of an African night.

"You were bloody lucky."

The PH was right. I'd sent Philip back to camp late in the afternoon. The bush was long in shadow. Alone, I trekked toward a small *vlei*, hoping to find a sable. Shy of the water, I came across the trail of elephants. Snapped limbs on twisted trees were stripped of leaves. Sand trampled in a wide swath bore tracks the size of dinner plates and manhole covers. The animals were going my way.

I found them in the *vlei*. There were many, well scattered and no longer traveling. The rumblings and trumpetings claimed ownership here. A red sun set at I looked for a way around the herd, now sifting into the bush on all sides. Bumping into an elephant in the dark held little appeal. The only thin spot was

behind four cows. I figured if they got my scent, they'd move enough to let me slip past. I eased upwind.

The effect was electric. Instead of moving away, they came. I read their intent clearly, dropped to my knees, and scurried as fast as I could crosswind, until a wall of thorn stopped me. Pressed to the earth, I heard the grass swish against their legs, their towering black forms obliterating an orange horizon. At 20 steps they stopped, trunks up, seeking. The wind held. After long minutes, they left. When later the Land Cruiser found its way through dark bush to find me, the herd charged it, driving it off.

I've since shot elephant, and stood for bluff charges to let young bulls grow bigger. I've not been so frightened as when prone in that long grass 27 years ago, heart hammering, powerless.

Yes, I did have a rifle, a Model 70 in .300 Holland. But it would hardly have stopped an elephant, let alone four. Its soft-nose bullets weren't meant to drive through thick skulls or break massive bones. The difference between stopping rifles and those for killing undisturbed game is significant. And for both, the ammunition can matter more than the rifle in putting animals down. Rifle, sights, and loads *all* contribute.

In stopping rifles, accuracy counts for little. We've come to disparage deer rifles that don't keep groups near a minute of angle (1.047 inches at 100 yards). But one MOA is more precision than you need in a tight place.

Recently, I fired a Merkel double rifle. At 100 yards, right and left barrels printed to point of aim vertically, four inches apart horizontally. The right barrel shot to the left of the left barrel. This isn't bad accuracy for

One advantage of the double rifle, a low line of sight. You point fast, as with a shotgun!

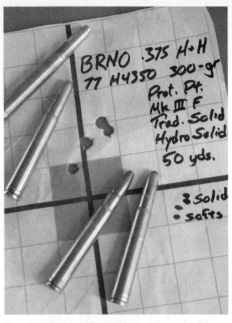

This .375 put four different loads, softs and solids, 1½ inches above point of aim at 50 yards. That's ideal, in Wayne's view. A stopping rifle should shoot "to the sights" from 20 to 100 yards.

a double. In fact, it's good. To shift impact points with doubles not so compliant, you start by changing loads. Should the rifle still not shoot to the sights, you must move the barrels relative to one another. My friend

Not long ago, I fielded a question on deer rifles: Is the 7mm Magnum adequate for hunting in the West? Well, deer now are a lot like deer felled by the gazillions with the .44-40, whose bullets trudged downrange at 1,300 fps packing 760 ft-lbs. A 7mm Magnum bullet leaves at a blistering 3,300 fps with a payload of 3,500 ft-lbs.

In similar fashion, the bar on stopping rifles has risen. John Taylor's 1948 book, *African Rifles and Cartridges*, hails the .375 H&H. It is, wrote Taylor, deadly on heavy game:

> *I've … fired more than 5,000 rounds of .375 Magnum ammunition at game … . One [rifle killed] more than 100 elephant and some 411 buffalo … .*

Graeme Wright explains all this in his fine book, *Shooting the British Double Rifle*.

The Merkel's four-inch horizontal dispersion is well within limits, because the bullet paths cross, left to right and right to left. To 80 yards, shots hit within three inches of each other—surely close enough to drop a beast the size of a golf cart. This rifle shoots where it should.

Sights for a stopping rifle must be easy to find quickly. I prefer a big, flat-faced or concave ivory bead in a shallow, fixed "V" or in a wide-open aperture sight. No folding leaves, please; open sights aren't for long shooting! A low-mounted scope with a bold, simple reticle also makes sense on a stopping rifle. So does a sturdy, compact red-dot sight from Trijicon or Aimpoint.

The .375 still quiets angry beasts. A wide variety of fine soft-point and solid bullets give it more versatility than its big-bore brethren. Manageable recoil allows riflemen to shoot it more accurately in rifles of modest weight.

VOICES FROM THE VELDT

John Hunter, whose career spanned the shift from commercial ivory hunting to sporting safaris, relied on "a .500 double-barrel hammerless ejector fitted with 24-inch barrels and weighing 10 pounds 5 ounces made by Holland & Holland." He insisted that it is unwise "to hunt elephant, buffalo, or rhino with a gun of less than .450 caliber." Like Taylor, John Hunter killed enough big game during the halcyon years of African hunting that his opinion matters. Gun bearers no doubt influ-

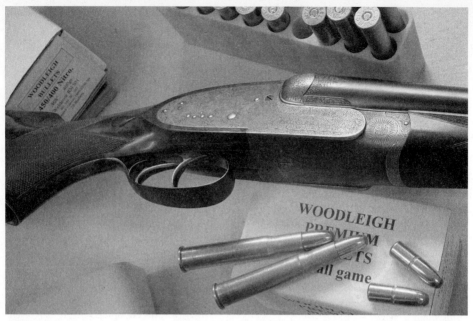

One of the most popular double-gun cartridges ever (though hardly the most powerful), is the .450/400, the cordite version introduced in 1896. Here it's chambered in a lovely Hollis double.

enced his charitable view of heavy rifles. In culling operations and chasing "problem" animals, he couldn't expect a sportsman's poke at undisturbed game. His bullets had to end hostilities instantly and reliably.

The .500 NE was like many big-bore British rounds that made the leap from black- to smokeless powders, during the late 1800s. The original .500x3-inch launched bullets of 380 to 440 grains at under 1,900 fps. When

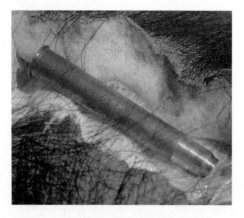

cordite replaced blackpowder, the .500 became a giant killer, hurling 570-grain bullets at 2,150. (Rifles designed for the blackpowder load should not be fired with modern full-Nitro ammo!)

The British decided early on that velocities of 2,050 to 2,250 fps were ideal for shooting Africa's biggest game. The bulk of .40- to .60-caliber rounds introduced or modified for smokeless powder near the turn of the last century deliver muzzle speeds in that bracket. The .416 Rigby drove its 410-grain bullet a bit faster, at 2,350. The .600 Nitro Express was a shot-put on steroids, its 900-grain pill clocking 1,900. Much thick-skinned acrimony has since been stopped with heavy-jacketed solids of 400 to 570 grains. Rimmed hulls suited to double rifles were joined early on by rimless rounds—the .404 and .500 Jeffery, the .416 Rigby, and .505 Gibbs—to better serve magazine rifles. The .375 Belted Rimless Magnum Nitro Express, or .375 H&H, appeared in 1912. It was then considered a high-velocity medium-bore round.

The inch-thick shoulder skin of an Australian buffalo is shown here cradling a .500 NE cartridge. Deep penetration is a must in any stopping rifle load.

Hunters comparing dangerous-game cartridges often talk of knockdown power. Actually, there's no such thing. A bullet does not "knock down" a big animal. The 5,000 ft-lbs delivered to an elephant by a .458 Magnum, for example, equals the bullet energy/body weight ratio of a .22 Long Rifle bullet hitting a big deer. Animals fall down when they lose bone support or nerve control or are dying from blood loss or damaged vitals.

Some time ago, a fellow decided to test the knockdown theory in person. He fired a .458 soft-nose against a thick steel plate. It did not penetrate, so he welded handles on the plate, then supported it in front of him on a table's edge and asked a pal to shoot the plate. It absorbed all 2½ tons of energy, but did not throw the fellow holding it off balance.

That exercise won't pass muster in Hunter Education classes. It did show, however, that even a bruiser like the .458 doesn't knock things over. It kills because it destroys organs. Any stopping value hinges on attendant shock. That big slug may not penetrate deeper than a steel-jacketed .303 British bullet, and either will kill instantly by entering a beast's brain. But the 500-grain .458 has a weight and energy advantage that helps it break shoulders and ring the bell of an elephant with a hit to the skull *alongside* the brain.

Adding energy boosts shock, but also recoil. The .45s and .50s—surely the Lott and Weatherby's .460, the .500 NE and .505 Gibbs—are brutal with full-house loads. Not long ago, a fellow who watched me fire a Gibbs asked for a turn at the CZ rifle. I handed him a Norma round with a 600-grain Woodleigh. At the shot, the big rifle flew out of his hands, as he staggered backward and fell.

John Taylor rightly noted that bullet construction has much to do with killing big game. He once shot a waterbuck bull at 40 yards with a 235-grain .375 bullet at 2,850 fps. The animal ran and had to be shot again, because the copper-pointed bullet "literally disintegrated against the spine … making [only] an appalling surface wound … ." Taylor liked the .375 with 300-grain solids, which gave "deeper penetration than any other bullet I have ever used." He warned against solids not hard enough to maintain their form.

The .470 Nitro Express, by Lang, became hugely popular in the early 1900s and is still a top pick in double rifles.

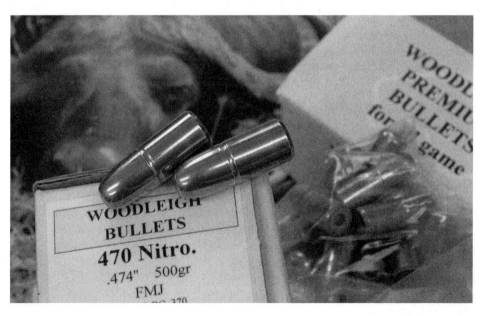

The first Cape buffalo I shot ran off, and I clobbered it quartering away with a German 300-grain solid from my .375. A couple hits later, the bull expired. Autopsy showed the second bullet had entered at the last rib, but instead of driving to the far shoulder had "gone banana," bending then carving a hooked path that ended just under the hide behind the *near* shoulder. Its arc kept it clear of the vitals. Not good.

Many years later, I shot a buffalo with my Montana 99 rifle in .375. The Trophy Bonded soft-nose landed just right and destroyed both lungs. But in true buffalo fashion, the bull ran. I swung with him and loosed a Federal TB Sledgehammer solid. It flew arrow-straight to the off-shoulder, tumbling the bull like a rabbit. Top modern bullets make stopping rounds of cartridges once questionable for heavy game.

A few seasons back, in Australia, I shot a buffalo with a Barnes bullet from a Savage rifle in .338 Winchester. The 225-grain Federal factory loaded TSX drove from just behind the near shoulder to the baseball-size knuckle at the point of the off-shoulder, shattering that massive knob. The impact also snapped the bone below, thick as a wrecking bar. Having delivered its two tons of energy, the TSX stayed nearly intact.

BEST BULLETS FROM DOWN UNDER

Last July, I returned to Australia's Northern Territories. I carried this time a fine Webley & Scott double in .500 Nitro Express. The buffalo that fell to it were not perfectly shot and required multiple hits. I'd have had better luck with a .375 bolt rifle, mainly because I'm used to shooting bolt guns and shoot them more accurately. The .500 has more energy than a .375, but, in my experience, does not penetrate as well. Inch-thick skin on a buffalo's fore-quarters, phone-book-dense muscle, and support bones the size of trolley

Wayne cycles a CZ Safari rifle in .416 Rigby. Note the Mauser extractor, a must by most stopping rifle standards. Practice reloading with your eyes on target can also give you an edge!

Geoff McDonald inspects one of the many double guns he uses to test his wide range of Woodleigh bullets. They're an industry standard for big-bores, loaded in Norma and Federal ammunition.

rails arrest dime-diameter soft-points. Even solids lose their enthusiasm in these great beasts; bullet tracks quickly become mere perforations in bushel-basket vitals.

While the .416s by Dakota, Remington, Rigby, and Ruger hurl bullets 100 grains heavier than the .375 H&H, I've used 300-grain solids to great effect on animals weighing tons. Norma's 350-grain Woodleigh load dropped an elephant for me instantly. While its solids drive through the toughest animals, the .375's 270-grain soft-points fly as flat as 180s from a .30-06. A cornucopia of loads for the .375 suit it to the big bears of the American North, as well as to Africa's thick-skinned animals heavier than a sedan. Norma offers a 270-grain TSX load, plus the 300-grain Oryx and Swift A-Frame. Bullet options for big-bore rounds are much more limited.

Current interest in powerful lever-action rifles has given rise to the .475 Turnbull. You could say its roots trace to the .450 Alaskan, a necked-up .348 developed for big, surly bears. CorBon was early out of the blocks with a 400-grain bullet for the Turnbull at an advertised 2,150 fps. Muzzle energy is 4,107 ft-lbs. Solids driven at that speed are now available, matching the punch of some traditional double-rifle rounds.

CHOOSE YOUR TOOL

In Africa, I usually carry a .375 by the Montana Rifle Company. Fitted with a 1.5-5X Leupold, it seems to hit everything just right. If ever I must stop a big, mean animal, I hope that rifle is close at hand! Another .375 in my rack is an early M70 Winchester with a Redfield receiver sight—my first "big" rifle. Still another is a Sako 85 Kodiak, uncommonly well proportioned and accurate. Like my Remington 798, a plain Jane but well-built .375 Mauser, it wears a laminated stock and intelligently designed iron sights.

For hunters who treat their stopping rifles like tools, it's hard to beat Ruger's Hawkeye Alaskan in .375 H&H, .375 Ruger (a tad more potent), or .416 Ruger. It handles better than it looks. The polymer stock and stainless steel will outlast you. Kimber's Caprivi, the Cooper 56, and Dakota 76 deliver a touch of class that won't impress a buffalo coming to grind you into the sand, but will make you feel wealthier than you are after you buy one.

I'm not a double-rifle shooter, partly because I can't afford to be. Honestly, though, while top-end doubles are seductively sleek and compact and point like shotguns, I hit as well with bolt rifles. Better, in fact. The way you hold a double differs from the way you hold a magazine rifle. Think of the difference between a longbow and a recurve. Both can be shot accurately, but not with the same technique.

Many doubles, particularly sidelocks, qualify both as sporting arms and art. A box-lock unadorned has the businesslike demeanor of a bolt rifle and is equally at home on treks through thorn. Not long ago, I carried a basic but nicely proportioned Heym in .470 NE. I surprised a kudu bull at 60 yards and dropped him with a soft-point. Just walking in Africa with a powerful double rifle is, well, special!

About as far as you'll get from the traditional double is Blaser's R8 straight-pull repeater. Still, it ranks among my favorite stopping rifles. Introduced in 2008, the R8 has many features that distinguished its forebear, the R93. Both models have hammer-forged barrels, telescoping, radial-head bolts, and single-stack magazines tucked into compact trigger assemblies. You run the bolt with a flick of your hand. No need to lower the rifle or lift the bolt knob. Cup your hand for a quick pull, then slap the bolt forward. A thumb-piece cocks the R8. Shove it up, and you're ready to fire. To de-cock, push it forward and ease it back. It is mechanically impossible to fire the R8 unlocked. The R93 and R8 are the only

bolt rifles I can think of that you can carry safely at the ready, because they're uncocked. This quick-pointing rifle is chambered for rounds as big and brawny as the .500 Jeffery! Triggers on R8s destined for the U.S. break at 2½ pounds. Like its R93 predecessor, the R8 has very fast lock time.

TESTED IN TEXAS

No thunder of hooves, but the buffalo is coming fast. Shoot! The Blaser bucks.

"Eight feet. He'd have skidded into you." Doug tapes the hole, centered below the horn boss. Nicely placed, but tardy.

The FTW Ranch in Texas Hill Country delivers a dangerous-game version of the mechanical moose in Scandinavia. Tim Fallon and Doug Pritchard hosted me last summer to blast paper targets of fearsome size up close. Easy shooting? Uh-uh.

Tim, who owns FTW, has traveled the world hunting. In military service, he and Doug trained snipers to hit at distance, so FTW has venues to 1,000 yards. But threading .308 bullets through mirage half a mile away can be easier than dropping elephants in steel-wool cover at spitball range.

"No penalties for late shots here," Doug grins. "But real beasts don't run on rails." Suddenly, two elephants tower, facing and quartering. "Hit the first in the brain, lung-shoot the next, then run in front of those buffalo!" Doug barks with an urgency he wants me to feel.

Thumbing the cocking piece, I shoulder the R8 and fire. The .458 Lott loads are full-house, with 500-grain solids. I rock with the recoil, cycle the bolt, and spin, as a hole appears in the tennis ball-sized brain zone. My second bullet drills the side-to tusker. I backpedal, swing the Aimpoint sight onto the near buffalo, now bearing down fast. *Bang!* Bolt-stroke.

Wayne downed this Australian buffalo with a Webley & Scott double in .500 Nitro Express firing Woodleigh bullets.

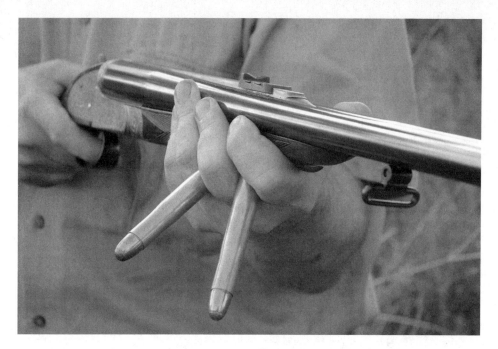

Bang! Both buffs brake at rail's end, almost close enough to touch. They have holes in their skulls. But, again, I'd been slow. Too slow?

Speed can be practiced—*after* you've a shooting routine you can maintain under stress and recoil. Accuracy comes first.

"And remember to spill those empties!" Doug says. "You don't want to die under a buffalo with your paws full of brass!"

We kill a paper lion with the Lott, a trio of elephants with a Blaser barreled to .500 Jeffery. Both cartridges test my concentration, even on the recoil-damped R8. A flinch comes naturally after a couple of swats from such heavies. Recovery is part of stopping-rifle practice. If one bullet fails to take effect, or if you must drop two animals, keeping your balance and getting back into the sights fast is an imperative.

A gazelle hangs from a tree in front of the blind. We wait and watch. With no warning a leopard swings silently onto a limb. The Zeiss 2.5-10X50mm finds it, and I trigger the .308. To my astonishment, the target has no hole.

"Forget to check zero?" Doug smiles, feigning innocence.

We'd just stretched this rifle to 600 yards. A

You can't have too much ammo. This hunter holds two ready to dump into the breech of his loaded double.

month later a hunter I know will be mauled by a real leopard after his client makes a bad shot. You needn't hit a leopard hard, but you must *hit* it. Once the cat has found cover and decided you're the source of its pain, the task becomes tougher. Leopards are so fast, your rifle feels like lead. And they're small, a blur beside which a Sporting Clays target from a tautly sprung trap looks sluggish. I was lucky, a couple years back, to nail a leopard crouched in tall grass a couple steps from natives on its track. I dashed through thorn to the shouts of alarm, firing offhand at a black rosette. A Trophy Bonded soft-nose from my .375 threaded both shoulders. The cat rocketed into the air, sunfished, and fell dead.

Stopping a leopard or an elephant or a brown bear can hinge on your ability to handle a rifle confidently and without mistakes, fire with dispatch and hit with certainty targets the size of a melon at 20 steps. That's why the hardware you choose matters less than how well you use it—and why practice gives you an edge that trumps every ballistic advantage.

CHAPTER 24

BARRELS, TRIGGERS, AND MAGAZINES

Rifles comprise parts that affect accuracy, function, and price. You're in closest touch with these.

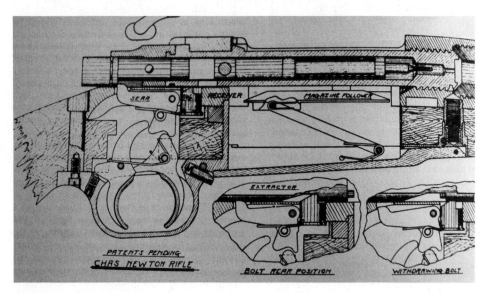

W ithout an accurate barrel, accurate shooting is impossible. But a barrel is also a pressure vessel. High-performance rifle cartridges can generate 60,000 psi, and a safety factor must be built into the barrel so a hot handload doesn't cause damage. Steel dimensions, type, and treatments all influence strength.

Most hunting rifles have barrels of chrome-molybdenum. Chrome-moly is the kind of steel used in truck axles and other high-stress components. It takes a traditional blue nicely. You'll often see chrome-moly designated "4140." Other four-digit numbers indicate a slightly different alloy; barrel maker Dan Lilja uses 4142. Stainless steel is increasingly popu-

This blue-print for a rifle designed by Charles Newton early in the twentieth century shows a higher degree of complexity than in Mausers of that day. Note the magazine springs.

lar in hunting rifles and it dominates in rifle competition. The stainless in barrels is not the same as in cutlery. Barrels of 416 stainless qualify as "rust-resistant." Their high chrome content increases hardness (and makes bluing difficult). Some shooters claim stainless is easier to clean and lasts longer than chrome-moly and, so, is worth its slightly higher cost. Very accurate barrels can be made from both chrome-moly and stainless steels.

Tensile strength and hardness affect barrel performance. "Tensile strength" is the force required to break a steel rod one inch in cross-sectional area by pulling from both ends. Generally, hardening steel increases tensile strength. But a tensile rating of 100,000 pounds for a rifle barrel is worthless if the steel is so hard as to be brittle. A hardness of 25 to 32 on the Rockwell C scale is a useful compromise. Heat-treating barrels leaves residual stresses that can be relieved by slow cooling after reheating the blank.

Barrel drilling and reaming haven't changed much over the last century, save for tooling. Carbide bits and reamers endure and deliver superior finish. The deep-hole drill traditionally used to perforate rifle barrels has a stationary bit; the barrel rotates around it at up to 5,000 rpm. The bit is mounted on a long steel tube with a groove for cooling oil. The hole is commonly drilled five-thousandths undersized so a reamer can finish the job, leaving the bore smooth and uniform.

Rifling the bore can be done with cutter, button, or hammer-forging machine. A cutter developed in Nuremburg in the late fifteenth century comprises a small hook in a hardened steel cylinder that just fits the barrel blank. The cylinder or cutter box moves through the bore on a long rod that pulls the hook against the barrel wall, removing about .0001-inch of steel per pass. After indexing so every groove is shallowly cut, the cutter box is adjusted to deepen the bite. Broaches with multiple hooks in steps speed the process. Rate of twist hinges on the pre-set rotation of the cutter box. Figure an hour to rifle a barrel with a single-point cutter. It's a low-stress process, but costly. John Krieger's best barrels are single-point cut.

Sako's plant, which also makes Tikka rifles, is noted for its accurate, well-finished barrels.

The T/C Icon here boasts "5R" rifling. Land and groove width and depth and the radius or angle between them, plus twist rate and finish, all affect accuracy!

Much faster is the tungsten-carbide button, with rifling in reverse. Mounted on the end of a high-tensile rod and rotated by a rifling head set to the desired rate of twist, the button is pushed or pulled through the finished bore by a hydraulic ram, "ironing in" the grooves. A thin-walled barrel is no candidate for a button. To prevent bulging, you must rifle the tube before turning thick walls down, which can result in distortion at the muzzle. Dan Lilja's barrels are button-rifled; he says the smooth interior and the uniform depth of the grooves give this method an accuracy edge.

A hammer-forging machine pounds the barrel around a mandrel with rifling in reverse. Because the barrel gets about 30-percent longer in this process, the blank begins short. The first hammer-forging equipment was developed in Germany to produce barrels for MG42 machine guns. Stainless barrels are difficult to hammer forge, because they're typically very hard. Substituting 410 for 416 stainless helps. Hammer-forging is fast, but leaves considerable radial stress, which is tough to remove.

Good barrels have been produced with all three rifling methods, though makers argue the merits of each. Button proponents even disagree on whether to pull or push the button—or whether it makes any difference! One thing is certain: cutters and buttons must move smoothly and at a constant pressure.

Accuracy depends a great deal on rate of twist, which must be tailored to the bullet. Fast-pitch or sharp-twist rifling is required for long bullets, especially at modest velocities. There's some latitude here: a 1:10 pitch (one bullet rotation in 10 inches of travel) works for a variety of loads in the .30-06. Barrels for .223s used in long-range shooting have a very fast pitch—1:9 to as sharp as 1:7—to stabilize 65- to 80-grain bullets. "Gain twist" is an increase in rifling pitch toward the muzzle. Dan Lilja discovered after many trials that it failed to yield measurably better accuracy than barrels with a uniform twist rate.

Generally, barrels with shallow grooves shoot tighter than those with deep grooves,

Hammer-forging pounds barrel blanks around mandrels with rifling in reverse. Here are laid out a couple mandrels with hammers.

The Blaser R8 has an ingenious detachable trigger group, which includes the magazine. The assembly is compact, lightweight, and sturdy. Trigger and magazine both function beautifully.

because they distort the bullet less. But shallow-groove barrels don't last as long. The bore's land size is a trade-off, too. Narrow lands distort the bullet less and create less drag, but also burn away faster. Reducing the number of lands, a maker can keep them wide, while minimizing distortion and drag. Rifling configuration has been long debated. Witness the two-groove Springfield barrel and Marlin's 16-groove Micro-Groove rifling!

A barrel's "groove circle" must be concentric with the bore, the land corners free of irregularities. Some *uniform* roughness in land and groove surfaces may actually prove a benefit, because glass-smooth surfaces hike friction that can pull jacket material from bullets, as do tool marks. Conventional wisdom is that a uniform surface ripple of 10 to 20 micro-inches produces best accuracy. Careful

lapping can deliver a properly smooth bore. Kenny Jarrett's super-accurate barrels are hand-lapped, a process that, in his shop, can take hours. But other makers say the process isn't necessary, given a careful rifling job.

A 75-power bore scope helps barrelmakers check inside finish. After rifling, bore uniformity can be measured with an air gauge, a probe moved through the barrel with air pressure recording variations. Shilen's air gauges are sensitive to 50 *millionths* of an inch! John Krieger recommends that every barrel be trimmed at least an inch at the muzzle when it is fitted, because the tooling used in bore finishing can leave a slight flare at the ends. Krieger barrels are lapped to just under 16 micro-inch in the direction of bullet travel. They're held to within .0005 over nominal groove and bore dimensions, which

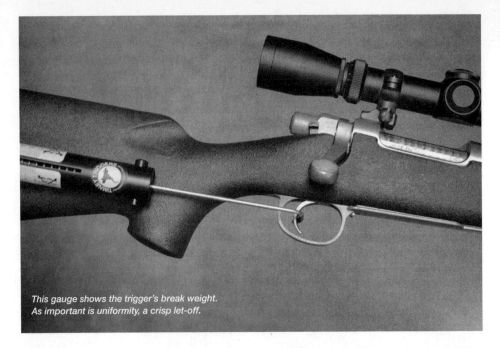
This gauge shows the trigger's break weight. As important is uniformity, a crisp let-off.

are *uniform* to .0001. Pac-Nor (a button-rifle shop) and H-S Precision (cut-rifled barrels) specify tolerances of .0003 for bore diameter. Pac-Nor limits variation in groove diameter to .0001.

You might also consider choking a barrel if you're shooting lead bullets, as in a rimfire rifle and competition air gun. Parallel bores are considered top choice if you shoot jacketed bullets.

Most well-known makers now have web pages, and some of these offer barrel-making insights. If you want to know where to buy the best barrels, shop Midway or Brownells. These shooter-supply outlets pay attention to the results of benchrest competitions that test barrel accuracy. In the 2003 USRA-IR50/50 Nationals, for example, 39 of 87 top competitors used Lilja barrels. Of the best 20 shooters in 10.5-pound centerfire benchrest competition, 16 favored Shilen barrels. Shilen also ranked most popular in the 13.5-pound class. Hart barrels showed up almost as often on the heavy rifles and have for decades been a top pick of smallbore shooters. John Krieger's cut-rifled barrels always finish near the top. Douglas appeared on both centerfire

and rimfire lists, in 50-foot matches to 1,000-yard competition. Some barrels, like those by Kenny Jarrett and H-S Precision, are less widely distributed, but one-hole accurate. Not all barrel shops market through big-box shooter-supply outlets, either.

HIGH CAPACITY IS OPTIONAL, NOT SO A CLEAN BREAK

Your first shot at game is almost always the best. If you get a better chance later, you probably shouldn't have taken the first when you did. Every first shot should be lethal. It is not a preamble.

Hitting your mark is mostly a matter of skill. But you're smart to insist on a trigger that breaks cleanly and consistently at a weight light enough that you don't disturb the rifle during the squeeze. I've come to appreciate very light triggers on prone rifles. In competition, in a solid position, you can control a sensitive trigger. The less pressure you need apply, the more precisely you can time a shot. A light touch won't move the rifle off target. In the hunting field, though, your fingers may be cold, and perhaps gloved. An urgent shot may deny you a solid posi-

A separate trigger tab adorns this Ruger American. Pioneered by Savage, the tab allows a light trigger pull without compromising safety. Internally, the mechanisms differ between makers.

trigger face collapses readily to your finger's pressure. It activates the trigger proper, which can be adjusted for light pull safely. A double set trigger is costlier and more complex. DSTs typically have long lock times. Single set triggers, like the Canjar you push ahead to set, still appear on match rifles.

Truly adjustable triggers can be manipulated for weight of pull, sear engagement and overtravel. Reducing sear engagement trims take-up or creep, which most shooters want minimized. Certainly, some fine shooting has been done with the long take-up built into service rifles to prevent unintended discharge by green recruits; zealous reduction of sear engagement can put the rifle at risk of firing when it sustains a blow.

tion. You may want to fire offhand or with the rifle moving. You may be breathing hard or fighting wind. A "hair" trigger doesn't make sense in these scenarios. If you can't rest your finger on the trigger, you can't apply the needed pressure gradually. Hunting rifles with a 2½-pound trigger behave best for me. The traditional three-pound pull is easy to manage. With practice, even a four-pound break will suffice. Consistency matters. Pull-weight variation is bad business, no matter the average weight. An increasing number of rifles have a mechanism similar to what Savage pioneered in its AccuTrigger. A tab in the

Every shot comes down to the last ounce on the trigger. Aftermarket triggers from Timney and others are available for rifles with disappointing, non-adjustable triggers.

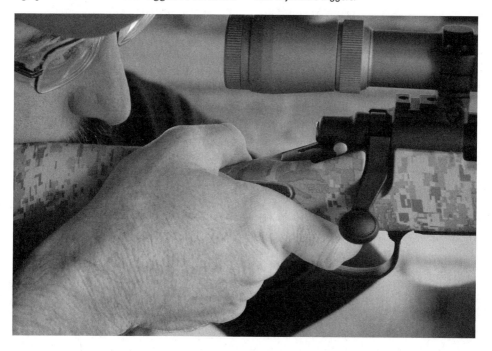

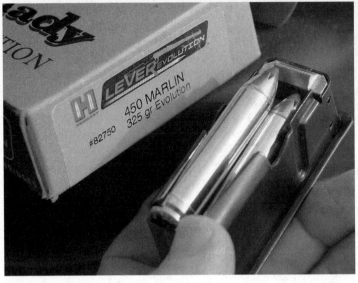

The detachable box magazine, here from a Browning BLR lever rifle, has a growing fan base. Shooters like its convenience.

But creep requires finger movement, which can move the rifle. In this litigious age, most factory installed triggers have lost their sear engagement screws. Even overtravel is now commonly factory set. Overtravel must be generous enough to ensure trigger movement past the break. Minimum overtravel puts your finger hard against a stop immediately after the break. That contact can move the rifle. I prefer enough overtravel to let my finger decelerate and give the rifle a chance to release the bullet undisturbed. While most hunting rifles have serviceable triggers, you can easily replace a problem trigger with an aftermarket version from Timney.

However good your trigger or how carefully you fire, a second shot can eventually prove useful. And, occasionally, a fast second shot can make the difference between a sure kill and abject failure. Because few of us care to squander the price of a new Land Cruiser on a double rifle, we rely on repeaters with magazines for follow-up shots.

Magazines are of two main types, tubular and box. Until Hornady came up with the FlexTip bullet and LEVERevolution ammunition, tube magazines in lever guns were limited to blunt bullets that rested safely against the primers of cartridges ahead. Lever guns with box magazines date to the

1895 Winchester, which Teddy Roosevelt liked very much. The 95 is among the most uncomfortable of rifles. The lever pinches my fingers, and the sharp, low comb pounds my chops. But it accommodates pointed bullets and chambers powerful rounds like the .303 British, .30-40 Krag, and .30-06 Springfield. Its box magazine, patterned after the Mauser box, also set a worthy precedent for lever-actions, one to be followed in the lighter, hammerless, and more comfortable Sako Finnwolf and Winchester 88. Browning's BLR features a silky rack-and-pinion mechanism and a detachable box. Savage's 99 and Ruger's 96/44 break the mold with their spool magazines.

The most common box magazine in my youth was the bolt-action's integral box, charged from the top and unloaded by operating the bolt to strip cartridges. Increasingly popular now is the detachable box, which can be inserted or removed, empty or loaded, as a unit. Detachable boxes can be loaded apart from the rifle. In fact, many are designed to be loaded *only* that way. Thumb in cartridges, snap the box home, and you're ready to chamber. When you wish to unload, press the catch and the box drops into your palm. I do appreciate boxes, like that of my Sako 85 Kodiak, which can also be loaded from the top, inside the rifle. It enables you to top off the magazine without pulling all the cartridges in reserve.

In states where firearms must be fully unloaded in vehicles, detachable boxes are hugely popular. Motoring from one woodlot to another to stage drives, whitetail hunters appreciate the quick, easy drop and insertion of self-contained boxes. Also, in cold climates, gloved hands and stiff fingers control full boxes better than they do individual cartridges!

Early detachable boxes were of stamped metal, feeding staggered stacks of cartridges. That's still the most prevalent type. But straight-up, single-column stacks have appeared in bolt rifles like the Tikka T3 and Cooper's high-power centerfires. I favor single columns for three reasons. First, the box is slim, which means the rifle can also be slim at the waist. With a single-stack box, less metal need be removed from the bottom of the receiver, and more steel means a stiffer receiver. Finally, a vertical column delivers each cartridge to the ramp exactly the same way as the last. When designing his first repeating centerfires, Dan Cooper told me the magazine was the most challenging component. "It looks so simple, and it's so frustrating!" He did, eventually, get it just right. My Coopers slick up cartridges as silkily as do original Mausers. Ditto Tikka's T3 with its straight-up box.

This Thompson/Center box fits the firm's Venture rifle.

Polymer is supplanting stamped steel in magazine boxes. While decades ago the use of "plastic" in rifles was derided, it's more accepted now. Honestly, I'd rather have a well-engineered, closely fitted polymer box than a stamping. It's apt to fit better, and it's quieter if there's any play. I've found polymer magazines as reliable as metal, and more durable. They don't dent. Polymer followers don't squeal.

Early detachable boxes protruded from the magazine well. Flush boxes and recessed front latches have trimmed rifle profiles; boxes are easier to insert and extract. Pump and almost all autoloading rifles have detachable boxes. An exception: the M1 Garand, a self-loader with a clever integral magazine.

By the way, a detachable box is not, properly, a clip. A "clip" is a cartridge carrier inserted into the rifle's receiver. There's neither lifting spring nor follower. Stripper clips used for 1898 Mausers and 1903 Springfields grip the cartridge bases and fall away as you press the stack down into the integral box. The Garand clip captures the body of the stack, too, and stays in the magazine well. As the last shot is fired, the Garand's mechanism ejects the clip automatically.

A traditionalist, I still prefer internal boxes with hinged floorplates, or those hollowed from the stock so there's no bottom metal. Such "blind magazines" were once reserved for low-cost rifles like the Remington 78 and Winchester 70 Ranger (inexpensive versions of the 700 and 70), and Savage's 110. But I'm told by people who manufacture rifles that a blind box and one with an alloy floorplate cost about the same to make. While a blind magazine cannot be emptied or cleaned from the bottom, it makes for a trim profile. With no bottom metal, your hand cradles wood, which stays warmer in cold weather. There are no edges to chafe your palm, no blued finish to fade as you cradle the rifle in sweaty hands.

CHAPTER 25

REAL RIFLE STOCKS

Polymers shed water. But for rifles of character, there's truly only one choice.

Fine French walnut, as on this Goudy-stocked Winchester M70, transforms rifles into art!

If you remember telephones with rotary dials, and sedans with four-figure prices, you may recall the real gunstock. It was walnut. It looked warm and felt like part of a real rifle. When I was a lad, you could buy a fancy American walnut stock blank for $25. I paid $7.50 for the plain but semi-inletted blank that graced my first deer rifle! Much more costly now, walnut has given way to polymers. The problem with walnut is that you can't make it. You must grow it. Growing walnut takes a lot longer than growing tomatoes. We're inletting wood from trees that may have been around before metallic cartridges, *before the Declaration of Independence*. Don't figure on cutting gunstocks from trees you're planting now.

In a cruel twist of circumstance, the people who discovered walnut had no guns to put it on. That was back in the thirteenth century, when Marco Polo allegedly brought walnuts from their native Persia to Italy. Nuts and seedlings eventually found their way to England, then to France and other parts of Europe. The scientific name for the species is *Juglans regia*, or "royal walnut." Though grain structure and color vary, *J. regia* is the same worldwide. Common names denote location, not genetic differences; English walnut is *J. regia*, so is French. When the tree wound up in California, it was adopted as "California English." Typically, California English wood grown from nuts has a tawny background with black streaking and less "marblecake" than England's English. Classic French is often red or orange. Most Circassian walnut I've seen runs heavy to black. It's named after a region in the northwest Caucasus, on the Black sea.

"The best *J. regia* walnut comes from Turkey and Morocco," the late Don Allen told me not long before his untimely death. Don knew more about walnut than anyone else I can name. Before establishing Dakota Arms, he built rifle stocks while finishing a career as a commercial pilot. He traveled all over the world to feed his passion for fine wood. "Top-rung Turkish walnut is superb," Don said. "Unfortunately, it's being sawed into dollars at an unsustainable rate. Age imparts color and figure to wood, but old trees take many decades to replace. We think some of the trees being cut in Turkey are 300 to 400 years old!"

Claro walnut, *J. hindsii*, was discovered around 1840, in California. Red in hue and open-grained, Claro was crossed with English to produce ornamental Bastogne walnut. Nuts from these shade trees are infertile, but fast growth and dense grain has made Bastogne a favorite of stockmakers. It checkers more cleanly than Claro and withstands heavy recoil. The best Bastogne has beautiful color and figure. Sadly, this walnut is getting very scarce, the limited supply diminishing fast under unrelenting demand. As with *J. regia*, the most desirable Bastogne comes from trees at least 150 years old.

American, or black, walnut, *J. nigra*, has been the mainstay of the firearms industry here since the first Kentucky rifles were built in Pennsylvania (though maple was also popular on those flintlocks). A warm brown color distinguishes typical American walnut, with just enough black to justify the moniker. The wood can be as plain as a power pole or richly patterned, depending on the tree's age and locale and the location and type of cut. Quarter-sawn walnut shows tight bands of color, because the saw runs across growth rings. Plane-sawed walnut has wide bands, the saw running tangent to growth rings. Either cut can yield a sturdy, handsome stock, but quarter-sawn walnut is most in demand.

Walnut must be dried before it is worked. Don Allen explained, "Immediately after a blank is cut, free water starts to escape. Think of a soaked sponge dripping. If water leaves too fast, the wood surface can crack and check and eventually crust, inhibiting movement of bound water from the core. Structural damage may result."

A kiln helps throttle the release of water.

"Most drying damage happens in the first weeks after cutting a blank. Moisture content

Ace riflemaker Patrick Holehan provided this laminated stock on a .25-06 he built on an early M70 rifle. It's more stable, durable than the one-piece walnut stock he also fitted.

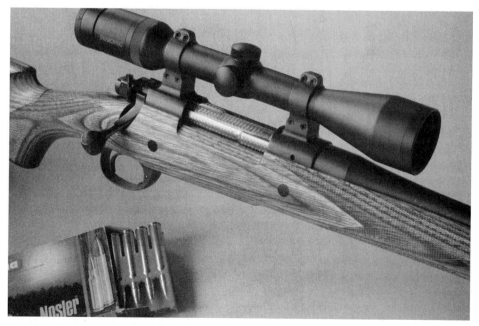

will then stabilize at about 20 percent, and the blank can be air- or kiln-dried without damage."

Don told me no special environment is needed to air-dry wood that's been properly brought to 20-percent moisture.

"Just avoid extremes of temperature and humidity. Weigh the blank periodically. When the weight stabilizes, the blank is dry enough to work."

Stockmakers commonly turn the blank to profile at this point, then let it dry another six months before inletting.

In France, walnut growers used to steam logs before cutting them into slabs or *flitches*. Steaming colored the sap, turning it from white to amber. It also wiped out resident insects.

Dakota rifles are renowned for their fine walnut. Dakota's wood room is one of few places where you handle high-grade walnut.

"Less than five percent of all walnut passes muster as fancy or exhibition grade," Don said. "Without sales of standard grade wood, big mills can't afford to deal in fancy walnut." Dakota Arms established a milling operation in New Zealand, still a source for dense, figured walnut.

To bolster Dakota's stock of exceptional wood, Don bought one of the largest Bastogne trees in the world. Very old, the lone tree towered over a surrounding prune orchard. Its trunk diameter measured 12 feet, its canopy spanned over 150 feet. Thirty feet above the ground, some branches were 20 feet round!

"It was a great find," said Don, "But then the work began! Even *limbing* proved a chore. Then we trenched around the stump. We didn't cut the tree down as you might a spruce. Instead, we cut the roots and *pushed* it over. Wood deeper than a foot underground is too soft for gunstocks; however, buttwood usually delivers best color. Figure can reach high in a tree; here, fiddleback ran all the way to the small limbs." That tree delivered 4,700 gunstock blanks, many with outstanding figure.

Don said that light-colored walnut is commonly assumed to be worthless.

"Truth is, many walnut trees contain *no* dark wood. Also, the best colors lie next to the core or sap pillar."

This Serengeti stock comprises two outside slabs of walnut sandwiching center laminates. It's stout, cheaper than one-piece figured walnut, and attractive! Kilimanjaro rifles feature it, too.

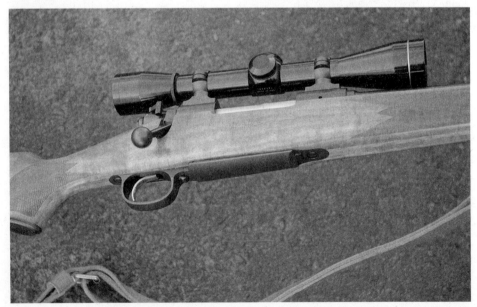

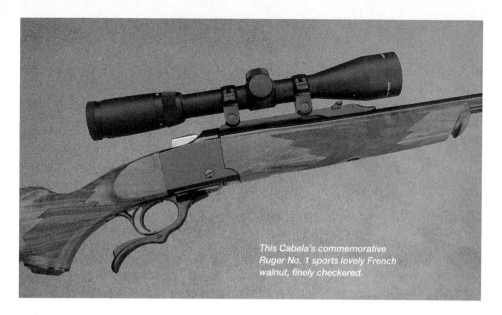

This Cabela's commemorative Ruger No. 1 sports lovely French walnut, finely checkered.

IT'S ALL IN THE CUT

Handsome walnut is of no value if it breaks. "Layout" is an important first step in stockmaking. The grain in a quarter-sawn walnut blank should run parallel with the top of the grip, when viewed from the side. That way, you'll get maximum strength through the grip, while keeping the fore-end stiff. Viewed from the top, wood grain should parallel the bore, to prevent side pressure on the barrel. Figure in the butt doesn't affect accuracy, but up front the knots and crotches that make for interesting patterns can twist the fore-end. Though figured wood is often dense, it is not as strong or stable as straight-grained wood.

Glass bedding strengthens wood but does not eliminate warpage. My own preference is for glass or epoxy in the recoil lug mortise, to prevent splitting through the magazine well and to give the metal firm and unchanging contact with the stock. With glass compound at the bottom of the mortise, you can tighten the front guard screw securely without compressing the wood. A smaller bedding patch under the tang makes sense, too. Aluminum pillars around the guard screws serve the same purpose, providing solid contact from bottom metal to receiver.

The best custom rifle stockers dismiss glass as a fix for shoddy inletting. They pride themselves in skin-tight fit of wood to metal, maintaining that a properly bedded stock won't split at the web or grip. While that's true for most rifles, the brutal kick of some modern magnums tests not just inletting, but the integrity of the walnut. That's why you'll see crossbolts reinforcing wood stocks on "safari" rifles.

Checkering helps you grip the stock. It also adds eye appeal, especially on plain wood. Once, all checkering was hand-cut. When such skilled labor became too costly, companies pressed or ironed panels into the wood. These appeared in the 1960s and looked as good on gunstocks as tire tracks on carpet. A decade later or so, machine-cut checkering became viable. It has since improved. While hand checkering by a talented hand still defines excellence, the best machine checkering is quite good. Its limits show up most clearly on curved surfaces—particularly the top of the grip.

The finer the checkering, the more demanding the work, because each diamond must be the same size as all the other diamonds and properly "pointed up." Hand checkering can be as fine as 32 lines per inch, though such tiny diamonds require

Walnut-stocked rifles can be accurate! This T/C Icon is, and helped Wayne center the vitals of this vaal rhebok at 250 yards in South Africa's mountains.

hard, uniform wood and are more cosmetic than functional. They appear most often inside skeleton grip caps and butt-plates. Grip and fore-end panels typically wear 18 to 24 lines per inch checkering. You'll get secure handling and pleasing appearance from 22 lines per inch panels. I prefer 24 lines per inch checkering, but it's exceedingly rare on production-class rifles.

A word on patterns. *Fleur-de-lis* panels probably owe much of their popularity to Al Biesen's use of them on Jack O'Connor's rifle. Oddly enough, the basic *fleur-de-lis* is easier to cut than even simple point patterns. That's because the *fleur-de-lis* is a fill-in job.

You scribe a border, then cut grooves to it. In a point pattern, the border is part of the checkering, not simply a frame. If you err a little on a fill-in effort, the border will still be right, and only close inspection will show the mistake. Scribe a line slightly off-kilter in a point pattern, though, and the problem follows you. In fact, its effect can be *magnified* in the final product. Of course, very fine ribbons in a *fleur* pattern can make fill-ins incredibly hard to do. Among the most skilled of contemporary stockers is Gary

Hooray for Mossberg! At this writing, it still produces an economically priced bolt rifle in a walnut stock!

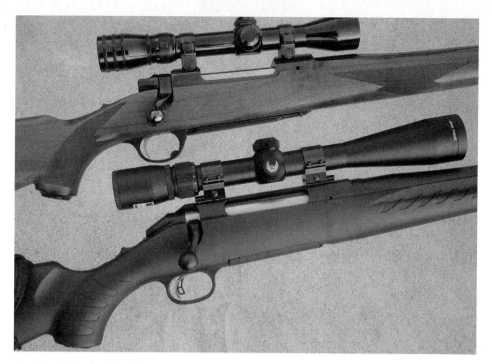

The Ruger 77 (top) dates to the 1960s. It's still available in walnut. The Ruger American appeared in 2011, a well-designed, accurate, affordable rifle. Walnut couldn't make the price point.

Goudy, of Dayton, Washington. He cuts ribbons as fine as flyline, uniform and unbroken by overruns. I can't tell you how he does that, because I don't know.

Checkering is best done after applying a stock finish, otherwise, finish gums up in the trenches. To finish fresh-cut panels, I use a toothbrush—which is also handy for cleaning the checkering of dried blood. Dip the brush in boiled linseed oil and scrub vigorously.

By the way, for a traditional stock finish, you can't beat boiled linseed oil (raw linseed oil won't dry before the next ice age!). Some commercial finishes offer nearly the same look in less time, because they contain drying agents.

Here's a method you can use with any oil-base finish. After dry-sanding, wet-sand with 400-grit paper to raise whiskers in the wood. Next, polish off the dust, then apply a base coat of spar varnish or rub in oil until it gets hot under your hand. When you're tired, wipe off the excess oil with a clean rag and set the stock aside to dry, preferably where conditions rival Death Valley in July. When the stock is *really* dry, wet-sand it, then apply more linseed oil. Multiple applications build up microscopically thin films of linseed oil. Open-grained wood takes longer to fill. To polish out trapped dust, rub in a slurry of rottenstone and oil, then wipe off the excess.

One benefit of a boiled linseed oil finish is easy maintenance. Because oil soaks into the walnut, scratches wipe away with an oily cloth. Dings can be steamed out with a flat-iron pressed over a wet washcloth. A quick rub with the rottenstone slurry will make the injury fade. Boiled linseed oil can be used with stain, but by itself it often brings out the most pleasing look. It is *not* a waterproof finish, but it does repel water quite well. Polymer coatings, such as those used on bowling pins, afford a more durable stock finish, but the look is neither warm nor natural. Polymers do excel as sealants and have a place on wood used in very wet climates.

CHAPTER 26

CARTRIDGES BY THE NUMBERS

If calculus soured you on digits, fear not. Caliber, cases, and powder charges make sense!

The versatile 7mm-08 Remington fires a 7mm (.284-inch) bullet from a .308 case necked down.

S ince their debut in the last half of the nineteenth century, metallic cartridges have been labeled for their dimensions. But because they don't all reflect the same dimensions, the numbers jungle is dark indeed! *Units* of measure vary, too. And, to avoid duplication in a field with hundreds of cartridges, the measures are rounded up and down, digits dropped and added, seemingly at random. Then there are numbers that have nothing to do with size. They tell of bullet weight, powder charge, even bullet speed. The .30-06, for instance, is named for the rifle's bore diameter and the cartridge's year of introduction! (As an aside, *Cartridges of the*

World, also published by Gun Digest, is an *excellent* resource for sorting through much of the confusion surrounding the naming of dozens and dozens of cartridges. Rife with the history behind each cartridge, the newest and completely updated *13th Edition* is available now at www.gundigeststore.com; 855-840-5120. I highly recommend you add this book to your reference library, whether you're a novice shooter, avid competitor, or a cartridge collector.)

Most commonly, the numbers indicate bul-

eter of the bore from land to land between the grooves. Bore diameter is always smaller than groove diameter, and either number could be used as "caliber." The .250 Savage and .257 Roberts, for example, have bullets of the same diameter: .257-inch. That's groove diameter. Both .250 and .257 rifle bores have a .250-inch land diameter. The .270 Winchester is .277-inch across the grooves, while .300s mike .308-inch across the grooves, as do the .308 Winchester and .308 Norma Magnum. Centerfire .22s, from the .218 Bee to the .225 Winchester, use the same .224-inch bullets. Bullets for the .303 British measure .311. Those for modern .338s and Weatherby's .340 Magnums mike .338-inch, for the .350 Remington and .358 Norma Magnums .358-inch.

let diameter or bore diameter. The two are *not* the same. Bullet diameter is more nearly the *groove* diameter of the barrel—its measure to the depths of the grooves cut during rifling. Bore diameter is *land* diameter, or the diam-

Woodleigh bullets, made in Australia but used worldwide, include those sized to match the myriad bore diameters of early British double rifles.

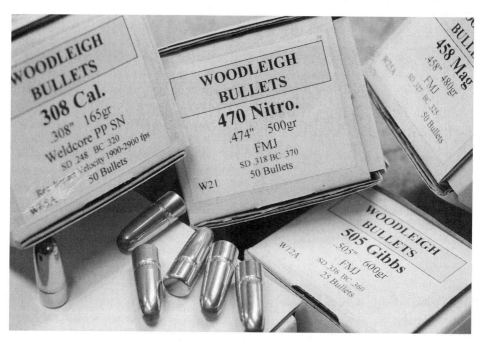

Two-digit designations simply indicate bore diameter in hundredths of an inch, rather than thousandths. Add a zero, and you'll often come up with the name of a similar cartridge and a good idea of the bullet diameter. Sometimes the rule doesn't hold. The .38 Special

At right, the .45-70, a U.S. service cartridge during Westward expansion, was designed with a rim for single-shot rifles. The .30-06, left, adopted by the Army in 1906, is rimless for bolt-action repeaters.

uses the same .357 bullet as the .357 Magnum! *Two* double-digit numbers usually mean the cartridge dates to blackpowder days, the second pair indicating grains of blackpowder in an original load. The .45-70 was fueled by 70 grains of blackpowder before smokeless replaced it. Incidentally, "grains" here is a weight measure, not a physical description as in grains of sand. There are 437.5 grains in one ounce. Some old cartridges wear a third set of numbers, designating bullet weight in grains, as in .45-70-405, a designation for the official U.S. Army cartridge from 1873 to 1892. Three-number sequences can also show caliber, bullet weight, and case length, as in .45-120-3¼ Sharps. The 3¼-inch case is long by modern standards, but many British rifle cartridges developed for African and Indian big game during the late 1800s had long hulls and were so designated.

The .25 Souper, one of Wayne's favorite cartridges, is a wildcat, i.e., not commercially made. It is a .243 necked up to take .257-inch bullets.

The .250-3000 Savage, developed by Charles Newton around 1913, did not burn 3,000 grains of powder! It featured an 87-grain bullet at an advertised speed of 3,000 fps. Savage wanted that velocity (high for the day) in the name. Starting to see a pattern? Starting to see there's *no* pattern?

In Europe, rifled bores are commonly measured in millimeters, not hundredths of an inch. Some American rounds have been labeled this way. The 6mm Remington uses a .243 bullet, the 6.5 Remington Magnum a .264 bullet (like Winchester's .264 Magnum). The various 7mms fire .284 bullets, the 8mm Remington Magnum a .323 bullet. Complete European designations include case length in millimeters: The 7x57 Mauser has a 7mm groove diameter, a case 57 millimeters long. As it also serves foreign powers, the .308 Winchester is known in military circles as the 7.62x51 NATO.

Cartridges not commercially manufactured but fashioned by handloaders have long been called "wildcats." Some, notably the .25-06 (a necked-down .30-06), and .22-250

(on the .250 Savage case), have gone commercial. Remington began producing .35 Whelen rifles and ammunition in 1988, many years after handloaders came up with the round (the .30-06 necked to .35 and named after Col. Townsend Whelen, a firearms authority in the decades between the World Wars). After long-range enthusiasts necked the *never* popular .284 Winchester hull to 6.5mm, they liked it so well that Norma, then Nosler, loaded it.

Many commercial rounds have other cases in their lineage. The 7x57 Mauser was revamped to produce the .257 Roberts and, later, the 6mm Remington. The .308 Winchester case fathered the .243 and .358, the 7mm-08 and .260, then the .338 Federal. The 7-30 Waters is a .30-30 case blown forward and necked to .284. The .30-338 resulted when shooters lusting for a short .300 seized on the .338 Winchester Magnum and necked it

The .250 Savage was developed, in 1912, by Charles Newton, who advised a 100-grain bullet. Savage chose an 87-grain bullet to hike velocity to 3,000 fps and called the round the .250-3000.

BELTS, BULK, AND BB CAPS

The rimfire stable has also grown. (The priming compound in rimfires lies in the rim itself, instead of in a separate, central primer). The patriarch of this family could be the .22 BB Cap, designed, in 1845, for what were known as parlor or saloon (salon) rifles. The "BB" stands for "bulleted breech." This round initially held no powder; the priming compound alone delivered enough thrust for indoor target shooting. During the 1880s, the CB (conical bullet) Cap appeared, loaded with 1½ grains of blackpowder. The .22 Short and Long came early, too. Originally, the Long Rifle had the Long's hull, but a heavier bullet, 40 grains instead of 29. A 37-grain hol-

down. The .300 Winchester and .308 Norma followed quickly. By the way, dual numbers on British rounds signify parent cartridge and bore in *reverse* order from American custom. A .450/.400 fires a .400-inch (actually .405) diameter bullet.

Some useful cartridges have died. The .33 Winchester, a potent round in its time, gave way to the .348 Winchester, which has since withered. Note the cast bullets in these cases. The original .33 factory load drove a 200-grain .338-inch bullet at an advertised 2,200 fps.

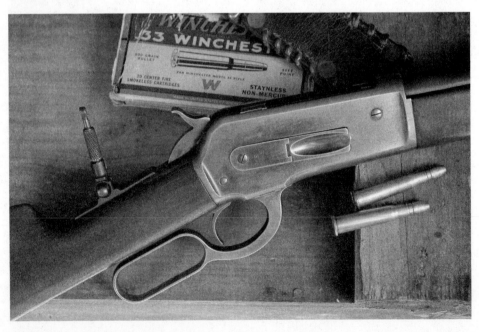

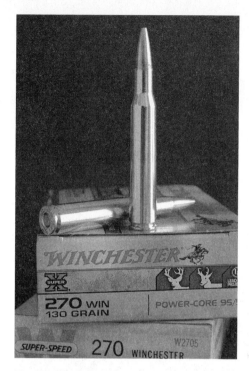

The .270 Winchester, introduced in 1925, was a fast-stepper for the time, with a 130-grain bullet at over 3,000 fps. Bullet diameter: .277.

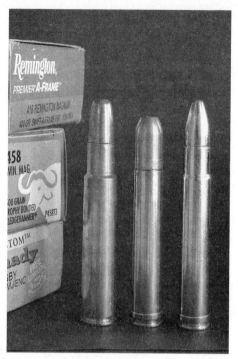

The stated diameter says nothing about case dimensions. Left, the .416 Rigby is an original. Right, the .416 Remington is on the .375 H&H case—as is the .458 (center), but shortened.

lowpoint followed. Some hyper-velocity .22 Long Rifle rounds now feature lighter bullets at higher speeds. The .22 Special is dead, but not the .22 WMR (Winchester Magnum Rimfire). Hornady's wildly successful .17 HMR (Hornady Magnum Rimfire) is based on that hull. The logical follow-up, the .17 Mach 2 (also by Hornady, on the .22 Long Rifle case) hasn't achieved the HMR's popularity.

Typically, the term "magnum" signifies high levels of power and/or speed. Some magnum rounds are not as potent as others with the same bore diameter. Some cartridges not called magnums (though they may come from magnum cases) outperform cartridges that carry the magnum label. Remington's 7mm STW (Shooting Times Westerner) derives from the 8mm Remington Magnum and has a bigger case than the 7mm Remington Magnum. "Belted magnum" refers to the belt ahead of the extractor groove, present on cartridges based, most famously, on the .375

H&H case, circa 1912. The belt is a head-spacing device; it really has nothing to do with case reinforcement. It is a stop, arrested by the chamber to ensure proper fit between case, chamber, and bolt head. The rim on a .30-30 and the shoulder on a .270 perform the same function: they prevent the case from entering the chamber too far. End play in a chambered cartridge can result in case separation on firing. Incidentally, magnum handgun rounds like the .357 and .44 magnums are much smaller than the .300 H&H and aren't belted.

The British equivalent of "magnum" might be "Nitro Express," which describes potent cartridges that came along at the end of the nineteenth century. The name followed "Black Powder Express" and derives from nitroglycerine, used in some gunpowders. It applies mainly to cartridges for heavy African game.

CHAPTER 27

PRIMERS AND POWDERS

Fire in the hole! Here's what you need to know about sparks, fuel, and the violence that follows!

Rifles designed for blackpowder cartridges can be used with smokeless—if they're loaded to original blackpowder pressures. The .577 Black Powder Express is not the .577 Nitro Express!

The percussion cap of the mid-nineteenth century spawned the modern primer. Drawn brass, solid head cartridge cases have no anvil, so, beginning in 1880 in the U.S., primer cups included anvils. Used in cases with a central flash hole, they're called "Boxer" primers. They come in two sizes for rifle rounds, two for pistol. Large and Small Rifle primers are the same diameter as Large and Small pistol primers, respectively, but the pellets inside differ. You need more spark to ignite heavy charges of rifle powders. The spark of magnum primers lasts longer than that of standard primers. By the way, a large rifle primer weighs about 5.4 grains and carries .6-grain of priming compound.

European cartridge designers followed a slightly different path, incorporating the anvil in the case and punching two flash holes in the primer pocket on either side of the anvil. This so-called "Berdan" design affords more room for priming compound, and flame can go straight through the holes, rather than having to scoot around the anvil and its braces. The Boxer primer is the clear choice of handloaders, who can pop the old primer out with a decapping pin while sizing the case in a die. Berdan primers must be pried out with a special hook or ejected by hydraulic pressure. Oddly, Hyram Berdan, whose design appealed to the Europeans, was American. Edward Boxer, for whom American-style primers are named, was British.

Early Boxer primers ignited blackpowder, but sometimes failed to fire smokeless. Adding more fulminate led to cracked cases. Blame fell on the propellant, but the real culprit was mercury residue from the primer. Absorbed by residual powder in the cases, mercury attacked the zinc component, causing the hulls to split.

The first successful non-mercuric primer for smokeless loads was the H-48, developed, in 1898, for the .30-40 Krag. Its primary detonating component was potassium chlorate—which, alas, could wreak havoc with bores by attracting water and causing rust. Hot water and ammonia, pumped through the bore on patches and followed by oiling, helped save barrels. Neglected cleaning doomed them.

In 1901, the German Company Rheinische-Westphalische Sprengstoff (RWS) introduced a primer with barium nitrate and picric acid, instead of potassium chlorate. These compounds did not induce rust. The Swiss followed with a non-corrosive primer, and German rimfire ammunition soon featured Rostfrei (rust-free) priming, which contained neither potassium chlorate nor the ground glass used in other primers to generate friction. Unfortunately, this mixture left a residue of barium oxide, which also scoured barrels.

Remington was the first U.S. firm with non-corrosive priming in sporting ammunition, promoted under the "Kleanbore" label, in 1927. Winchester caught up with "Staynless," Peters with "Rustless." All contained mercury fulminate. German chemists Rath-

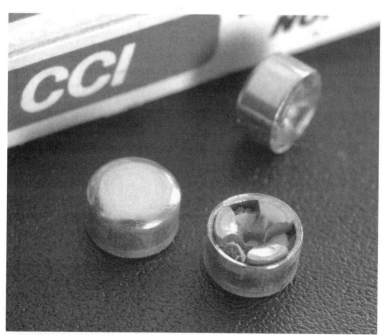

The modern Boxer primer contains an anvil set against priming compound. Cup sizes and the amount of priming differ between Large Rifle, Small Rifle, Large Pistol, and Small Pistol.

burg and Von Hersz later managed to remove both potassium chlorate and mercury fulminate from primers. Again Remington took the lead with the first U.S. version of a non-corrosive, non-mercuric primer. The main ingredient: lead tri-nitro-resorcinate, or lead styphnate. It remains an important component in small arms primers today. The U.S. Army adopted non-corrosive, non-mercuric primers, in 1948.

Development of big, flat-shooting cartridges during the 1940s called for slow-burning powders that required friskier ignition. More priming compound could shatter powder directly in front of the flash-hole, causing erratic pressures and performance. But Dick Speer and Victor Jasaitis, a chemist from Speer Cartridge Works, had a better idea. They added boron and aluminum to make the primer burn longer. The result was more heat, more complete ignition before primer fade. Other munitions companies

followed suit. Speer primers are still made in Lewiston, Idaho, under the CCI brand (Cascade Cartridge Industries).

While machines that produce primers are more sophisticated now, primer manufacture is much the same as it was at the outbreak of the second World War. Huge batches of primer cups are still punched and drawn from sheet metal and indexed on perforated metal tables. Perforated plates are smeared with wet priming compound the consistency of fresh dough and laid precisely on the tables so the mixture can be punched down into open-faced cups; sometimes the cups are filled by workers brushing the compound across the face of the table. Next comes a foil disc or shellacked paper. Anvils are inserted as the plates line

When you pull the trigger, the hammer or striker crushes the explosive compound on a primer's anvil. Pressures in modern cartridges can exceed 60,000 psi almost instantly, as the powder charge burns.

up. Priming mix is stable when it is wet, but extremely hazardous to work with when dry. No mix is allowed to dry in primer rooms!

Long before primers became practical, gunpowder presented its own hurdles. From its inception in the fourteenth century until the middle of the nineteenth, blackpowder generated the gas that pushed bullets out of gun barrels. "Black" is essentially a blend of fuels and oxidants. Nitroglycerine, discovered, in 1846, by Italian Ascanio Subrero, promised higher performance. A clear liquid of nitric and sulfuric acids plus glycerin, nitro is an oxygen-rich compound just waiting to rearrange itself into more stable gases. It does not need a spark to change; a little jolt will do. With age, nitro becomes less stable and more dangerous.

In 1863, Swedish chemist Emmanuel Nobel and his son Alfred learned how to put this touchy substance in cans. That made it easier to handle, but no less hazardous. After the Nobel factory in Germany blew up, Alfred found that soaking the porous earth Kieselguhr with nitro rendered the chemical less sensitive to shock. Dynamite followed, in 1875.

Blackpowder has competition from modern substitutes, which are cleaner burning and, in pellet form, more convenient. Dan Pawlak pioneered Pyrodex. Tragically, he died in a plant explosion.

DON'T TRY THIS AT HOME!

Meanwhile, Swiss chemist Christian Schoenbein had discovered that cotton treated with sulfuric and nitric acids formed a compound that burned so fast the cotton would be consumed without igniting blackpowder heaped on top of it! John Hall and Sons then built a guncotton plant in Faversham, England. It blew up. So did most other guncotton plants. Chemists concluded this substance had little use as a propellant, because it burned too fast and was too unstable. Eventually, bright people figured out how to harness these frisky compounds. During the 1850s, J.J. Pohl developed a fuel he called "white powder." It comprised potassium chlorate, yellow potash, and sulfur. Though a second-rate propellant, it served the Confederacy during the Civil War, when blackpowder became unavailable. Wartime backyard powder mills turned out propellants of widely varying compositions and behaviors.

In 1869, German immigrant Carl Dittmar erected a plant to make "Dualin," sawdust treated with nitroglycerin. A year later he introduced his "New Sporting Powder." By 1878, he was building a mill in Binghampton, New York. It blew, taking part of Binghampton with it. When Dittmar's health failed, he sold what was left of his firm. One of his foremen, Milton Lindsey, landed at the King Powder Company, where he worked with president G.M. Peters to develop "King's Semi-Smokeless Powder." The patented 1899 formula contained saltpeter, wood cellulose, charcoal, and sulfur. Dupont's "Lesmoke" came along soon thereafter, with roughly the same composition. Fouling remained a problem, but the residue didn't harden like that of blackpowder—an asset not shared by early smokeless, which left nothing to dilute or carry off the corrosive primer salts. "Lesmoke" was more hazardous to produce than smokeless, however.

Paul Vieille of France is generally credited with the first successful smokeless powder. "Poudre B" comprised ethyl alcohol and celluloid. But, in the 1870s, a decade before Vieille's triumph, Austrian chemist Frederick Volkmann patented a cellulose-based powder. Unfortunately, Austrian patents were not acknowledged worldwide. By 1887, Alfred Nobel had found he could employ his blasting compound as a propellant. A year later he introduced "Ballistite." This double-base powder (it had both nitrocellulose and nitroglycerin), was similar to a new powder developed at the same time by Hiram Maxim of machine-gun fame. Concurrently, the British War Office began looking for a more effective rifle powder and came up with "cordite," named for its spaghetti-like form that was first called "cord powder." The formula of 58-percent nitroglycerine/37-percent guncotton was later changed to 30-percent nitroglycerine/65-percent guncotton, plus mineral jelly and acetone. Nobel and Maxim sued the British government for patent infringement, but got nowhere.

As forward a step as the new smokeless powders were, they had their problems. Variations in load densities plagued handloaders. "Bulk" powders could be substituted bulk for bulk for blackpowder. "Dense" or gelatin powders could not be safely measured by bulk, because their energy/volume ratios were higher. The shooting industry marked shotgun loads in "drams equivalent"—in performance, these matched shotshells loaded with the marked number of blackpowder drams (the antiquated "drams equivalent" term prevails on shotgun shell boxes to this day). Rifle and pistol shooters were advised to treat smokeless as an entirely new powder with new measures.

The first military round designed for smokeless powder was the 8mm Lebel, adopted by France, in 1886. England followed with the .303 British, in 1888, Switzerland with the 7.5x55 Schmidt-Rubin a year later. By the mid-1890s nearly all nations that could muster an army were equipping soldiers with smallbore bolt rifles firing smokeless cartridges. The new propellant boosted bullet speed by a third and didn't give away a rifleman's position with lingering clouds of spent saltpeter. Oddly, most powder companies of this era failed. Fierce competition, substandard product, and the hazards of powder manufacture made this a tough business. Firms blossomed and faded.

During the Great War, Hercules manufactured cordite powder for the British government—up to 12,000 pounds a day. The company also sold three million pounds of small arms propellants and 54 million pounds of cannon powder. The conflict spurred improvements in powders and their manufacture. Plagued by copper residue in cannon bores, U.S. munitions experts took a tip from the French, adding tin to their propellants. DuPont's No. 17 became No.

17½. No. 15 became No. 15½. Tin levels were halved when dark rings appeared in the bores of National Match rifles, a result of tin cooling near the muzzle.

Now, myriad powders spanning a range of burning rates serve ammunition firms and handloaders. Single-base smokeless uses only nitrocellulose to generate pressure; double-base powders have the added kick of nitroglycerine. That extra oomph makes double-base powders a logical choice in cases of modest capacity. VihtaVuori's double-base 500-series powders, for example, deliver more energy than 100-series single-base powders that burn at equivalent rates. Nitro also reduces the tendency for grains to draw moisture. Its drawback: residue. Double-base powders don't burn as cleanly as single-based.

SPAGHETTI WITH ENTHUSIASM

Smokeless powder starts out as nitrocellulose, vegetable fiber soaked in nitric and sulfuric acids. Guncotton, a special kind of nitrocellulose, has slightly higher nitrogen content and lower solubility. Like other forms of nitrocellulose in powder production, it comes from crude cotton fibers or "linters," which are boiled in caustic soda to remove oils. Water formed in nitrating is absorbed by sulfuric acid, preventing decomposition by hydrolysis. A centrifuge strips excess acid. Then the linters are rinsed and boiled 48 hours to purge the acid, which can cause spontaneous combustion. The cotton is beaten and boiled again. Agitators fluff it.

Magnum cartridges resulted from the development of progressive-burning "stick" and ball, or spherical, powders. Thank high but controlled pressure curves!

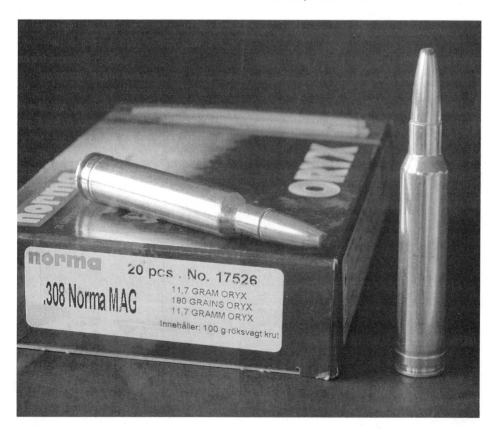

Washed in solvent, it is then heated to evaporate the solvent. Hard grains of powder (and water) remain. Ether is used to dissolve the fibers in nitrocellulose marked for single-base powders, acetone for double-base (and, again, adding nitroglycerin produces the double-base powder).

At this point in production, the powder is an unstable soup. Mixing turns soup to jelly, which is squeezed through dies (extruded) to form slender tubes. Rollers push these tubes through a plate, where a whirling knife shears them into measured segments. The resulting grains still contain ether. They're sent to a warm, solvent-recovery room and there soaked in water for about two weeks. The wet single-base and freshly sheared double-base powders are then air-dried, sieved, and polished in drums that coat them with graphite. Tumbling smooths edges that might produce friction. Graphite further reduces friction while imparting a slate color. Uncoated powder is yellow.

In 1933, Western Cartridge Company introduced the first successful ball powder. Nitrocellulose intended for ball powder goes through a hammer mill that grinds it to a fine pumice. Blended with water and pumped as a slurry into a still, the nitrocellulose combines with chalk added to counteract the nitric acids. Ethyl acetate dissolves the nitrocellulose, producing a lacquer. Agitation and heat break the lacquer into small particles, or it is pressed through plates much like extruded powders and chopped by whirling knives. Tumbling leave the grains round. The ethyl acetate is distilled off; salt draws out moisture. In a water slurry, the grains pass through sizing screens, then to a heated still where nitroglycerine is added. Deterrents come next, to smooth the pressure curve by controlling burn rate. A centrifuge removes excess water. The grains are tumbled in graphite, then sized again. Some ball powders are measured blends of sizes. Some are purposefully rolled or crushed to manipulate burning characteristics.

Extruded powders look like segments of dry spaghetti. The central hole controls the burn rate and pressure curve. Powders whose grain surface area diminishes during the burn are classified as "degressive." Ball and flake powders are like this. Powders whose grain surfaces stay about the same size through most of the burn are said to be "neutral." A one-hole extruded powder falls in this category, because as flame eats away at the outer surface, it also consumes the grain from inside out. At that final point of gas release, of course, grain size shrinks rapidly. Large powder grains may have multiple holes—typically seven or 19—that help them burn "progressively." Progressive or neutral powders deliver sustained thrust, the launch needed for heavy, small-diameter bullets fighting lots of bore friction. But ball powders can work in this arena, too, with additives that throttle burn rate and gas release. Nearly all smokeless fuels have three additional components: a stabilizer to prevent decomposition of the nitrocellulose; graphite to make handling easier and boost electrical conductivity so static electricity doesn't pose a threat; and a flame retardant to reduce muzzle flash. Additives have a negligible effect on bullet velocity.

Whichever powder fuels the ammunition in your rifle, efficiency runs only to about 30 percent. In other words, only a quarter to a third of the energy released by the propellant actually pushes your bullet. About the same amount is lost as internal heat during firing. Nearly 40 percent jets out the muzzle as hot—and useless—exhaust! By the way, only about .1-percent of the powder's energy reaches you as felt recoil.

CHAPTER 28

THEY PUT THE *OOMPH* BEHIND BULLETS!

Some of the names have faded, but without them,
your rifle has all the utility of a garden stake.

In 1802, E.I. DuPont de Nemours established its first factory on Delaware's Brandywine River. French immigrant Eleuthere Irenee DuPont had assured Alexander Hamilton, "I can make better blackpowder than what your country now has in its magazines." Soon the enterprising DuPont built a plant in Wilmington. Gunpowder remained the firm's primary product for most of the nineteenth century. In the 1880s, DuPont added a plant at Carney's Point. During World War I, 25,000 people worked at this Brandywine facility, providing more than 80 percent of powders used by the Allies (the British and French, the Danes and Rus-

DuPont established its first powder factory on Delaware's Brandywine River, in 1802. IMR (Improved Military Rifle) powders replaced the MR series, in the 1920s.

sians, as well as U.S. troops)! Following the transition from black to smokeless powders, "MR"—for Military Rifle—began appearing on cans of DuPont powders. The IMR stable of Improved Military Rifle powders came along in the 1920s, four-digit designations replacing two-digit numbers at DuPont. The first entry: IMR 4198.

Meanwhile, many competing firms arose. Some tenures were brief. The Giant Powder Company vanished in an explosion, in 1898, four years after Tennessee's Leonard Powder Company folded. Laflin & Rand pursued Ballistite, but considered Nobel's price of $300,000 plus royalties too steep. Ballistite manufacture later came under DuPont's wing, which contracted that job to Laflin & Rand. Lightning, Unique, Sharpshooter, and L&R Smokeless powders also came from Laflin & Rand.

The Robin Hood Powder Company of Vermont became the Robin Hood Ammunition Company, before it sold, in 1915, to the Union Metallic Cartridge Company. The American E.C. & Schultz Powder Company was acquired by DuPont, in 1903, then became part of Hercules, when DuPont was split by court order, in 1912. DuPont and the California Powder Works began serving U.S. soldiers, in 1897, with nitro fuels that resembled cordite. DuPont's IMR (Improved Military Rifle) 4895 later became the powder of choice for the .30-06 M2. Even after Hercules started up its operation in Kenville, New Jersey, DuPont dominated the market in small arms powder; it manufactured up to a ton daily. By the onset of World War I, Her-

cules had established a factory in Parlin, New Jersey, there making nitrocellulose and popular rifle and pistol powders, including Bullseye, Infallible, and HiVel. But DuPont got the big war contracts. It established plants in Old Hickory, Tennessee, and Nitro, West Virginia. Combined capacity: 1.5 million pounds per day! After the war, DuPont bought the town of Old Hickory to build a rayon factory. One day, in August 1924, powder magazines on the premises caught fire. More than 100 buildings and *50 million pounds* of powder disappeared in a horrific fire.

DuPont weathered not only the Depression, but scathing political attacks from some U.S. senators, who accused the company of war-mongering. As Hitler revved up his war machine, the U.S. prepared to re-arm, and DuPont boosted its production capacity. But the company's relationship with Congress throttled its investments. Rather than build new plants, the firm contracted to operate government facilities for a dollar a year. That way, it could not be said to have a stake in the hostilities. DuPont subsequently supervised construction of seven new factories. Another went up in Canada. At the height of the second World War, these operations shipped a million pounds of powder a day.

DuPont made powder for troops in Vietnam, as well. In the summer of 1978, DuPont contracted with Valleyfield Chemical Products, in Quebec, to produce smokeless powder. The Valleyfield plant (built in the 1940s), was run by CIL, or Canadian Industries, Limited, a branch of the government. Valleyfield was bough, in 1982, by Welland Chemical, which became EXPRO. Late in 1986, DuPont sold its smokeless powder business to EXPRO. The IMR Powder Company established itself as a testing and marketing arm. IMR's lab and office, in Plattsburg, New York, gen-

Hodgdon's LEVERevolution and Superformance powders, developed by Hornady, bring the performance of those factory loads within reach of handloaders.

Handloading can improve accuracy in rifles that print ho-hum groups with commercial ammo. (This T/C Venture also shoots factory fodder very well.) RL-22 has a burn rate like that of H4831.

erated ballistics data for IMR powders and distributed them. With an annual manufacturing capacity of more than 10 million pounds, EXPRO made powders for Alliant and other brands. Though DuPont owned 70 percent of Remington for decades, it also provided powder for competing ammunition firms.

TWENTY-FIVE TONS OF INSURANCE

In mid-country, another powder dynasty grew. Half a century ago, blackpowder drew almost no interest from sportsmen. As World War II ground on, powder mills fueled its rifles and machine guns with smokeless. In 1945, huge stocks of powders remained in government arsenals. An ambitious Bruce Hodgdon thought he could peddle it to handloaders.

Brewster E. Hodgdon was born in Joplin, Missouri, in 1910. After business studies at Pittsburg State College, then at Washburn, he married high school sweetheart Amy Skipworth. In the mid-1930s, Bruce worked as a gas appliance salesman. Later, he and Amy bought a small farmstead in Johnson County.

When he sold a life insurance policy to buy 50,000 pounds of powder, Bruce knew it was a gamble. Sure, this was 4895, a popular fuel for the favorite .30-06. And it came really cheap. But Bruce had nowhere to store such a quantity, and no market. He bought a derelict boxcar and moved it to a rented cow pasture. He placed a one-inch ad in the *American Rifleman*. Mail-order price for that first Hodgdon powder: $30—*for 150 pounds*! As demand grew, Bruce's powder supply dwindled. To get more, he went to an Australian factory with a sample of the remnant. It was 4831, produced by DuPont for cartridges bigger than the '06.

Long ago, I was shown a keg of Hodgdon 4831 powder.

"It's still gray," said its owner, unwrapping the tape securing the cardboard lid. He set the lid aside and plunged his hand into the silvery, slippery kernels. "See. No red dust." I didn't have enough .270 cases to use 50 pounds of powder. I bought it anyway. Thirty-five years later, I fired a group with cartridges I'd loaded with that H4831 in the 1980s. The holes touched.

Hodgdon couldn't have chosen better powders, and he was quick to seize on the warm reception they got from handloaders hungry for fuel. He enlisted his family's help to build the business.

"Early on, the powder cans were metal," says son J.B. "My brother Bob and I glued on the labels and built shipping boxes from orange crates. On our way to school, we drove tons of 4895 to REA and Merriam Frisco terminals in the trunk of a 1940 Ford."

Amy became bookkeeper. Orders soon included other shooting supplies, eventually rifles and ammunition. Copper-lined kegs were later replaced by cardboard.

"We sold the salvaged copper for more than those first batches of powder," recalls J.B.

By 1952, brisk powder sales prompted Bruce to quit his appliance job in Kansas City and funnel all his energy into the powder business, B.E. Hodgdon, Incorporated. J.B. and Bob joined him after finishing school in 1959 and 1961. Industry colleagues helped Bruce lobby the Interstate Commerce Commission to change the classification of some powders to "Flammable Solid." Containers under eight pounds each, in shipments totaling less than 100 pounds, could then be delivered by common carrier. In 1966, the family separated the powder enterprise from its firearms business to form Hodgdon Powder Company. It would come to include powder magazines and packaging facilities on 160 acres six miles west of the office.

From his headquarters at Overland Park, Kansas, Bruce Hodgdon sold about four million pounds of surplus powder, mostly H4831. This powder suited the belted magnum cartridges just beginning to catch on.

"We got some surplus H4831 fresh," J.B. says. "Some came from disassembled ammo. To sell it fast, we offered primers with it, in a package deal. Primers weren't easy for han-

Hodgdon's Hybrid 100 is one of many progressive-burn powders developed to serve a growing number of high-velocity magnum cartridges.

Accurate 2015 is an efficient powder that burns relatively fast, by modern standards. It's a top pick for the .35 Whelen and other medium-bore, mid-capacity rounds.

Scandinavian imports have much to offer riflemen, from Norma ammunition to Lapua brass and bullets and VihtaVuori powders.

Western Powders, in Montana, markets an extensive line of useful propellants. It also has the Montana Extreme stable of gun-cleaning supplies.

the .308." WC 852 took on a new moniker, when Bruce found it gave excellent results in his .22-250. "He used 38 grains behind a 50-grain bullet for 3,800 fps," Ron tells me. "The powder became H380."

By 1959, surplus stocks had run dry. The Hodgdons sought commercial sources. During WWII, the U.S. government had subsidized Olin and DuPont. The French-owned Australian Thales factory that currently manufactures Hodgdon's extruded powders also got its start as a U.S.-funded project.

"After the war," explains J.B., "countries transferred ownership to commercial firms. One of our first non-military sources was a plant in Scotland established to supply powder to the British."

The Hodgdons bought ball powder, pioneered by John Olin in 1933, from the Olin Corp. At first Bruce called ball powders ball powders. "But we soon learned Olin had registered that name," says J.B. "so we changed our designation to 'spherical.'" Olin's Winchester powder is currently made by St. Mark's, an industry supplier owned by General Dynamics and operated at a Florida location of that name. Since 2005, Hodgdon has marketed Winchester canister powders under a licensing agreement. Though DuPont decided not to sell powders to Hodgdon in the 1960s, Hodgdon now owns DuPont's IMR business! It also distributes Finland's VihtaVuori line. Hodgdon does not itself manufacture powder.

Brewster E. Hodgdon died, in 1997. He lived modestly and seldom traveled. His interests included goose hunting and small-bore rifle competition. He taught his sons from the Bible. When he turned the firm over to them, in 1976, it was with no strings. The company he started by trading a life insurance policy for 25 tons of powder now markets 80 types of propellants.

dloaders to find then. One of Dad's packages included a 150-pound keg and 15,000 primers for $49.95." Or you could get a 50-pound keg with 10,000 primers, or a 20-pound keg with 5,000. "Bob and I screened that powder with a double-mesh drum cranked by hand.

At this writing, Ron Reiber has worked at Hodgdon for 20 years. He remembers early powders no longer available, and some with new names. "H335 was first designated WC 844, a powder for the 55-grain .223 load in the M16. It followed BL-C2, developed as WC 846 for a 147-grain hardball in

CHAPTER 29

SHORT MAGNUMS, BELTED AND OTHERWISE

On the highway, these hot rods would draw flashing blues.
In rifles, their performance sets the bar.

From left, .458, .338, and .264 Winchester
Magnums. They were fashioned in the late 1950s
from the .375 H&H case shortened to 2.50 inches,
in order to function in .30-06-length actions.

My first elk rifle, a Henriksen-built 98 Mauser, was chambered in .300 Holland. At last light in a darkening Oregon meadow long ago, I turned to find myself eyeball to brow tine with a six-point bull. A Speer bullet brought him down. Since then, many of the elk I've shot have fallen to .300s. Winchester's .300, introduced in 1963, has become very popular across the country. In a decade guiding hunters, I've also seen more elk killed with that round than with any other.

Now, of course, Winchester has another potent .30. The .300 Winchester Short Magnum (WSM) appeared in 1999. It measures just 2.76 inches *loaded*, compared to 3.31 inches for the .300 Winchester Magnum. The roots of both go back to a .30-caliber rifle cartridge developed by the brilliant inventor Charles Newton. Alas, even when loaded by Western Cartridge, no commercial firm other than Newton's chambered rifles for it. Western dropped the loading, in 1938. Meanwhile, the .300 H&H joined Western's catalog. A long, belted round designed for cordite powder, the "Super .30," as it was called at its 1925 U.S. debut, duplicated .30 Newton performance. But, like the Newton, it suffered from a dearth of commercial rifles Stateside. The Holland's 2.85-inch hull required a long action, like the costly magnum Mausers'.

In 1937, Winchester offered the .300 H&H in its Model 70. By the time Remington added it to the 721, in 1949, Roy Weatherby had fashioned a line of cartridges based on the Holland hull. Unlike the .257, .270, and 7mm Weatherby, their 2.5-inch cases sized for .30-06-length actions, the .300 Weatherby was as long as its parent—just blown out to hold more powder. Meanwhile, American wildcatters Charlie O'Neil, Elmer Keith, and Don Hopkins came up with the .333 OKH, essentially a .30-06 necked for .333-inch bullets. To give the Kynoch 300-grain steel-jacketed round-nose bullet higher speed, the three experimenters put it in a necked-up .300 H&H case. Not surprisingly, these long bullets, designed for the .333 Jeffery, came apart in tough game. Later OKH rounds were necked to .338 so they could use American bullets. Results: the .338-06 and .338 Winchester Magnum.

The .338 Winchester didn't arrive until 1959, three years after the firm announced its first short belted round. The .458 Winchester Magnum became the first U.S. cartridge to compete with British Nitro Express ammunition. The standard load, a 500-grain solid at 2,130 fps, delivered 5,040 ft-lbs of muzzle energy. (Those initial figures were later trimmed to 2,040 and 4,620, and many hunters claimed factory .458 loads fell short of 2,000 fps.) The compact 2.5-inch case de-

manded compressed loads of some powders, resulting in ignition problems. Still, many professional hunters in Africa favor the "four-five-eight," especially for culling operations, where magazine rifles offer a firepower advantage over doubles.

FASTER, FLATTER ... AND VERSATILE!

Winchester couldn't have expected to sell truckloads of rifles firing thumb-size bullets. Besides, at $310, a Model 70 in .458 cost nearly double what you'd pay for a .30-06. But sales apparently satisfied the Olin accountants, so another magnum went on the drawing board.

Like the .458 and Weatherby's short magnums, the .264 Winchester derived from the .300 H&H case. News of the .264 came in 1958, the 26-inch barreled Model 70 dubbed "Westerner" appeared a year later. Winchester cataloged 100- and 140-grain soft-points at 3,700 and 3,200 fps, respectively.

The .264 used huge charges of slow powder and soon earned a reputation as a barrel-

Essentially a short .338 Winchester Magnum, the .325 WSM arrived late in that series. Its 200-grain bullet leaves the barrel at 2,950 fps.

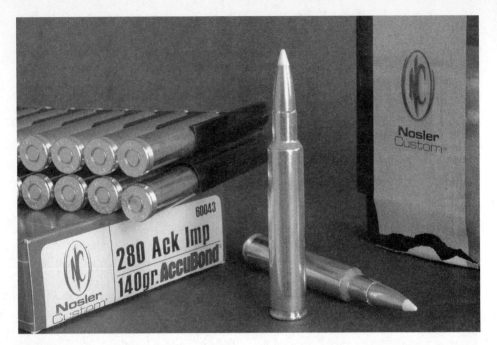

Early attempts at boosting velocity resulted in "Improved" cartridges. P.O. Ackley reduced body taper and sharpened shoulder angles for more capacity. Here we see a .280 Improved, now loaded by Nosler.

burner. It made lots of noise and kicked harder than the more efficient and hugely popular .270. When Winchester revised the .264's 140-grain velocities down to 3,030 fps, this cartridge lost what little traction it had. Actually, it is among the best choices for long shooting at deer and elk. My handloads push 140-grain bullets well past original catalog velocities, but without undue pressure.

You'd think the deep affection shooters had for the .30-06 and .270 Winchester would have put the East Alton team on the trail of a .300 or 7mm magnum. Instead, they followed their .264 with the .338 Magnum. Even by today's standards, the .338 Winchester is on the brawny side of versatile. It kicks 200-grain bullets along at 2,900 fps and 250s at 2,700. At the muzzle, 225- and 250-grain spitzers register over 4,300 ft-lbs. Some .338 loads hit *much* harder.

The cartridge got a slow start at market. Recoil from the Model 70 Alaskans that Winchester first offered for the .338 impressed riflemen already familiar with the .30-06. The violence might have been expected. After all, the rifle's name conjured visions of seven-foot moose and brown bears the size

of Volkswagons. Few hunters shot animals that big, and elk were falling regularly to the .30-06. Like the .264, the .338 also suffered from a limited selection of bullets available in factory loads.

Regrettably, I've sold my Alaskan, a marvelous elk rifle. I recall a bleak afternoon on the trail in Montana's Bob Marshall Wilderness. Suddenly, across a steep draw, a five-point bull galloped into view and toward timber. I swung off my pony, yanked the .338 from its scabbard, and sprawled against a log. A 200-grain Power Point caught the elk in the slats as it vanished into the shadows. We found it dead, the bullet balled up against the off shoulder. Another time, in an Oregon thicket, three bulls tried to slip out behind me as cows crashed away. I turned just in time to fire at the biggest elk and drop him. He rose and pressed on. I fired twice more. My last 250-grain Speer kept him down. Elk adrenalin is powerful stuff.

Oddly enough, the first .30-caliber cartridge designed on a short magnum case hailed not from the Winchester shop, but from Norma of Sweden. The .308 Norma case measures 2.56 inches, slightly longer than the .338, so it did not fit rifles chambered to the wildcat .30-338 developed in the 1960s by shooters tired of waiting for Winchester to field a .300 magnum. But Norma blunted its entry into the U.S. market by first offering only *cases*. A year and a half later, ammunition appeared. "Re" on the headstamp meant the brass was Boxer-primed and reloadable.

Winchester's momentum sustained a bigger blow, in 1962, when Remington announced its 7mm Magnum. There's only .020-inch difference in bullet diameter between .264 bullets and 7mm bullets. But the public that had shunned Winchester's fast 6.5mm embraced Remington's 7mm. The reasons? A sympathetic press and company advertising that cleverly billed the new cartridge as a deer/elk round. The .264 had, tragically, been offered up as a deer/*varmint* cartridge, a niche already filled by the less violent .243 and .25-06. The 7mm Remington Magnum also piggybacked on the debut of the sleek Model 700 rifle.

Winchester's response to Remington's belted 7mm appeared in 1963. Shooters had expected the .300 Winchester Magnum. But it was not the necked-down .338 they anticipated, nor a clone of the .308 Norma. Winchester, instead, delivered a case 2.62 inches long, with a neck shorter than bore diameter. It held more powder than Norma's hull, though in standard actions you couldn't use the extra capacity, because you had to seat bullets deep to clear the magazine. Still, the .300 Winchester Magnum steadily ate market share from the 7mm Remington Magnum. In my surveys of elk hunters during the 1990s, the .30-06 and Remington's 7mm Magnum shared the popularity prize; the .300 Winchester owned third place.

VELOCITY VS. EFFICIENCY

For more than two decades, the .300 Winchester and 7mm Remington Magnums satisfied hunters having a thirst for power. Subsequent rimless

From left: .300 Remington Short Action Ultra Mag, .300 Winchester Short Magnum, .300 Ruger Compact Magnum, all recent and about equal ballistically. The WSM arrived first, still sells best.

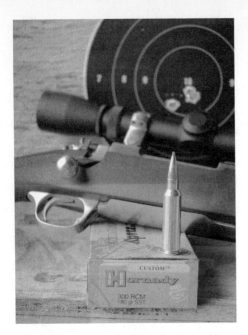

magnums—long and short—by Don Allen, John Lazzeroni, and Remington upped the ante. Not to be outdone, Weatherby weighed in with its .30-378 and was soon scrambling to fill orders from shooters craving a .300 the size of an aspirin bottle. Norma couldn't make Weatherby cartridges fast enough.

The only cartridge to ballistically challenge the .30-378 Weatherby Magnum is John Lazzeroni's 7.82 Warbird, a rimless round fashioned from scratch, but similar to the .404 Jeffery. The .404 also served as raw material for Remington's Ultra Mag, 13-percent bigger than the .300 Weatherby. You won't get 13-percent more velocity from the Ultra Mag, though, because as case volume grows, cartridges become less efficient. For each additional increment of performance, you need more powder than you did for the last increment. And therein lies the beauty of the .300 Winchester Magnum. It is less efficient than the .30-06, but you get a lot more performance with manageable recoil.

Years ago, climbing out of a canyon, I saw other hunters flush a bull elk on a ridge above. Quickly I sat, snugged the sling, and triggered my .300 as the crosswire passed the bull's chest. He tumbled like a shot hare.

Started at 3,100 fps, a 180-grain Nosler Partition through the front ribs has dramatic effect. My favorite load of 75 grains H4831 is also accurate in the rifles I've used.

You don't need a magnum to kill any North American big game. Controlled-upset bullets have scotched the fragmentation that once plagued cartridges like the .30-06 and have made them more deadly on elk-size animals. Still, a 7mm or .30 magnum is ideal for long shooting at tough game. Though I have friends who've loaded VLD (very low drag) bullets in the 7mm Remington Magnum and achieved most impressive results at distance, my vote goes to the .300. Of the big .30s, I most favor the .308 Norma, as it seems so beautifully designed. In truth, any .30 driving a 180-grain bullet at 3,000 fps is as lethal. There's plenty of energy left at 400 yards to kill elk, moose, or big bear. And today's bul-

The .300 Winchester Magnum, introduced in 1963, has more steam than its longer parent, the .300 H&H Magnum. Hunters and long-range target shooters have embraced the .300 Winchester.

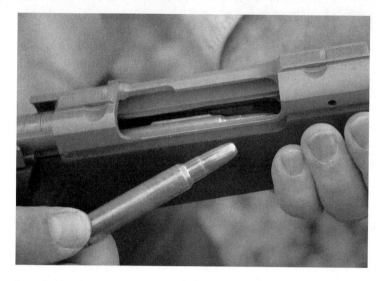

The .375 Ruger, a rimless round, packs a tad more punch than the longer, belted .375 H&H.

let selection is staggering. Finally, while 30 ft-lbs of recoil will certainly wake you up, it's not a brutal blow. You can fire a high-octane .30 in a lightweight deer rifle without having to explain the decision to your psychiatrist.

Arguably even better than the belted 2½-inch .30s and the .300 WSM are the rimless magnums that arrived while WSMs grabbed headlines. One is Remington's .300 Short Action Ultra Mag. As you'd expect, it's a short version of the leggy, clavicle-cracking .300 Ultra Mag. Its case closely resembles that of the .300 WSM, but it's slightly shorter. It fits handily in Remington's compact Model Seven action, but gives up no performance in doing so. It's a ballistic twin to the WSM. Only hair-splitters will tell you the WSM has slightly more case capacity and can edge the SAUM in handloads. One of my favorite rifles is a Custom Shop Model Seven in .300 SAUM. With it I bagged, by all accounts, the first elk taken with the round. The Idaho bull fell in a thicket just a few yards from the muzzle.

Similar in many ways is the .300 Ruger Compact Magnum, introduced by Hornady, in 2006. More than a thinly veiled copy of the .300 WSM or .300 SAUM, it and a companion .338 RCM were designed to wring magnum velocities from 20-inch barrels. Mitch Mittelstaedt, who headed the project, explained to me that, with new proprietary pow-

ders, his team was able to "tighten" pressure curves so the .300 RCM performs like ordinary .30 magnums in ordinary barrels, but doesn't lose as much enthusiasm in carbines. Lab tests showed velocity losses of 170 fps, when .300 WSM barrels were chopped from 24 to 20 inches; RCMs lose about 100.

Inspired by the 2.58-inch .375 Ruger, the .300 and .338 RCM share its .532-inch head. WSM rounds are bigger, with rebated .535-inch heads. RCM shoulder angles are 30 degrees. Case capacities average 68 and 72 grains of water to the mouth. For comparison, Remington .30-06 hulls hold 67 grains, Winchester .300 WSM cases 79 grains. Ruger Compact Magnums cycle through WSM magazines, but you can sneak four RCMs into most three-round WSM boxes. They're loaded to the same overall length (2.84 inches).

With chronograph guru Ken Oehler, I chronographed .300 RCM loads from the 20-inch barrel of a Ruger carbine. The Oehler 35 gave me readings of 2,840 fps with 180-grain bullets.

Winchester was inexplicably late marketing a short .30 magnum. But, more surprisingly, no other firm rushed to fill that void. Today, the .300 Winchester Magnum and .300 WSM are the most popular of their type, a pair of cartridges that even fans of the slick-feeding .300 Holland can cuddle to.

CHAPTER 30

THE BEST CARTRIDGES DURING THE DEPRESSION STILL ARE

Curmudgeons take note! You were right all along!

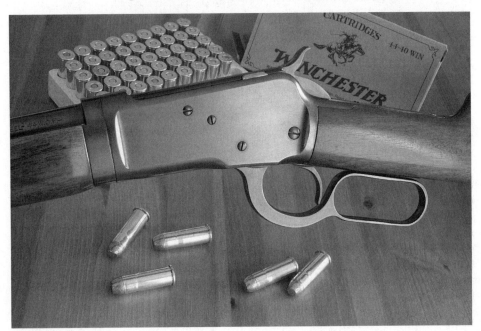

This lovely Winchester 53, a version of the Browning-designed Model 1892, is bored to .44-40, pioneered in the 1873 Winchester. Smokeless loads are still popular in rifle and revolver.

Many dozens of rifle cartridges have appeared since the development of smokeless powder. Most are unnecessary. Most, also, have endeared themselves to shooters who don't care if they're unnecessary. Your favorite may have come with an heirloom rifle, or killed your first deer, or drilled the tightest group you've ever shot. Cartridges that endure in a competitive market are ably promoted; but they must also give good account of themselves afield. While Jack O'Connor's enthusiasm for the .270 surely gave that round a boost, the cartridge also delivered in the field. Timing matters, too. The .270 came along when such rockets were poised to replace deer cartridges on the template of the .30-30.

Failure at market—and bare survival—can credit the same fickle factors. The .30-30 appeared in a Browning-designed rifle that became instantly popular and eventually sold six million copies. The first sporting cartridge for smokeless powder, it outperformed its competition. A century later, Remington's .300 Short Action Ultra Mag struggled. It is an efficient cartridge and fits comfortably in short actions.

It shoots as flat as a .270, with little more recoil than a .30-06. Its punch nearly matches that of the much bigger .300 Winchester Magnum. But Remington announced it on the heels of Winchester's .300 Winchester Short Magnum, which immediately sucked all the oxygen from the room. A flood of other short magnums washed ashore at the same time. The fertile, vacant, editorial soil that welcomed the .270 had shrunk and become crowded with other nascent candidates, all vying for attention.

My picks for the most useful and appealing rifle cartridges since the 1890s would include scores of popular rounds. Most would be recent, but many would also be redundant. Long ago, before the advent of non-corrosive primers or fog-proof scopes, before television and jet engines, shooters had pretty good ideas about cartridge design. If you were now limited to rifle rounds available during FDR's first term, you'd be well served. Here are five that, in my view, haven't been eclipsed. You'll pardon my omission of the .250 and .300 Savage, the .257 Roberts, 7x57 and .300 H&H. They merit page space I don't have!

The .30-30 Winchester, or .30 WCF, was our first smokeless hunting round. Thanks largely to Winchester and Marlin carbines, it's still popular, an excellent woods cartridge for whitetails.

.30-30 (.30 WCF)

Arguably the best-known rifle cartridge under the Winchester label, the .30-30 made its debut in 1895. Known early on as the .30 WCF (Winchester Center Fire), it was first loaded with 30 grains of smokeless powder and a 160-grain bullet that clocked 1,970 fps. This, our first commercial smokeless cartridge, earned a following in the John Browning-designed Winchester 1894 rifles and carbines. It later appeared in the Models 64 and 55, which have the same action. Mar-

.30-30 Ballistics

■ 150-grain Winchester Silver Tip (zero: 100 yards.)

	MUZZLE	100 yards	200 yards	300 yards	400 yards
velocity, fps	2390	2040	1723	1447	1225
energy, ft-lbs	1902	1386	989	697	499
arc, inches	-1.5	0	-7.5	-27.0	-63.0

■ 160-grain Hornady LEVERevolution FTX (zero: 100 yards.)

	MUZZLE	100 yards	200 yards	300 yards	400 yards
velocity, fps	2400	2150	1916	1699	1503
energy, ft-lbs	2046	1643	1304	1025	801
arc, inches	-1.5	0	-6.0	-20.9	-47.7

■ 170-grain Remington Core-Lokt SP (zero: 100 yards.)

	MUZZLE	100 yards	200 yards	300 yards	400 yards
velocity, fps	2200	1895	1619	1381	1191
energy, ft-lbs	1827	1355	989	720	535
arc, inches	-1.5	0	-8.8	-30.9	-71.1

lin picked up the .30-30 for its 1893 rifle. It proved by far the most popular offering in the firm's subsequent Models 36 and 336. Savage cataloged it for many years in the Model 99 and in the 170 pump gun.

Few hunters these days think of the tried and true .30-30 as a bolt-action cartridge, but Winchester chambered it in the Model 54, and Savage designed its inexpensive 340 for the round. You'll also find the .30-30 in well-known single-shots—Winchester High Walls and Remington Rolling Blocks. Modest pressures suit it well to hinged-breech firearms, from H&R rifles to Thompson/Center handguns. As a smokeless round, the .30-30 established itself with 150- and 170-grain bluff-nose bullets. Velocities: 2,390 and 2,200 fps.

The .30-30 has enjoyed great popularity in central and South America and even in Europe, where it is known as the 7.62x51R. It excels in combination guns. In 1979, Remington loaded it with a 55-grain .22-caliber bullet in a seven-grain plastic sabot. This .30-30 Accelerator load clocks nearly 3,400 fps. Hornady's soft polymer FlexTip-pointed bullets in LEVERevolution cartridges have given the .30-30 new life. Remington added a Managed Recoil load, with a 125-grain bullet at 2,175 fps. It's a good pick if you're introducing a youngster to a deer rifle, especially Grandpa's carbine with that steel buttplate.

The .30-30 has been called the quintessential whitetail round. In iron-sighted carbines, it's served hunters waiting beside deer trails, easing through poplars, or combing cedar swamps in short drives. While many deer are still shot close, rifle preferences have changed. Many hunters watch crop fields instead of trail intersections. And the deer have expanded their range into more open country, especially in the West. The .30-30 carbine remains a convenient saddle gun.

I've shot deer, pronghorn, black bear and elk with the .30-30. Inside 150 yards, it's adequate for all, though elk and big bruins can test it. I decline all but ideal shots at very close range. LEVERevolution ammunition turns the .30-30 into a 200-yard deer and pronghorn round. Hornady 160-grain FTX bullets at 2,400 fps get there with 1,300 ft-lbs, almost as much as standard 170-grain bullets bring to 100 yards! Because the .30-30 arrived in lever-action rifles designed for blackpowder, commercial loads hew to a 42,000-psi pressure ceiling.

.30-06 SPRINGFIELD (.30 GOV'T '06)

The .30-06 cartridge was conceived, in 1900, when engineers at Springfield Armory

From left: The .300 Savage came in 1920, ballistically a notch below the .30-06. The .308 arrived in 1952, one of the world's most versatile cartridges. But the .300 Savage lacks little to match it.

.30-06 Springfield Ballistics

■ **150-grain AccuTip** (Remington) — *zero: 200 yards.*

	MUZZLE	100 yard.	200 yards	300 yard.	400 yards
velocity, fps	2910	2686	2473	2270	2077
energy, ft-lbs	2820	2403	2037	1716	1436
arc, inches	-1.5	+1.7	0	-7.4	-21.5

■ **165-grain Barnes Triple Shock** (Federal Premium) — *zero: 200 yards.*

	MUZZLE	100 yards	200 yards	300 yards	400 yards
velocity, fps	2800	2560	2340	2120	1920
energy, ft-lbs	2870	2405	2000	165	1350
arc, inches	-1.5	+1.8	0	-8.4	-24.2

■ **180-grain AccuBond CT** (Winchester Supreme) — *zero: 200 yards.*

	MUZZLE	100 yard.	200 yards	300 yards	400 yards
velocity, fps	2750	2573	2403	2239	2082
energy, ft-lbs	3022	2646	2308	2004	1732
arc, inches	-1.5	+1.8	0	-7.9	-22.8

began work on a battle rifle to replace the .30-40 Krag-Jorgensen. Their prototype emerged in 1901. Two years later, the Model 1903 Springfield appeared. Its .30-caliber rimless cartridge headspaced on the shoulder, like the 8x57 Mauser. A 220-grain bullet at 2,300 fps made the .30-03 a ballistic match for the 8x57, and a 236-grain bullet went out at 2,125.

A year after the .30-03's debut, Germany switched to a new 154-grain 8mm spitzer at 2,800 fps. The Americans countered with the Ball Cartridge, Caliber .30, Model 1906. It hurled a 150-grain bullet at 2,700 fps. Someone decided to shorten the case by .07 to .494. All .30-03 rifles were recalled for re-chambering.

The first .30-06 bullets were jacketed with an alloy of 85-percent copper/15-percent nickel. It did not hold up at .30-06 velocities, and fouling rendered rifles inaccurate. Tin plating reduced fouling, but, over time, tin "cold-soldered" to case mouths and could cause pressure spikes. An alloy of zinc and copper, 5/95 or 10/90, solved this problem. It became known as "gilding metal."

After World War I demonstrated the val-ue of high ballistic coefficients, the Army replaced the 150-grain '06 bullet with a 173-grain spitzer at 2,646 fps. This M-1 round pestered troops to 5,500 yards. It hiked recoil, too. In 1939, the Army adopted the M-2 load. With a 152-grain spitzer at 2,805 fps, it saw U.S. troops through World War II. By conflict's end, two generations of riflemen were hopelessly in love with the .30-06.

As a hunting cartridge, the .30-06 is a fine choice for any North American big game and for all but a few ponderous beasts abroad. It is chambered in more rifles than any other round save, now, the .308. During the first 25 years of Model 70 production, Winchester sold this rifle in 18 chamberings. More than a third shipped (208,218) were .30-06s! You can buy '06 cartridges in more places than any other rifle ammunition. Such ubiquity endears the round to any traveling hunter who has lost luggage.

Ballistically, the .30-06 is a near match to the 7mm Remington Magnum. Given identical bullets and 200-yard zeros, the '06 hits within two vertical inches of the .300 Winchester at 300 yards.

.375 H&H MAGNUM

The English gunmaking firm of Holland & Holland introduced the .375 Belted Rimless Nitro Express, in 1912. It came to the U.S., in 1925, when Western Cartridge Company began loading it. Known Stateside as the .375 H&H Magnum, it fathered a necked-down version, the .300 H&H Magnum. About 1926, up-scale New York gun-builder Griffin & Howe began chambering the .375 in magnum Mauser rifles (as had Holland & Holland). In 1937, Winchester put the cartridge on its charter list of Model 70 chamberings. Remington offered it in the Model 725 Kodiak, fewer than 100 of which were built and all in 1961. Even Weatherby took an occasional order for a .375 H&H rifle, though the Weatherby line of high-velocity rounds included a blown-out version of the cartridge.

Because its hull measures 2.85 inches and factory loaded cartridges 3.6 inches, the .375 requires a long bolt and magazine. Steep case taper with a shoulder angle shy of 13 degrees are said to have prompted the belt to ensure positive headspacing. Holland & Holland in-

The grandfather of modern magnums, the British .375 Holland & Holland Magnum debuted in 1912. Western Cartridge started loading it Stateside in

.375 H&H Magnum Ballistics

■ **260 Nosler AccuBond** (Federal) — *zero: 200 yards.*

	MUZZLE	100 yards	200 yards	300 yards	400 yards
velocity, fps	2700	2510	2330	2160	1990
energy, ft-lbs	4210	3640	3130	2685	2285
arc, inches	-1.5	+2.0	0	-8.5	-24.5

■ **270 Winchester Fail Safe** (Winchester) — *zero: 200 yards.*

	MUZZLE	100 yards	200 yards	300 yard.	400 yards
velocity, fps	2670	2447	2234	2033	1842
energy, ft-lbs	4275	3590	2994	2478	2035
arc, inches	-1.5	+2.2	0	-9.5	-26.8

■ **300 Hornady FMJ** (Hornady Heavy Magnum) — *zero: 200 yards.*

	MUZZLE	100 yards	200 yards	300 yards	400 yards
velocity, fps	2705	2386	2089	1817	1568
energy, ft-lbs	4873	3792	2908	2198	1637
arc, inches	-1.5	+2.3	0	-10.1	-31.3

The .300 H&H, a necked-down .375, appeared in the Western Cartridge line, in 1925. It was a charter chambering in the Winchester M70. Roy Weatherby blew out the shoulder to form his .300 Weatherby

The original light-bullet load, a 235-grain soft-nose at 2,800 fps, is long dead, but few mourn its demise. Modern 260- and 270-grain bullets beat it in flight and deliver better terminal performance. Nosler's 260-grain Partition and AccuBond bullets fly as flat as 165-grain spitzers from a .30-06 and deliver more punch at 200 yards than the '06 musters at the muzzle. Drop at 300 yards is essentially the same. Though used primarily at modest ranges, .375 rifles can well handle a 200-yard zero.

Part of the .375's enduring popularity has to do with the people who have used it. John "Pondoro" Taylor praised it in his 1948 book *African Rifles and Cartridges*. Describing a buffalo hunt, he wrote, "I gave him the left barrel fairly in the center of his great chest … [the effect being] as though there had been a steel hawser stretched across his path just the right height above the ground to whip the forelegs from under him. He crashed on his nose … dead."

Jack O'Connor called the .375 H&H the queen of the medium-bores "and probably the best all-around cartridge ever designed." He wrote that were he to hunt all over the world with only one rifle, it would be a .375. He used the round for brown bears, lions, and "one very large tiger."

.270 WINCHESTER

The .270 Winchester dates to 1925, but its roots run deeper. Paul Mauser developed the 7x57 in the early 1890s, on the heels of the French 8x50R Lebel (the first smokeless military cartridge). The 7x57 launched a 173-grain bullet around 2,300 fps. It was adopted by many European and South American governments. Hunters found the 7x57 ideal for deer, mountain game, and antelope the world over.

troduced a flanged (rimmed) version of the .375 for double rifles. This option has faded, as belted hulls work fine in hinged-breech mechanisms. The .375 H&H is one of few cartridges widely chambered in both bolt rifles and doubles.

While some professional African hunters rate it as marginal for elephant and close-cover buffalo, the three-seven-five has floored many thousands of both. I killed an elephant with a frontal brain shot that drove the 350-grain Norma-loaded Woodleigh solid to the opposite flank. The bone-mashing momentum of controlled-upset 300-grain softpoints from Nosler, Barnes, Hornady, Winchester, and Trophy Bonded suits the .375 for shoulder shots on buffalo. The cartridge also has a big fan base in Alaska, where hunters trail brown bears into alder thickets.

Universally acclaimed as the top all-around cartridge for heavy, soft-skinned game, the .375 H&H appeals, as well, to hunters with no need for a "stopping rifle."

In 1917, the brilliant Wilhelm Brenneke introduced his 7x64, which drove a 173-grain bullet 500 fps faster than the 7x57. Eight years later, Winchester announced the similar .270, essentially a necked-down .30-06. The .270's .277-inch bullet is just .007-inch smaller than that of 7mms. The Winchester name helped endear it to hunters Stateside. So did Jack O'Connor, who began his career as a gun writer during the .270's infancy. When, in 1937, it made the list of charter chamberings in Winchester's Model 70, the .270 became even more popular. Only the .30-06 has enjoyed a larger production run in this rifle.

Initially loaded with 130-grain bullets at 3,000 fps, the .270 gained a reputation for destroying meat. Hunters accustomed to the modest damage inflicted by .30-30 bullets called for a milder load. Winchester complied with a 150-grain offering at 2,675 fps. Nobody bought it. Stronger bullets that opened predictably and drove deep at high impact speeds later gave the .270 more appeal.

When Roy Weatherby announced his .270

The .270 Winchester, here with a Browning X-Bolt, was introduced in 1925 and became a hit. Jack O'Connor wrote glowingly of it. Modern bullets make it even better.

Weatherby Magnum, in 1943, hunters were slow to embrace it, even though the belted round beat the .270 Winchester out the gate by 200 fps. Most shooters wanted high performance, but in affordable rifles that used ordinary ammunition. In 1957, the wildcat 7mm-06 became the commercially loaded .280 Remington. Stoked to 47,000 psi to function in Remington's pump and autoloading rifles, it got a peppier 150-grain load, in 1979, when it became the 7mm Express. The name didn't stick, and Remington revived the .280 designation. Ballistically, it's a .270. The 7mm Remington Magnum, which arrived in 1962, beats the .270 with heavy bullets, but no beast that falls to a 140-grain 7 Magnum bullet will survive a 130-grain .270.

Despite the .270 Winchester's success, there aren't a lot of factory-loaded .270-bore alternatives. The wildcat list includes the

.270 Winchester Ballistics

■ **130 Ballistic Silvertip** (Winchester) — *zero: 200 yards.*

	MUZZLE	100 yards	200 yards	300 yards	400 yards
velocity, fps	3050	2828	2618	2416	2224
energy, ft-lbs	2685	2309	1978	1685	1428
arc, inches	-1.5	+1.4	0	-6.5	-18.9

■ **140 SST** (Hornady) — *zero: 200 yards.*

	MUZZLE	100 yards	200 yards	300 yards	400 yards
velocity, fps	3090	2894	2706	2526	2353
energy, ft-lbs	2968	2603	2276	1983	1721
arc, inches	-1.5	+1.3	0	-6.1	-17.6

■ **150 Nosler Partition** (Federal) — *zero: 200 yards.*

	MUZZLE	100 yards	200 yards	300 yards	400 yards
velocity, fps	2850	2650	2460	2280	2110
energy, ft-lbs	2705	2345	2020	1735	1485
arc, inches	-1.5	+1.7	0	-7.4	-21.7

.270 Titus on the .300 Savage case, and the .270 Redding on the .308 Winchester hull but with a 30-degree shoulder. The long, rimless, .270 AHR appeared in the 1990s, designed by Ken Howell and offered in bolt guns by Ed Plummer under the banner of American Hunting Rifles. The .270 Winchester Short Magnum came later; it nearly matches .270 Weatherby performance.

The .270 Winchester is arguably the best open-country deer cartridge ever developed. Perhaps the best sheep round, too. I've shot elk with .270s. O'Connor used his on moose. Alaskan guide Hosea Sarber is said to have killed grizzlies with a .270. Modest recoil is a plus; almost anyone can learn to shoot a .270 well. With a 2.54-inch hull and 17½-degree shoulder, the .270 fits neatly in rifle mechanisms developed for the .30-06. Graceful in form and function, the .270 favors mid-range powders like RL-15, IMR 4895, and H380 with 130-grain bullets. I prefer RL-19 and 4350, but have charged many cases with surplus H-4831. No powder scale? You can dump H-4831 into a .270 hull and card it off the mouth.

.22-250

If you barged into the studios of CNN, grabbed a mike, and barked into the cameras that the .22-250 was, by golly, the best .22 centerfire cartridge ever, you'd still get thrown out of the studio. But a lot of shooters chomping chips in front of the tube would cheer. Most who disagreed would slink off to nurse their wounds over brass with other headstamps.

The .22-250 is now almost an octogenarian, but no other high-performance .22 has yet upstaged it. Not the .220 Swift, the .225 Winchester, the .224 Weatherby, or the .223 WSSM.

The .22-250's parent case is the .250 Savage, developed by Charles Newton, in 1913. During the 1930s, Harvey Donaldson, J.E. Gebby, J.B. Smith, John Sweany, and Grosvenor Wotkyns necked the hull to .22. A version by Gebby and Smith, circa 1937, became the "Varminter." Gebby copyrighted the name. But not until 1965 did the cartridge go commercial, when Remington began loading it and chambering the fast-stepping round in its still-new Model 700 rifle.

.22-250 Remington Ballistics

■ **50-grain AccuTip** (Remington) — *zero: 200 yards.*

	MUZZLE	100 yards	200 yards	300 yards	400 yards
velocity, fps	3050	2828	2618	2416	2224
energy, ft-lbs	2685	2309	1978	1685	1428
arc, inches	-1.5	+1.4	0	-6.5	-18.9

■ **60-grain SP** (Hornady) — *zero: 200 yards.*

	MUZZLE	100 yards	200 yards	300 yards	400 yards
velocity, fps	3090	2894	2706	2526	2353
energy, ft-lbs	2968	2603	2276	1983	1721
arc, inches	-1.5	+1.3	0	-6.1	-17.6

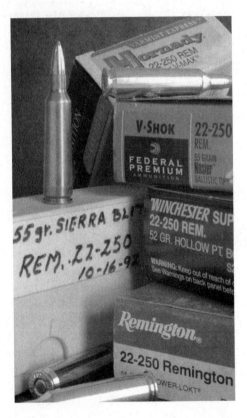

The .250 Savage came from the bench of inventor Charles Newton, in 1912. Wildcats on that case didn't make headlines until the 1930s, but no doubt some 'chuck hunter necked it to .22 earlier.

It is astonishing that, for 30 years, the .22-250 trundled along as a wildcat, while the Swift quickly appeared in the M70 Winchester. Even as Swift shooters lamented short case and throat life, the .22-250 remained in its shadow. The larger Swift managed 4,110 fps with 48-grain bullets. But the Varminter was close on its heels and, with modern powders, can match that speed.

Now the Swift has faded, while the .22-250 enjoys international acclaim. It's chambered in every varmint-class rifle I can think of, domestic and foreign. It was modified to join Remington's EtronX line of electronically ignited cartridges. That project failed, but the .22-250 is stronger than ever!

With a 50-grain bullet at 3,800 fps, the .22-250 brings more than 500 ft-lbs of energy to 400 yards—a knockout blow to any coyote or rockchuck! That bullet starts as fast as a 40-grain spitzer from a .223, but it bucks wind better and, at 400 yards, outpaces the .223 by 270 fps. A 60-grain .22-250 bullet at 3,600 fps beats a 75-grain .243 bullet off the blocks by 200 fps and is still faster at 400, where it dumps 627 ft-lbs to the .243's 768. A Varminter soft-point through the slats is deadly on deer, if not everywhere legal.

Handloading the .22-250 is easy. Choose from myriad bullets of 40 to 60 grains and powders in the mid-range of burning rates, such as AA2520, H335, IMR 3031, RL-15, Viht 140 and Varget.

CHAPTER 31

REDEFINING RIFLE AMMUNITION

Hornady Superformance ammo excels with less powder, less recoil.
Short barrels welcome!

L ike many of Hornady's 260 employees, Dave Emary is an active
rifleman. His high-power skills once
earned him a spot in the President's Hundred
at Camp Perry. Before joining Hornady's
engineering staff, he worked with artillery,
launching five-pound bullets at 7,000 fps
from 90mm cannons. He's shooting lighter
bullets now, but more efficiently.

"It's true. We get higher velocity under
SAAMI pressure limits. We don't compress
the powder. We lose just 18 fps per inch when
we chop down a .300 Winchester barrel."

Steve Hornady looked me in the eye.

"No other sporting ammo can come
close. Our Superformance delivers higher
speeds, flatter flights, less recoil, and low-

*While exploring more efficient powders for hunting
ammunition, Hornady re-defined the standard for
target and tactical loads.*

er pressures. It's as accurate as any ammo
we've ever made, less temperature sensitive,
and better in short barrels. It'll cost less than
souped-up cartridges."

That conversation took place early in
2011. The line of Superformance ammunition
then comprised 28 loads, from 95-grain .243
to 225-grain .338 Winchester Magnum. All
shared the feature that sets this line apart: ball
powders chemically and physically treated
to deliver the smooth, steep, but flat-topped
pressure curve that pushes bullets quickly
from the case, accelerates them smoothly
down the bore, then drops off decisively.

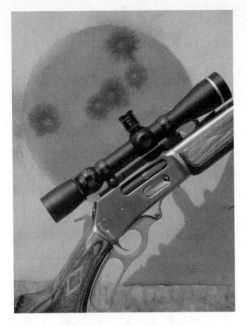

Heavy Magnum ammo, but with charges 10- to 15-percent lighter—and not compressed.

"Our tests show an increase of up to 300 fps over standard loads," said Steve Johnson, my contact at Grand Island back then. "We compared Superformance with two other brands of ammo in a Model 70 .270. Our SF got 3,100 fps from 130-grain bullets in that 22-inch barrel. The competition clocked 2,920 and 2,780."

Trials in temperatures from -15 to 140 degrees Fahrenheit confirm that Superformance powders don't care a great deal about temperature. According to Dave Emary, some loads show no velocity loss with a drop in the mercury to below zero.

"We've even found SF less sensitive to variation in bore diameter."

The Superformance line has grown, because those advantages are significant. In carbines, the low muzzle pressure of what Hornady catalogs as SF cartridges means you get less blast, and less energy is wasted at exit. Superformance loads equal the ballistic thrust of Hornady's earlier Light and

Hornady's Neil Davies tested Superformance loads in the field. He killed this kudu with one shot from a T/C Icon rifle.

Powders used in Superformance ammunition were not initially sold to handloaders, but Hodgdon soon offered a Superformance propellant, manufactured by St. Marks, in Florida (home of Winchester ball powders, also sold by Hodgdon).

Most SF ammunition is loaded with Hornady's polymer-tipped SST bullet and its lead-free GMX (gilding metal expanding). The GMX is not solid copper, but an alloy: 95-percent copper/five-percent zinc.

"It's the material we've used for years in Hornady bullet jackets," explains Jeremy Millard, who headed the GMX project, in 2007. He says the alloy keeps bore fouling to a minimum. GMX bullets are cut from wire

Hornady match ammunition developed for the M1 Garand excels in sporting rifles like the Ruger American. Wayne used it effectively on basketball-size gongs to 700 yards.

and swaged to shape. Because gilding metal is lighter than lead, GMX bullets hold to the low end of weight ranges for the caliber. This bullet relies on a unique cavity for upset in game. The front is parallel-sided to accept the tip; the cavity then tapers to its terminus even with the base of the ogive. That's where expansion stops. "We get 99-percent weight retention in ballistic gelatin," Jeremy told me. "All we lose is the plastic tip."

Loaded, a GMX looks just like an SST. The shank, covered by the case neck, differs. "We gave the GMX two cannelures to reduce bearing surface and allow metal displaced by the lands a place to go. The tapered heel is like the SST's. Ballistic coefficients are almost identical. You can use SST data."

"You'll see bigger velocity differences between lead-core and solid-alloy bullets in

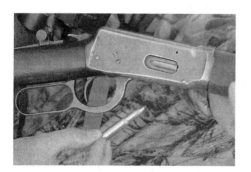

Hornady LEVERevolution cartridges with pointed FlexTip bullets brought many .30-30s out of the closet. Loads are friskier than ordinary ammo too, boosting effective range to over 200 yards.

The LEVERevolution line expanded beyond traditional deer-rifle cartridges to include rounds like the .450 Marlin and Hornady's own .308 and .338 ME. Superformance ammo for bolt rifles followed.

small cases," Dave explained. "That's because, in small hulls, the bullet represents a bigger percentage of total charge or ejecta weight." He added that, in developing the GMX, Hornady's team tried one, two, and three driving bands, settling on two, because "there was no significant drop in pressure with three."

My rifles drilled tight groups with the first batches of GMX bullets. I tested the bullet's lethality on a moose hunt with my friends and outfitters Lynn and Darrell Collins, in central British Columbia. Late in the hunt we spied a bull moving through open timber. When he stopped, I triggered my Ruger Hawkeye in .300 RCM. The 150-grain GMX bullet flew 105 yards and drove through the animal's shoulder. The bull fell backwards and did not move.

ACCURATE FROM THE START

Questions on bullet manufacture had triggered my first visit to Hornady's Grand Island, Nebraska, plant nearly 30 years ago.

"We shoot four five-shot groups with rifle bullets," I was told. "The average must pass muster. For .30s it's .6-inch at 100 yards, for .17s it's .4-inch. The 6mms come in at .45-inch, the .338s at .75-inch." Match bullets get no slack: .22 Match must nip into .35-inch, while .30 Match is tested at 200 yards to meet a .8-inch maximum.

Joyce Hornady insisted his rifles shoot accurately. He concluded that only uniform bullets would give him the "10 shots in one hole" he sought. In 1949, he decided he could make a bullet good as any he could buy. Other riflemen apparently agreed; his first year's production brought $10,000 in sales.

War in Korea interrupted Joyce's budding bullet business. In 1958, he built an 8,000-square-foot factory. The Secant Ogive soft-point has since distinguished Hornady hunting bullets. ("Secant" and "tangent" refer to the point from which an arc, measured in calibers, defines the bullet nose. The tangent measure is taken perpendicular to the bullet axis at the cylinder/cone juncture. Secant measure is based farther back.)

In 1964, Joyce Hornady entered the am-

Wayne killed this New Mexico pronghorn with a Hornady LEVERevolution load in .338 ME, plus iron sights.

munition business with his Frontier line. He used canister powders in once-fired brass, and his own bullets. Initial offerings were .243, .270, .308, and .30-06. When the Vietnam War choked off brass supplies in 1972, Joyce began buying new cases. Then son Steve moved back from Lincoln, where he'd been working for Pacific Tool. He brought that company with him.

Joyce Hornady lost his life in a plane crash, in 1981, en route to the SHOT Show in New Orleans. In 1983, Hornady Bullets, Frontier Ammunition, and Pacific Tool Company were absorbed into Hornady Manufacturing Company. They retained autonomy as Hornady Bullets, Hornady Custom Ammunition, and Hornady Reloading Tools. A year later, the enterprise was making its own cartridge cases in-house and loading them. Expanding its operations, Hornady launched itself as a major player in the ammunition field. It introduced the Light Magnum line, in 1995. Heavy Magnum ammo for belted cases followed. But rimfire ammunition was hardly on its radar.

The .338 Marlin Express is a .30-06 equivalent in traditional lever guns. It was developed by Hornady on the heels of the .308 ME. Its propellant technology led to Superformance ammo.

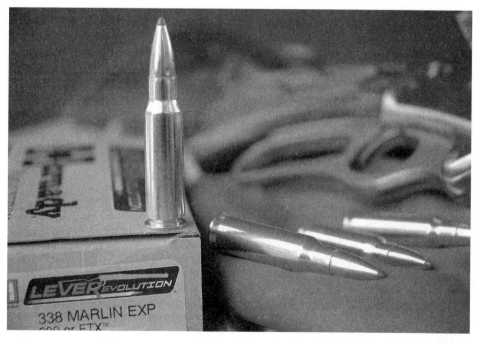

"Dave had worked out many of the early problems with sub-caliber rimfires," Steve recalled. "He got me excited about the .17 HMR, a .22 WMR case necked down. I phoned Darrell Inman at CCI to see about loading it. Darrell told me I had to order five million cartridges and pay for tooling! It was a dare. I took it."

Just weeks after it appeared, sales of .17 Hornady Magnum Rimfire ammunition rocketed past first-year projections. Hornady doubled its order for cartridges (still the only ones to bear Hornady's name). When, in 1998, I reported on the first .17 HMR rifles, ammo backorders totaled *12 million rounds*!

Meanwhile, sales of three million 33-grain bullets for the .20 Tactical hinted of strong interest in sub-.22s. With Ruger, Hornady assembled a scorching load in a modified .222 magnum case, a 32-grain V-Max .204-inch bullet at 4,200 fps. Negligible recoil allowed riflemen to see bullet impact through the scope. The .204 Ruger resulted. It quickly became popular for prairie dog shooting, selling briskly.

Dave Emary's interest in old lever rifles soon led to another development. The blunt bullet noses required in the tube magazines of those guns to prevent accidental ignition also throttled downrange performance. Solution: a resilient polymer nose that would "give" under the jar of recoil but spring back into aerodynamic shape. At .330 and .300, the ballistic

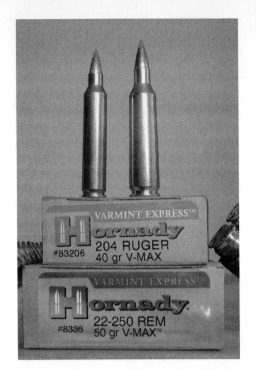

Hornady developed the .204 Ruger (left) with Ruger. It kicks Hornady bullets out at more than 4,000 fps, but with little recoil, so you can see the hit through the scope. In reach and effect, it's much like the .22-250.

coefficients for new .30-30 and .35 bullets were 20-percent higher than for blunt bullets. But nose-to-primer stacking under spring pressure produced no shock-induced ignition. The Hornady crew didn't stop there. Loading a 160-grain bullet ahead of new propellants in the .30-30 gave it 2,300 fps—close to .300 Savage performance. At 250 yards, the 160-grain FlexTip (FTX) spitzer hit half again as hard as flat-nose bullets from traditional loads.

NEW LIFE FOR LEVERS

LEVERevolution ammo revived America's favorite deer cartridges and boosted the fortunes of new ones like the .376 Steyr, .450 Bushmaster, and .30 T/C. Dave Emary next applied the technology to a round that would shoot like a .300 Savage in exposed-hammer ri-

Dave Emary, who developed LEVERevolution ammo, cycles a Marlin rifle chambered in .308 Marlin Express. The cartridge outperforms the .300 Savage.

fles, or do what the .307 Winchester might have done with pointed bullets not so deeply seated.

"We shortened the .307 hull from 2.015 to 1.92 inches," he told me then. "A mix of deterred and undeterred powders gave us a short, efficient curve for carbine barrels."

Dave called this cartridge the ".308 Marlin Express." It carries .300 Savage punch in a semi-rimmed case. But pressures above 47,000 psi could cause extraction problems in some levers, so Hornady throttled the .308 ME to 46,500. The 160-grain FTX developed for the .30-30 flew more accurately than the 165-grain spitzer intended for the new round. A redesign resulted in a 160-grain with long ogive, the Interlock band pushed forward to boost weight retention. The .308 ME's .395 ballistic coefficient gave it great reach. Exiting at 2,660 fps, it was still traveling at over 2,000 at 300 yards.

That fall, I shot the first elk to fall to the .308 ME, a New Mexico six-point whose antlers I lost to a thief in a motel parking lot on the way home.

Dave figured he could now fashion a lever-gun round to trump all others, "One to match the .30-06." With Mitch Mittelstaedt and other Hornady colleagues, he studied the .376 Steyr hull and tweaked it. A thicker web added strength. They gave the 200-grain .338 Winchester Magnum bullet a flexible tip and a thinner jacket to ensure upset at long range. The .338 Marlin Express measured 2.60 inches, loaded. At 2,565 fps, the pointed 200-grain bullet matched the exit velocity and energy of the .348 Winchester flat-nose, then left it behind. It hewed closely to the arc of a 210-grain Partition from the .338 Federal and a standard 180-grain bullet from the .30-06. At 400 yards, the 200-grain .338 ME and 180-grain .30-06 bullets both land with about 1,760 ft-lbs.

While raising the bar on lever-rifle performance, Hornady was also quietly at work on new bolt-action rounds. Development of powders that would later fuel Superformance ammunition proved the key to more efficient rounds for short-action carbines.

"Typically, we sacrifice 160 fps when we whittle a .30 magnum barrel from 24 to 20 inches," Mitch Mittelstaedt explained. "The .300 and .338 Ruger Compact Magnums leak only 100 fps in those four inches."

On a range with chronograph guru Ken Oehler, I set up one of his fine 35P instruments to check bullet speeds in Ruger rifles with 20-inch barrels. A trio of 180-grain .308 SST bullets averaged 2,840 fps. The Ruger in .338 RCM (Ruger Compact Magnum) sent 225-grain soft-points out the muzzle at 2,675 fps. Groups measured just over an inch.

"The RCMs are really short versions of the .375 Ruger," Mitch told me. "The .300 and .338 cases have .532-inch rims, mike 2.100 and 2.015 base to mouth. We load both to 2.840 inches, putting the shoulder of the .338 hull well back and keeping the case short, so we could use current .33 bullets. A 2.100-inch case would have put the mouth in front of cannelures and beyond the shanks of some bullets."

Just a couple years after RCMs debuted, Superformance ammunition replaced the charter loads. RCMs remain among the most efficient—and underrated—hunting cartridges.

CHAPTER 32

A CASE FOR METALLIC SIGHTS

Rifle scopes are like sunglasses: sometimes useful.
Simple sights can still be your best pick.

Tang sights were popular on early Savage 99s, as well as on Winchesters and Marlins.

A century ago, you'd have seen few rifles with optical sights. Though scopes appeared in combat as early as our Civil War and on hunting rifles during Westward expansion, they weren't widely used then. Target rifles accurate enough to warrant scopes wore iron sights through the famous long-range matches at Creedmoor, then into the smokeless era. Because iron sights have remained standard issue on infantry rifles from the Krag to the Springfield to the Garand and M14, they're still required in National Match competition. U.S. snipers have relied almost exclusively on opti-

cal sights since the first World War, and now ground troops are equipped with the likes of Trijicon's ACOG (Advanced Combat Optical Gunsight) and Leupold's HAMR (High Accuracy Multi-Range), both illuminated and designed for the M16 and kin. But even these rugged sights won't soon replace irons. For durability and quick aim at bayonet distance, a big aperture sight and a stout blade in front are hard to beat, and they don't take up a lot of room.

The same can be said of iron sights on hunting rifles. For decades after scopes got good enough to be practical, hunters mounted them on detachable or "pivot" mounts, "just in case." They wanted fast access to those iron sights. As late as the 1930s, rifles designed for all-around big-game hunting had no provision for scopes. During its first years of production, before WWII, Winchester's Model 70 lacked drilling on the rear bridge for a scope mount. Lever rifles developed in the 1890s had to be modified to accept optics. Double-barrel rifles built in England and on the Continent are still expected to be used only with open sights, though many now accommodate scopes. Honestly, iron sights are capable of remarkable precision—assuming your eyes haven't lost all their youth—and remain the most effective sights for some types of game, especially in tight cover.

You'll get the best accuracy from iron sights on a hunting rifle if you pair an aperture or "peep" rear with a fine bead up front. A long sight radius (distance between the sights) increases precision. The closer the aperture is to your eye, the smaller it can be, another boost to accuracy. Field of view, depth perception, and brightness all increase as your eye crowds the aperture. So it's no wonder rifles for nineteenth century Schüetzen matches had tang-mounted rear sights. Winchester and Marlin lever rifles and single-shot hunting rifles routinely wore tang sights before scopes upstaged them; now cowboy action shooters have rediscovered the value of these long-stemmed Marbles and Lyman aperture sights. Cocking-piece sights on bolt-action rifles have become as rare as crank-handles on automobile engines—but they're still among my favorites, because they're close to your eye and compact.

ABOUT APERTURES

On modern bolt-action target rifles, a receiver-mounted aperture sight complements a globe front with an insert that's the equivalent of a scope's reticle. For years on the small-bore circuit, my insert was an orange plastic disc with a hole in the middle just big enough to admit a narrow rim of white around the black target. The hole's bevel appeared dark, for a crisp sight picture.

An aperture rear sight on a hunting rifle must have a bigger hole to help you find the target right away, and to bring more light

Open sights look good on (and add utility to) big-game rifles used in a variety of places. This beautiful switch-barrel Mauser has QD scope mounts, for instant access to its iron sights.

to your eye. Afield, you may be shooting in shadow or at dusk. I've taken the aperture out of the Redfield sight on my Model 70 in .375, and the threaded hole now serves as aperture. It is more precise than it appears, because my eye automatically puts the front bead in the middle, as that's where most of the light is. Its position on the rear of the receiver puts needed space between eye and sight, to ensure the recoil doesn't plant the aperture in my brow. (This is a real hazard with uphill shooting and positions that deny a firm grip on the rifle.)

My first hunting rifle, a restocked .303 SMLE, had a barrel-mounted Williams open sight with a shallow "V" "African" notch. It proved faster than the popular "U" or deep "V" notches of the day and didn't obscure the target as much as buckhorn or semi-buckhorn sights then still common on lever rifles. I like the shallow "V," with or without an eye-catching white center line. It's popular on double rifles. So is the multiple-leaf "Express" sight with a series of folding sights, typically perched on a quarter-rib. But the no-

The smaller the aperture, the more precise (albeit slower) your aim. Tiny holes must be very close to your eye, so they aren't appropriate on hard-kicking rifles. This tang sight is on a .22.

tion that these give you an instant choice of sights zeroed for different yardages is weak indeed. Few riflemen can shoot accurately with open sights beyond 150 yards or so. I prefer a single fixed leaf filed to a 100-yard zero. Then there's no choosing the wrong leaf or having the right one collapse during recoil or rough handling. An open sight is properly a close-range sight. With a single rear notch, you should be able to hold center and count on lethal hits as far as you can center the vitals of big game.

Whether you choose an open sight or aperture sight on a hunting rifle, the front sight should be big enough to catch your eye right away. You'll trade some precision for speed of aim. There's no magic bead size, because barrel length affects *apparent* size and target subtention. There's no ideal bead color, either. I prefer ivory, except in snow. Gold

The cocking-piece sight on this lovely Springfield sporter by Nate Heineke is very close to your eye for aim, but drives forward with the striker, so it doesn't scar your brow. It folds flat, doesn't interfere with a scope. Such sights are scarce now, and expensive.

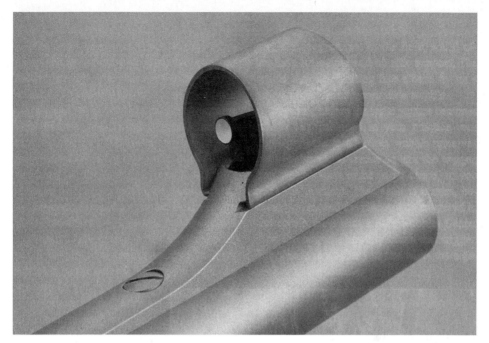

works well against a variety of backgrounds. Fluorescent sights are very fast, but get fuzzy under bright conditions; in shadows they can deliver a halo effect, like that of street lamps at night.

Too much brightness not only blurs sight edges, it can hide the target. Even metal beads can degrade a sight picture by scattering light. Avoid spherical bead faces, as they reflect incident light off the edge, shifting the bead's apparent position and causing you to miss. A bead should be flat-faced but angled toward the sky to catch light.

Redfield's Sourdough front sight featured a square red insert, angled up. You could em-

Wayne thinks this bead on his Sako Kodiak is one of the best front sights around. It's big enough to see easily and is also concave, so light doesn't reflect off an edge. White shows nicely in most cover.

ploy it as a bead or a post. It showed up better in timber than a black steel post. Thick black posts that work well for black bull's-eyes on white target faces don't do as well afield, not only because they get lost in shadow, but because they subtend much of your sight picture and require a six-o'clock hold. One of the best front sights I've seen lately is the concave white bead on my Sako 85 Kodiak in .375. It is easy to see but unreflective, with a clean profile.

Someone is always cooking up new iron sights. Bob Fulton equipped his Ruger No. 1 in .411 Hawk with a globe front sight holding a clear plastic insert etched with a crosswire. The rear sight is a modified Krag. At the end of the 27-inch barrel, the flared end of the globe sight fits almost perfectly in the aperture of the rear sight. There's a thin ring

Big-bore double rifles are properly fitted with an open rear sight with a wide "V," plus a big, easy-to-see bead up front. A low line of sight speeds your shot.

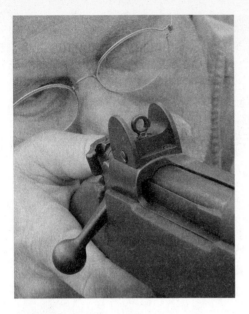

at 70. A scope would have allowed me to shoot at longer range—but would also have denied me the thrill of a sneak. Iron sights afford closer contact with the game, more intimate than one artificially conjured in a lens.

Years ago, a tall, big-boned Texan handed me a Marlin lever rifle with a perforated peg perched on the receiver. Its stem threaded into a small block that dovetailed into a larger base and moved across it for lateral adjustment. To raise or lower the sight, you screwed the ring out or in.

of daylight around the globe, so you can tell instantly if it's out of center.

"It works well against mottled backgrounds," Bob told me. "Unlike a blade, the vertical and horizontal wires obscure almost none of the target. You get a scope-like sight picture."

Bob installed a barrel-mounted aperture sight on his Winchester 95. A platinum-lined ring arcs over the factory notch.

"It's the fastest sight I've ever used. When I was stationed in the Southwest and surplus '06 ammo was cheap, that 95 accounted for many, many jackrabbits!"

FASTER, STURDIER, STILL PRECISE

Some innovative sights have gone commercial. The "Little Blue" peep was a small folding aperture that screwed to the back of a Redfield scope base. Alas, this clever auxiliary sight is no longer made.

Standard Lyman, Redfield, and Williams receiver sights have accounted for truckloads of big game. On one of my trips to Alaska, I carried a re-stocked 1903 Springfield with a Lyman rear aperture. A fine gold bead up front gave me excellent accuracy to 200 yards or so. With that old .30-06, I made a one-shot kill on a moose at 120 yards and toppled a Dall's ram

Seeing Right

■ Focus on the front sight. Your eye can't focus at three distances simultaneously, so it's best to get a sharp view of the middle image. That way, you won't put two fuzzy images together. The rear sight can be out of focus, the target not quite as clear as you'd like. You'll still hit close to center if the front sight is distinct and in the proper relationship to the other two images.

■ The sight picture is a crucial component of every shot, but it's not the only one. If you follow a fine sight picture with a sloppy trigger pull, your results at target will disappoint—but you *won't* know if the sights were properly aligned or not. Eliminate variables by eliminating flaws in your routine. Good results at the target bring confidence. Confidence leads to better shooting.

■ Don't assume a scope will always improve your accuracy. Scopes help mainly when a target is too small or indistinct to see clearly. Iron sights take weight off the top of your rifle, improving its balance and enabling you to aim more quickly. Irons are also less affected by the snow and rain that cloud scope lenses. If your eyes are reasonably sharp, you can probably shoot very well with irons at the ranges most big game is killed. But you won't learn to shoot well with them if you stay glued to glass sights.

The shallow "V" sight factory installed on this Ruger M77 Hawkeye in .375 Ruger is just the ticket for fast shooting in alder thickets or African thorn.

Open sights on this Marlin in .45-70 make for quick shooting in this British Columbia bush.

"How about that, partner?" he bellowed. "Slick, huh?"

It was indeed. So was the front blade, angled like a Sourdough, but all the way to the base and with a white line down its middle. Ashley Emerson went on to found Ashley Outdoors. The firm has grown and now goes by the name of XS Sights. It builds aperture sights and front blades for all manner of rifles. They excel in cover and perform surprisingly well at distance.

The key to hitting with *any* sight is practice. The key to effective practice is replicating the correct routine *every time you fire.* Keep these things in mind:

Remember that the world's best-known hunters used iron sights almost exclusively. Jim Corbett, for instance. The famous slayer of man-eating tigers began his career waiting for jungle fowl on the bank of a ravine. Suddenly, he spied movement close by. A leopard! It sprang. Jim fired as the cat sailed over his head and vanished in brush. Jim reloaded and followed the trail. So confident was he of his rifle and his ability that, when he spied the leopard's tail, he grabbed it and pulled the dead animal from a thicket! Such cool, deliberate action up close would save him many times later, when, at night, he sat alone near tiger baits. Jim killed the great Muktesar man-eating tiger at a range of just two yards!

In Africa, every dangerous-game hunter of note has used iron sights. So have the most celebrated exhibition shooters, who've hit targets as difficult as airborne aspirins and .22 cases, and achieved the precision to split playing cards edge-on. Sometimes scopes are simply superfluous!

CHAPTER 33

ALL THE GLASS YOU NEED

More lens is better if you're gazing at stars.
Not so if it burdens your rifle or slows your aim!

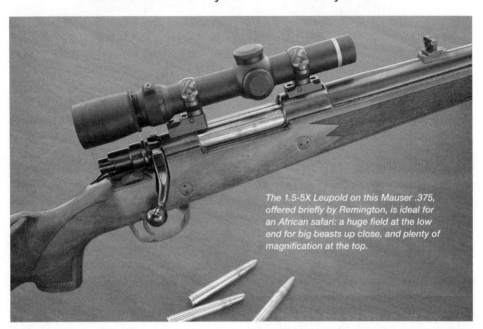

The 1.5-5X Leupold on this Mauser .375, offered briefly by Remington, is ideal for an African safari: a huge field at the low end for big beasts up close, and plenty of magnification at the top.

If bigger were always better, we'd eat Cheerios from punch bowls. For most things, there's an efficient size. Efficiency is aesthetically appealing. That's partly why a Porsche coupe looks good to just about everybody. So I'm puzzled by the trend toward bigger riflescopes.

A big scope is heavy.

A big scope has lots of inertia, which can cause it to slip in the rings during recoil.

A big scope must be mounted high above the bore, forcing you to crane your neck to aim.

A big scope doesn't fit in saddle scabbards designed for more useful sights.

A big scope costs more than a small scope of the same quality.

Almost all big scopes are of high magnification, which restricts field of view and limits eye relief, the distance from your eyeball to the ocular lens. It's easier to make scopes with generous, non-critical eye relief if magnification is low. Modest magnification delivers a bigger "exit pupil," too, that pencil of light you see in a scope held at arm's length. You figure EP this way: Objective lens diameter divided by magnification. So, the higher the power, the smaller the EP, unless you use bigger lenses up front. Because exit pupil diameter is a measure of light transmission, low power gives you a brighter image for any given objective diameter.

High magnification does deliver more detail to your eye, and big glass affords higher resolution, all else equal. But the magnification that divulges detail also puts more wobble in the sight picture. No, it's not *creating* that wobble, it's just showing you what's not visible at low power. But seeing the reticle dance wildly slows your shot as you try to bring that movement to heel. Some you can control; much of it you can't and you waste time trying. Your muscles tire and a good shot becomes harder. That fine detail you wanted to see is, in the final sift, useless. The out-size objective lens that delivers it in high resolution adds weight to your rifle. To clear the barrel, that scope requires high rings, which lift the rifle's center of gravity and force your head off the stock when you aim.

Though I use a 20X scope in rimfire prone competition and see the utility in high-power variables for varmint shooting, I've stuck with low-power, fixed-power models for big game. I have shot one deer with a 20X scope. It was a Coues buck, a dainty creature the size of a collie. It appeared in the purple light of dawn on a distant hill, ghosting through desert scrub. I dropped to my belly, snapping the bipod legs out on the David Miller rifle. Through a narrow shot alley, I guessed

the range at 400 yards. As the deer stepped from the brush, the vertical wire came even with his first rib. I nudged the intersection up nearly a foot and a half and fired. The 168-grain Sierra from the .300 Weatherby hit just a couple inches from where I'd planned, 410 paces away—that would have been a tough shot with a 4X scope. If you're hunting game of this size at long yardage, you'll naturally want high magnification at hand. In my view, though, more power than 8X is hardly ever necessary.

I once shot an elk at a measured 603 yards, about twice as far as any other I've killed. Ordinarily I'd decline such a poke, but conditions were perfect. Tight in a sling, prone over my pack, and with a red sun illuminating the elk, I couldn't feel a breath of wind. Also, I'd been shooting this Magnum Research rifle on steel plates to 500 yards. The GreyBull/Leupold scope dial was calibrated to the arc of my 6.5mm Creedmoor load. I had no approach option; night was coming on, and a valley of thick brush lay between my hillside perch and the elk. I turned the scope to 14X and waited for the bull to show me his forward ribs. A second after the trigger broke,

Wayne killed this Utah elk with a Remington CS Model Seven in .308 wearing a Weaver 1.5-5X scope. It's as versatile a sight as you'll likely need for elk hunting.

The Sightron 1.5-5X on this Ruger Hawkeye Alaskan gives you fast aim, with plenty of eye relief to stop the .375's recoil short of your brow.

the elk whirled. Blood glinted in the oblique light. He galloped in a small circle and nosed into the sage. My Hornady had struck within a hand's width of where I'd aimed.

YOU'LL WANT LESS THAN YOU THINK!

While I welcomed the high magnification available to me for that shot, I can't envision shooting game that far very often, if ever again. Mostly, I've found 4Xs more useful than 14Xs. In open country I'll use a 6X Leupold or crank variables to that number. Sometimes I've wept with other hunters who've lost a shot because they had too much scope power. In fact, it happened just weeks ago as I write this.

Night was zipping up the sun. We had minutes left.

"There!"

"I can't see him!"

I could, following our tracker's hand. But not much showed. A sliver of dun, a light stripe, the base of the kudu's long black curl. All in deep shadow, all screened by steel-wool thorn.

"Everything's a blur!"

The details *were* indistinct, even in my Zeiss binocular. But to me they didn't blur, as I'd focused the glass precisely. Sadly, the view through the hunter's scope amounted to little more than a gray smear. The adjustable objective of her 6-18X had been focused at 100 yards. Chasing the crippled kudu, we had closed to 30 yards. Peering into dark thickets, even a veteran hunter would have had trouble focusing. With no image to focus *on*, the lady was at a loss. A scope field of just six feet wasn't helping her. We got the bull, but the finishing shot proved not at all easy.

Having grown up when only about half the hunting rifles wore scopes, I've seen huge progress in scope design. Early on, reticles moved out of center when you adjusted the windage and elevation dials. Wet weather fogged the tube. Uncoated lenses robbed lots of light. Recoil tore apart spider-web crosshairs. A cottage industry in hinged and detachable scope mounts eased the transition to optical sights. Skeptical hunters had no intention of relinquishing their access to iron sights!

The first variable scopes seemed to some a step in the wrong direction. Why tempt fate with still more complexity?

This cutaway of a Kahles 2-7X variable shows the complexity of a modern scope. Much of the cost lies in hewing to close tolerances with the many machined parts, and in glass and coatings.

Bill Weaver's 3X Model 330, which he built by hand at age 24, in 1930, had prompted many hunters to try glass sights. At just $19, complete with a "grasshopper" mount that resembled a big paper clip, the 330 was much less costly than Zeiss scopes of the day (the 4X Zeilvier retailed for $45 in 1926). Weaver had equipped the ¾-inch tube with internal adjustments: one-inch increments for windage, two-inch for elevation. A flat-top post was the standard reticle, but you could order a crosswire for $1.50. The 330 defined scopes for hunters brought up on iron sights. Those who learned to use it would graduate to Weaver's K2.5 or K4, perhaps a Noske, a Lyman Alaskan, or a Redfield Bear Cub (then manufactured by Kollmorgen). A series of improvements enticed more shooters to install scopes throughout the 1950s, though

variable power had little appeal—why would anyone want *that*?

At the risk of sounding daft, I must say that question was and remains reasonable.

The earliest variables offered a meager choice of magnification. One, with the dial atop the turret, gave you 2.5X *or* 5X—nothing in between. Continuous or zoom power-change followed. As the one-inch tube became standard for riflescopes, so did 3-9X magnification. Also winning approval: 40mm objective lenses, a useful diameter that permitted low scope mounting on most rifles, but delivered as much light to the eye as it could use.

EXIT PUPIL IS OVERSOLD!

Now, half a century later, the 3-9X40mm has yet to be eclipsed as a hunting sight. At least some of us think so. The crowd clamoring for more and more power in scopes and

This CS Model Seven Remington took the first elk ever shot with the .300 SAUM round. It wears a 2-7X33mm Leupold, lighter and sleeker than the more powerful variables now in vogue.

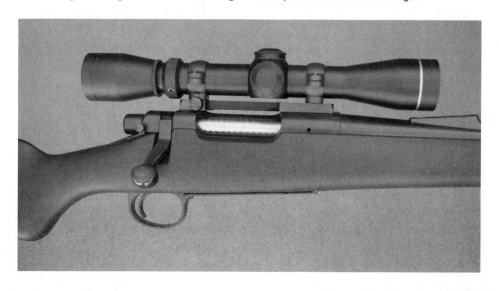

bigger glass claims a 40mm front lens limits light transmission. Well, it does *not*—at least not until you dial to 8X or higher and conditions are so dim that your eye has fully dilated. Your eye can open to seven millimeters in total darkness; figure five or six millimeters in timber at last legal light, less if you're gray enough to recall Clint Eastwood as Rowdy Yates. A scope with a 40mm objective has a 5mm exit pupil at 8X. In bright daylight, as your eye's pupil shrinks, even the 4.5mm shaft of light from a 3-9X40mm scope *at 9X* is bigger than your eye can use!

Given a maximum useful exit pupil of six millimeters, I'd be well equipped with 24mm front glass in fixed-power 4X scopes. The lens in a one-inch tube without a front bell measures about 21 millimeters. So I'm happy with scopes like Leupold's old M8 3X, with its sleek, straight tube. Such scopes look good on all rifles and add little weight to them. They sit low and slide easily in and out of cases and scabbards. I've shot game as far as 300 yards with 2.5X and 3X scopes.

A few years ago, I stalked a herd of elk spread across a steep burn. Wind and scatterings of cows prevented me from closing on the bull on the herd's far side. I backed out, climbed a parallel ridge, and slinged up prone. When the bull fed into my crosswire, he was 300 yards away. I could have cranked my 3-9X Leupold above 3x, but didn't. Instead, I held the Duplex reticle just shy of the bull's backline and squeezed. The .358 Norma bellowed. In the settling scope field, I watched the elk collapse. The 250-grain soft-point had struck within a couple inches of where I'd intended. I *could* argue the front bell and all that scope's magnifying power from 4X to 9X were essentially useless.

At 3X, most scopes deliver a field of 33 to 35 feet at 100 yards. That's generous enough to corral a bounding buck when you must shoot quickly. It's also a deep field, so you'll see detail in sharp focus, near to far. At 3X you get helpful magnification to find a shot alley through thickets or confirm an antler is not a branch. I don't want less power than 2.5X in a scope, and 3X is fine. That's why I'd be equally pleased with a 2.5-8X36mm or a 3-9X40mm. Below 2.5X, you might find the sight picture deteriorates. Field curvature increases. If your rifle has a front sight, it becomes visible in the field. At very low

The Zeiss 3-9X40mm Conquest on this Ruger American .30-06 ranks as one of the best buys in versatile hunting scopes. The 3-9X40mm is the classic variable and still as practical as ever.

This Browning BLR wears a cantilever mount on its barrel, with a low-power IER, or intermediate-eye-relief, scope. It retains zero after assembly because it's never removed.

the moon can bring you to grief when game pops up near enough to hit with a stone. Years ago, a pal and I sneaked over the lip of a basin toward a bull elk we had spied from afar. He saw us. As he left, five more bulls suddenly appeared. Two sported enormous antlers. "Shoot!" I shrieked. At 8X, my friend's scope afforded a field of just 10 feet. He could see only one elk at a time, and the bulls were moving with purpose. In short seconds, all had vanished.

Variable scopes driving the market these days have 30mm tubes with four, five, even six times magnification ranges. That is, the top power is four, five or six times the *bottom*. So, instead of a 3-9X40mm, you can have a 2-12X42mm (Leupold) or a 2.5-15X44mm (Swarovski). They're both brilliant scopes, as are other current top-end offerings from Zeiss, Leica, Nikon, and value-oriented lines by Alpen, Burris, Bushnell, Minox, Vortex, and others. But most of these sights exceed 17 ounces in weight, and some scale 20. The Nightforce 3.5-15X50mm specs out at 30 ounces. That heft adds substantially to your rifle's weight. The high mounts needed to bring the front bell clear of the barrel lift the center of gravity and alter the geometry of your shooting position.

power (1 or 1.5X in so-called "dangerous-game" variables), the target image can seem to diminish in size, compared to what you see with the naked eye; aiming can take split seconds longer if you must sift the target from a herd or the brush around it. The notion that wider fields are *always* better doesn't make sense to me. With even a little practice, any shooter can point a rifle accurately enough to put a target near the center of the scope field instantly. You needn't include the landscape.

Afield, I carry my variable scopes set at 3X or 4X (a 4.5-14X at 4.5X). Guiding, I've encouraged other hunters to do the same. "You won't have time to fiddle with that scope if we see something close," I explain. "For long, deliberate shots, there's almost always time to dial *up*."

Optics dialed high enough to see life on

LOSE THE WEIGHT, KEEP THE EYE RELIEF

Most 3-9X40mm scopes with one-inch tubes weigh less than 15 ounces. One of my favorite scopes, the Swarovski AV 3-9X36mm, scales 11½, same as another fine choice, Leupold's VX 2 3-9X40mm, and the well-proven Weaver 3-9X38mm. At just over 13 ounces, Trijicon's 3-9X40mm offers the advantage of an illuminated reticle without batteries. Incidentally, there's no ideal weight for a riflescope. My rule of thumb: a hunting scope *with mount* should weigh no more than 15 percent of the rifle's bare weight. So, on a

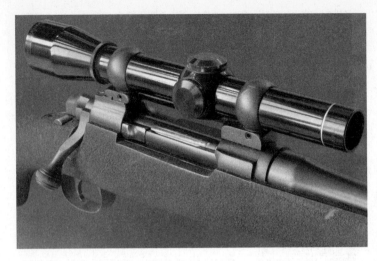

The M8 3X Leupold on Wayne's modified Springfield in .30-06 Improved is one of his favorite scopes. It has returned as a Custom Shop offering at Leupold. This rifle took a big Wyoming elk.

seven-pound rifle, you're allowed a sight that weighs up to 16.8 ounces. Trim rifle weight to six pounds, and you get a ceiling of 14.4 ounces. Steel bases and rings add several ounces; alloy mounts like Talley's one-piece base-and-ring weigh as little as an ounce apiece.

These days, eye relief among variable scopes is greater and more constant than was the case early on. You'll want eye relief of at least 3½ inches, and as much at the top end of the power range as at the bottom. Commonly, you'll see a slight reduction in eye relief as you boost magnification. The *latitude* of eye placement also diminishes, that is, the eye-to-lens distance at which you see the full field becomes more critical. An advantage of the 3-9X40mm over more powerful scopes is that eye relief is generally neither as short nor as critical. Fast aim is easy across the power range.

Most 3-9Xs still come with one-inch tubes. Manufacturers use bigger, 30mm pipe to increase range of magnification. A 30mm scope also permits greater latitude in windage and elevation adjustment, if the erector assembly inside is the same diameter as in one-inch scopes. If it's bigger, you trade that extra span of adjustment for (theoretically) sharper images. But unless you re-zero frequently for very long distance, or the mounting holes on your receiver are misaligned with the barrel, you won't need greater adjustment range than provided with most one-inch scopes. And my eye can't detect any differences in image quality between an erector assembly of ordinary proportions and one developed to take advantage of the bigger cavity in a 30mm tube. So, the lighter, typically less expensive one-inch scope gets my vote.

As for reticles, the medium crosshair and

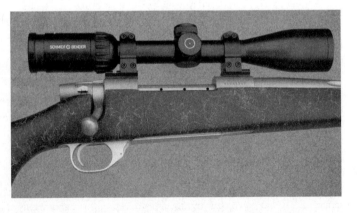

Renowned for its tactical and sophisticated hunting scopes, Schmidt & Bender courted the American hunter recently with this relatively lightweight 3-9X with one-inch tube. Superb optics!

post-and-crosshair standard during the 1950s still make sense. The Lee Dot is less common now, and admittedly less versatile. Where available, it's commonly an extra-cost option. The Plex strikes me as the best choice for all-around hunting, though the German No. 4—essentially a three-legged Plex—appeals, too. Illuminated dots look fetching; I've used them to shoot elk and moose in dark cover, but mostly I've found them unnecessary.

You could argue that the 3-9X40mm is outdated—so is the pre-'64 Winchester 70 and Shelby's Cobra of that decade. Not long ago I hunted with a .500 Nitro Express double built in 1910. We revere what we call "classics," because they have a timeless quality. Not to dismiss improvements—electronic ignition is less trouble-prone than the distributors firing the engines of my youth. But muscle cars of that day now bring many times their initial value at auction. Besides, technical advances needn't compromise classic form. Such is the case with the 3-9X40mm scope. Fully multi-coated optics, fog-free lenses, crisp, finger-friendly adjustments, and bomb-proof construction make new 3-9Xs a top choice for any hunting rifle.

The 2.5X fixed-power Sightron on this McMillan rifle is no longer available. But it's a fine all-around hunting sight—bright, compact, lightweight, and inexpensive!

One more plug. "I sell more 2.5-10X42mm scopes than any other," a dealer told me recently. That's partly due to an inventory heavy to the type. The 3-9X is losing its grip as *the* top-selling variable. You'll do well to consider, though, how its long popularity affects pricing. Every major scope manufacturer I can think of catalogs a 3-9X40mm. Sales volume keeps retail prices low, compared to less active scopes of similar quality. Zeiss offered special introductory pricing for its superb 3-9X40mm Conquest and sold it to the walls. You can get a 3-9X at just about every price point and be assured it will be a good value.

A lot of game is killed with rifles wearing big scopes. Almost all of it could be taken with smaller scopes that cost less and make rifles carry easily and point faster. The one-inch 3-9x40mm is as common in deer camps as cold coffee and old boots. If you don't own one, it's about time you did.

CHAPTER 34

THE LITTLE RED DOT

Sometimes you don't need a bigger image,
just a distinct sight. And why limit eye relief?

T all dark firs dripped audibly in air too
still to move the mist—*pip, pip, pip.*
I shifted the rifle, a Blaser in .30-06.
The faint moan of a hunting horn came many
minutes into my vigil. Not long after came
the whoops and chatter of the Danes, cheer-
ful drivers pushing the highland. I dabbed the
sight's rear lens with a saturated Kleenex. A
dark flicker of movement winked between alders on the swamp's edge.

The moose had ghosted past me, 90 yards
out, before I saw antlers. A good look mattered. Here cows were legal game, but only if

*At the FTW Ranch in Texas, hunters get a chance
to test a variety of rifles and sights on game of
imposing size. Some, on rails, come at you. A red
dot sight, as on this Blaser, gives fast, precise aim.*

they were without calf. A bull with fewer than
five total points could be shot, but not one
bearing six to ten points. The long legs scis-
sored to a halt as the animal cocked its ears to
the cacophony of the drive, still distant, but
coming. I eased against a tree, found a shot
alley to the ribs. The dot glued itself to the
shoulder, and I triggered the .30-06. Instantly

the bull lunged ahead, a rear hoof coming up just a little higher than normal.

Cycling the bolt, I waited. In Sweden you didn't leave a stand until the drivers converged or you heard the final three blasts on the hunting horn. The mist changed to rain. Finally, red jackets and orange ribbons winked through the trees. I walked to where the moose had stood and saw the great animal dead a few yards down the trail. It was the first moose of the day at Claestorp, the first game I'd shot in Europe.

The notion of shooting driven game held little appeal at first. I don't like to stand still. But those huge, brooding tracts of timber soon held me under their spell. I knew they weren't empty. The trees hid big animals. Color, sound, and action would wash like a wave through the forest. I couldn't predict when it would arrive. Chances to fire would come and quickly go. On stand, I found the anticipation gripping. I saw moose sneak away from the drivers and sprint between the standers. A huge wild boar, which would have been the hunt's finest trophy, seemed to vanish in the mist.

Swedes hardly need to apologize for shooting a few moose. A few years ago, when the big-nosed deer were at a population peak, there may have been more moose in Sweden than in all of North America! Roughly the size of California, Sweden had to trim moose numbers. With typical Scandinavian caution, it did. Closely managed on privately controlled ground, moose thrive north of the coffee-colored soils that nurture sugar beets to the sunrise side of a line between Malmo and Hoganas.

Not surprisingly, the favorite moose cartridge among Swedes is the 6.5x55mm. Next comes the .30-06, then the .308. Almost all of Sweden's moose are taken with one of these cartridges. Big scopes have a big fan base here, too. Hunting wild boar at the edge of night, Swedish hunters value pie-plate objectives.

"But you don't need high magnification on drives," one rifleman told me before the moose hunt. "In fact, I like an Aimpoint red dot sight with no magnification at all, even for the qualification target."

The qualification target was the life-size print of a moose on a frame that ran under motor power along a track. Scoring rings on the vitals were invisible from the line, 100 yards distant. The drill: Load with four rounds. Call for the target and fire once as the moose pauses. Then cycle the bolt and fire as it scoots along the track. Repeat the target call, then shoot once more at the standing moose and again as it races in the opposite direction. You fire all shots offhand, for a possible score of 20. I managed 18 once.

There's no reason you shouldn't net 20. Unlike a real moose, the target runs smoothly and at a set speed. There's no brush in the way. But the Swedes assured me that many hunters failed to keep all shots in the scoring rings. Offhand is evidently as tough a position in Scandinavia as it is Stateside.

I found in shooting the target, then in killing moose, that my pal had dispensed good advice. Here a red dot sight makes a lot of sense. In the dim forest, that dot shows like the North Star on a frosty night. It's easy to pick up, and no matter where it appears in the field of view, the bullet will go there. I proved that at the range, moving my head to different positions. I found the key to precision was keeping the dot at its lowest visible brightness setting. Many shooters dial up brightness to give themselves the equivalent of a brake light. As the dot gets brighter, it appears bigger, hiding the target. There's also a halo effect that reduces resolution around the dot, and your eye's pupil shrinks, impairing its ability to see anything *but* the dot. Dark conditions call for a low setting—No. 3 was my choice on the nine-station dial of the Aimpoint—while in bright light a higher setting is required if you're to see the dot at all.

A TUBE WITHOUT A VIEW

Frankly, I hadn't given red dot sights much thought until the trip to Sweden. But, after a couple days at Claestorp, I was convinced this sight is one of the best you could choose for a whitetail rifle. Red dot sights are available from several companies now, but the idea was pioneered in Sweden, back in 1975, by Gunnar Sandberg, inventor and entrepreneur. Sandberg formed the Aimpoint company shortly thereafter. In 1976, it comprised four people. One of them was Kenneth Mardklint, who graciously agreed to talk with me at Aimpoint's modern Malmo facility. It's an upscale place.

"The first red dot sight we called the 'single-point sight,'" said Kenneth. "You saw the dot with one eye and the target with the other. You couldn't see *through* the sight at all!"

In 1975, the first-generation Aimpoint Electronic appeared, with windage and elevation adjustments under the ¾-inch tube, so it sat high on Weaver-style bases.

"Its five light settings were all too bright for a dark day," Kenneth laughed. "We produced only 2,000 of them."

Two years later, an improved version came out, with more latitude in the brightness dial and no detents. A year later, the second generation of Aimpoint sights made its debut. They featured a better diode and a detachable 3X or 1-4X lens. It was the first Aimpoint sold in the U.S.

Early red dot sights were heavy and hard to mount. Detachable magnifiers added length and heft and decreased eye relief. In the rear focal plane, they magnified the dot, too! Battery life was limited. But the Aimpoint XD brought a wider field to the line—and reduced weight. Aimpoint's 7000, a handsome sight, sported a diode that offered 20 times the battery life of previous LEDs. A 3V lithium camera battery gave you a visible dot for *20,000 hours* on the low setting. That's a lot of hunting! The newest

Aimpoints deliver up to *80,000* hours per battery!

While many other companies now sell red dot sights, not all have adopted Aimpoint's compound objective lens, which corrects for parallax. A single lens still reflects the dot produced by the diode in the rear bottom of the tube, but the angle of reflection varies. The Aimpoint's doublet brings the dot to your eye in a line parallel with the optical center of the instrument. The reflective paths of a single lens spread fan-like, on the other hand, as your eye changes position behind the sight. Result: If the dot isn't centered in the sight, you'll have parallax error at distances other than the one for which the sight was parallax-corrected. The farther your eye is off-axis, the greater the error. With an Aimpoint, if you see the dot, the bullet goes there.

Aimpoint 1X red dot sights impose no limits on eye relief. Your eye can be two inches back or 10, and you see the same field. The dot is there in the same apparent focal plane as the target. With the dot's brightness at a low setting, you get scope-like precision. My shooting suggests that 200-yard kills should be easy. That's about as far as you'll zero a big-game rifle, or as far as you'd fire at animals without the benefit of magnification.

The Aimpoint's straight tube was not designed to maximize field. The current Micro series, the Pro and the Comp M4, M3, and M2 Aimpoints, continue with popular 1X(zero) magnification, and a field about like that of a 4X riflescope. It's more than big enough for close shooting in cover, and because the Aimpoint sight affords both-eyes-open aim, it's faster than the scope.

No Aimpoint sights are nitrogen-filled.

"It's not necessary," Kenneth told me. "Our sights have long been submersible. First with caps on, then with caps off. Aimpoints do not fog."

Having hunted with them in very wet

conditions in varying temperatures, I'll concur. The only moisture problem I've seen in an Aimpoint came late in an afternoon, in a swale overhung by dripping conifers. Sweden's October rain drove through them, and I tucked the Blaser under my arm. My body heat eventually fogged the outside of the lens—but I didn't think about that until a branch snapped. Moose! The animal paused behind a big fir 70 steps off. Hastily I thumbed the condensation off. Still, it was like looking through a pond: black moose in black timber curtained by rain thick enough to part with a power saw. A crosswire would have vanished in the murk. But that red dot stood out. I fired. The moose bolted back toward the drivers.

Many optics firms now build red dot sights. Most are compact and lightweight, as useful on slug-shooting shotguns and hunting handguns as on rifles for fast shooting.

When the Danes appeared, I expected them to have found a kill. None had. "We'll bring the dog." Tracking dogs are not only popular in Sweden, the law requires that big-game hunters have quick access to them. Still, I paced in the wet as the handlers waited an hour for the woods to "get quiet." Meanwhile, rain washed the trail and darkness descended. "If you hit the moose, the dog will find it," a Swede assured me, then admonished "Don't go near where the moose was. Your scent will confuse the dog."

It was flashlight-dark when we harnessed up a couple Norwegian hounds. The older dog went to work like a setter on a hot pheasant track, over a knob, down into the swamp. Then she hooked toward where I'd shot the moose. But surely the drivers would have seen a carcass there.

"She's here." The dog handler pointed. In a narrow, water-filled depression lay a big cow moose, belly down, her hump blending with the swamp grass and hidden from the side by brush. I'd never have found her. She'd fallen where even seasoned woodsmen only a few yards apart had passed her by.

The dog tore a little hair from the hump. I let her.

CHAPTER 35

GETTING TO ZERO

The sight must follow the bullet before you can hit where you look!

When zeroing, keep every detail the same, shot to shot, including fore-end placement, hand support, and cheek pressure. Here a rifleman zeroes a T/C Dimension with the bag under the recoil lug, no left-hand contact.

S hivering in the November dawn, the kid was also shaking from excitement. He couldn't steady the crosswires, even when he leaned against the fence post. It would be a very long shot; the deer looked small in the K4. He'd have to hold high. His reticle bobbing above the buck's shoulder, the kid yanked the trigger. *Bang!* The buck kept eating. Two more shots brought no more reaction. The deer might as well have been cropping wheat on the moon.

Magazine empty, the youngster dug his last cartridge from his pocket and held right on the buck's ribs. When the .264 bounced, the deer collapsed. The kid was astonished.

Oddly enough, finding the dead deer proved as difficult a task as shooting it. The boy scoured the shin-high Michigan stubble

for 20 minutes before he found the animal only 160 yards from where he'd shot.

Since then, I've carefully avoided aiming too high, though I must admit that I've sent an embarrassing number of bullets over the backs of animals near and far. I've threatened to get a tattoo on the back of my trigger hand: "Your barrel is already pointing up."

It's true. When you zero a rifle, you're adjusting the sight line to intersect the bullet's path twice in its gentle arc downrange. The yardage at which the rifle is said to be zeroed is the second intersection. The first occurs close to the rifle—35 yards or so, depending on the height of the sight above the bore. Because a bullet starts dropping *as soon as it leaves the muzzle*, the barrel must be elevated above a distant target to put a bullet it its center. You look straight to the target, but the bullet's trajectory—ever the downward arc from the elevated barrel—cuts through the sight line, then drops back to it

"Point-blank range" is the distance at which a dead-on hold brings desired results. In smallbore rifle competition, I adjust my sight or scope to plant bullets exactly in the middle at the appropriate distance (50 feet, 50 yards, 50 meters, or 100 yards). Only center hits keep you at the top of the scoreboard. Most hunting rifles in my rack are zeroed at 200 yards, not because I shoot that far most of the time, but because, for many cartridges, a 200-yard zero yields a long *effective* point-blank range on big game. Arbitrarily and historically, we hunters have accepted three inches of vertical deviation from center, that is, we consider a hit up to

three inches low or high as still lethal. Given the size of the average whitetail deer's vitals, it's a useful assumption.

Popular big-game cartridges like the .270 and .30-06, the .243 and .308, the 7mm Remington and .300 Winchester Magnums, will land bullets within three inches of vertical center to between 250 and 300 yards if you zero the rifle at 200. At 100 yards, figure on bullet strikes two to three inches high. Because most big game is shot closer than 200 yards, you could zero for, say, 100. While you'll hit spot-on at that range, and probably closer to center throughout your hunting career, you'll have to aim high for shots beyond 200 yards—and, depending on the load, perhaps even at shorter ranges. The 200-yard zero takes full advantage of your load's potential. Some fast-stepping, ballistically gifted bullets merit an even longer zero, mid-weight

Schmidt & Bender's turret dials show where in the adjustment range your reticle lies, so you know if you must adjust the mount to keep the scope's optical axis near center.

spitzers in the .300 Weatherby, for example, or the 7mm Remington Ultra Mag. But beware stretching any zero too far. If mid-range trajectory (the point at which the bullet's arc carries it farthest above sight line), exceeds three inches, you're setting yourself up to shoot over your target. Most game dies not beyond zero range, but closer.

Remember that a bullet's arc is parabolic; the highest point above sight line is not in the middle of that arc, but beyond it. For example, the .270 Weatherby zeroed at 300 yards with a 130-grain, pointed bullet will print 3.3 inches high at 100 yards and 3.8 inches high at 200, where it is nearer its zenith. Four inches is, to my mind, too much lift to ignore. It is silly to zero for extreme range, where you'll seldom shoot, if by doing so you incur a midrange gap that forces you to adjust your aim.

PITFALL OF THE LONG ZERO

Part of the reason many hunters like to zero long is that they overestimate yardage in the field. One fellow told me that his .30 magnum could outshoot any rifle to 900 yards and that he'd toppled a huge buck at 700 steps by holding a tad over its withers. Now, I'm a country boy, but even a congressman would have blushed spinning that yarn. The flattest-shooting cartridges around lob their bullets nearly *three feet low at 500 yards* when zeroed at 200. To keep a 130-grain .270 Weatherby bullet from sagging more than a foot at 700 yards, you'd have to zero at beyond 600. That would put the bullet about two feet high at 300 *and* 400. The bullet would be plunging so rapidly at 800 that, if you misjudged range by 50 yards, you'd miss the deer's vitals!

A few cartridges are best zeroed at 100 yards, because most of the shooting they're designed for will be at that range, or because they lack sufficient energy to be effective much beyond 150 yards. The .30-30 is a woods cartridge. So are the .35 Remington, the .444 Marlin, and the .45-70. Even rifles chambered for 200-yard cartridges can benefit from a shorter zero; the .250 and .300

Assemble a variety of loads before you zero, to check impact points and compare group sizes. Refine your zero to the best ammunition.

Savage come to mind. Iron sights don't affect bullet performance, but they can reduce effective range by limiting precision.

Because I've guided many hunters whose rifles were poorly zeroed, I came to ask up front, "Why don't we fire that rifle, to make sure it's hitting where it should?" This tactful opener prompted one of three responses:

A. "Good idea! It might have been bumped in transit. Besides, I could use a warm-up myself."

B. "Well, okay. Ammo's expensive, and I'm sure it's right on, but I suppose one or two rounds won't hurt."

C. "Naw. This rifle has shot down the middle since '73. I don't want to mess with it."

All these fellows would eventually punch a paper target. I gave them no alternative. Commonly, the man most reluctant to step to the bench turned in the worst performance. It became an easy call. Any hunter unwilling to test his rifle or himself either has something to hide or holds a distorted view of shooting. One such perception: Shooting prowess is a measure of manhood, of competence in a field in which every man is assumed to be competent. The pitiable souls who hang their egos with the targets are bound to be humbled.

Truly, shooting is a skill that must be learned and honed. It cannot be inherited or bought. Hunters who prefer to talk up their prowess without putting holes in paper are, almost without exception, unskilled. Any rifleman can make a poor shot; an accurate rifle can print a loose group. But there are lessons in errant bullets. An accomplished shooter learns from them and loads up for one more string.

Zeroing, or sighting in, is every marksman's first step. Here's how:

Check your scope bases to ensure they are tight to the receiver. You may have to remove your scope to do this. Taking the bases off lets you check for rust. To remove rust, scrub lightly with a brass brush and solvent. Finish with an oily cloth, then a dry one. Use a close-fitting screwdriver to tighten each base down, cinching screws alternately to evenly distribute pressure. Greasing the dovetail cuts on Redfield-style bases eases ring installation.

Space the rings to support both ends of the scope well. This is especially important if your scope has a big objective bell or the long, heavy ocular housings of some variables. Extra weight and length on an end adds leverage to any blow or force that might strain your scope tube and affect zero. Accidental bumps and long days in tight scabbards can make your rifle shoot where you're not looking. Most scopes tolerate lots of punishment, but an extension base or ring can be useful for long scopes. Short-coupled variable scopes may require an extension base or ring reversed, so the power-dial clears.

Many hunters mount their scopes too far back. They install it on a table or a shooting bench, not in the woods after a fast shot at a

whitetail or on the steeps following an uphill poke at a ram. When you fire at game, you'll likely lean into the sight; prone, sitting, and uphill shots put your face even closer to the sight. If you must pull your head back to see a full field or prevent the ocular ring from dinging your brow, the scope is too far back. The scope must be mounted so aim comes naturally and immediately from a range of field positions; you see a full field at first glance, as soon as the stock hits your cheek. So, as you mount the scope, snug the rings gently, then throw the rifle up as if snap-shooting. Kneel, sit, flop prone on the ground. Chances are you'll push that tube forward before you tighten those screws!

Once you've established eye relief—and before cinching those screws—hold the rifle out in front of you and rotate the scope so the vertical crosswire is plumb with the buttpad. A scope level can help "square up" the reticle. You can also check by looking over the top of the scope, with the muzzle just visible over the front bell. The top turret cap should center itself over the bell and the barrel. Any tilt should be apparent.

Sandbags have no adjustments but give you all the support of mechanical rests. Make sure they don't leak or shift shot to shot. For hard-kicking rifles, grip the sling affixed only to the front stud.

TARGETS AND THE FIRST-SHOT IMPERATIVE

Cinch ring screws as you would the lug nuts on an automobile wheel, opposites in turn. You don't need goop on the threads to keep screws from backing out, nor should you apply so much muscle that they leave the screwdriver handle's imprint in your palm. I wipe most scopes with a tack rag before installing the rings, then with a dry cloth. A dry, clean scope stays in place best.

Scope weight has much to do with the load on rings. Big objective lenses and 30mm tubes boost weight and inertia, so, when the rifle recoils, it has a hard time getting the scope to come along. When rings lose their grip, you lose your zero. A gunsmith pal who has mounted dozens of scopes met his match when he tried to affix a husky German variable to a rifle in .458 Lott. The scope kept slipping in recoil, even when he used tape to boost gripping power and tightened the rings so they dented the steel tube! He finally punted, talking the customer into a smaller scope.

Once your scope is mounted, you'll want to bore-sight the rifle, which is aligning the axes of scope and bore without shooting. If you have no straight-through access to the breech, as with autoloading or pump or lever rifles, you'll need a "collimator." This device has a spud that fits in the muzzle, a screen that appears in front of your scope. You aim at a grid on the screen, adjusting the sight so the crosswire quarters it.

If yours is a bolt rifle or dropping-block single-shot, bore-sighting is easier. Remove the bolt or drop the lever and set the rifle on sandbags. Center a distant object in the bore. Without moving the rifle, adjust your reticle so it quarters that object. I bore-sight indoors by placing the rifle in a Battenfeld gun cradle and looking through the bore out the window at a rock on a distant hill. The farther the object, the more useful the result. *Bore-sighting is not zeroing*. It's simply a preliminary step, a quick way to align bore and scope so you don't waste ammunition trying to "get on paper" at 100 yards. After bore-sighting, you *must* shoot.

On the range, I use cardboard boxes as target boards. My targets are notebook paper-sized to give me the sight picture I prefer. Medium

Once you've zeroed, fire from field positions, with sling or bipod if you use either on the hunt. Point of impact may not match bench results. Wayne fired this knot from a sling-assisted sit with a Winchester M70 Cabela's commemorative. Neither he nor the rifle ordinarily shoot this well.

crosswires in a 4X scope call for a six-inch-square target at 200 yards. A 6X scope offers the best picture with a four-inch square. It's important that the white squares be big enough to accommodate the movement of your reticle, small enough to help you discern differences in the size of each quarter. High magnification calls for small targets, heavy reticles require bigger ones. For iron sights with a bead in front, big circular targets make sense. The light-brown cardboard backer and white target both show bullet holes clearly. My 25X spotting scope picks up .243 holes at 200 yards easily, unless mirage is strong. If you use a black target, or one with black printing, you'll have to walk

forward often to check for bullet holes you can't find from the bench.

Zeroing is a bench project, because you want to eliminate as much as possible the human factor that affects accuracy. Use sandbags or a mechanical rest (the latter not with a fixed buttstock holder; heavy recoil can split a stock if you prevent the rifle from moving to the rear). The object is to align scope or iron sights so your sight line intersects the bullet path at predetermined points. You must hold the rifle so it doesn't bounce off the rest, and trip the trigger without disturbing your aim. Actually, the fundamentals of zeroing are the same as those for shooting a tight group: Pick a calm day; take your time, and be sure the rest supports the stock the same for each shot.

For big-game rifles, place targets at 100, 200, and 300 yards. The 100-yard target is to check bore-sighting. Adjust the scope so bullets strike about two inches above center. Then switch to the 200-yard target. Fire three rounds between sight changes, giving the barrel time to cool between rounds. I allow 30 seconds between shots in a group. Hot days are poor times to zero, because the barrel heats fast, cools slowly.

A sitting position may not give you bench-tight groups. But you'll want them centered on point of aim at your zero range, say, 200 yards. If the field position moves the group, adjust the sight! A taut sling pulling on a barrel-mounted stud can depress point of impact.

When you've nudged point of impact to center at 200 yards, let the rifle go cold, clean it, then fire another group. Mark the first shot from the cold, clean barrel, because that's the most important shot you'll fire on a hunt. Keep the target. Use it later for first shots on other days. If clean-barrel shots leak out of the subsequent group, you might want to try another load or hunt with a fouled bore.

At 300 yards, a practical maximum shooting distance for most big game, you'll want those bullets to land a hand's width below point of aim. That means four to eight inches drop, depending on the cartridge. The more shooting you do at distance, the more precision you'll bring to your sight adjustments. Shooting only at 100 yards and estimating bullet drop beyond that range is bound to bring you to grief. Refine the zero far away, then check it at short range.

When you're done zeroing, get off the bench and practice from field positions. Zero will carry you only so far.

CHAPTER 36

EXTRAORDINARY MARKSMEN

Rifles accurate enough to hit tiny targets have no value
until fired by shooters who can.

Wayne fired these 50-yard five-shot knots in competition with his McMillan-barreled M37 Remington. Such accuracy wins matches, titles. Let one shot leak, however, and someone may beat you!

Few people young enough to have avoided cod liver oil have watched an exhibition shooter from bleachers. That era passed during my youth, as Herb Parsons gave his last demonstrations. With a dozen guns on a table, he'd tell the people how those guns worked and how to handle them safely. Still talking, he'd start tossing things in the air, where he'd blow them apart with whatever rifle or shotgun came to his shoulder. Some didn't get that far; he'd blast cabbages from the hip, seemingly without looking at them. Potatoes didn't have a chance. Shattering eggs with .22 bullets required more precision—still, Herb spent little

time in the sights. It was obviously huge fun for one so skilled, inspiration for those of us determined to practice until we, too, could milk seven rounds from a Model 12 in a burst so fast it sounded like a roll of thunder, leaving only smoke floating where seven clay birds had hung briefly in the sky.

Some truly gifted shooters have cropped up lately. They heave tall stacks of clay disks aloft and, if the spread is favorable, reduce them to dust with staccato bursts from repeating shotguns with extended magazines. They fire the guns upside down, shoot ejected empties out of the air, shoot until they're ankle-deep in red plastic. They are entertainers as well as crack shotgunners. Their videos appear everywhere.

Rimfire rifles—.22s—used to get equal play. Back when glass balls, not pitch saucers, served as aerial targets, gifted marksmen awed the bleacher-bound. By current standards, those rifles were hardly accurate. But exhibition shooters didn't have to nip quarter-minute groups at 50 yards— blasting an aspirin out of the air at 15 feet sufficed! The routines demanded more of the shooters than the rifles.

One of the most celebrated shooters of that time was Annie Oakley. Born Phoebe Ann Moses in a log cabin in Darke County, Ohio, in August 1860, she had a hard childhood. Subsistence hunting would not only feed her family, but propel her to fame. She killed her first game, a squirrel, at age eight. Natural talent with a rifle led to market hunting. Then Annie began shooting quail on the wing with her .22. She not only won local turkey shoots, she dominated every event. At one match, she soundly thrashed visiting sharpshooter Frank Butler, who apparently did not know, at first, that his opponent was a 15-year-old girl! A year later they married, and Phoebe joined Frank's traveling show under the stage name Annie Oakley. Chief Sitting Bull called her *Watanya Cicilia*— "Little Sure-Shot." When exhibition shooter Capt. A.H. Bogardus left Buffalo Bill's Wild West Show, Annie joined the docket, aiming in a mirror to shoot over her shoulder at glass balls Frank threw in the air.

Petite at 100 pounds and sweet-tempered, Annie became an audience favorite. Germany's Crown Prince, later to become Kaiser Wilhelm II, asked her to shoot a cigarette from his lips. She did, allowing after World War I that a miss might have changed history. Annie shot coins from Frank's fingers

and split playing cards edgewise with bullets. In 1884, using a Stevens .22 at an exhibition in Tiffin, Ohio, she hit 943 glass balls out of 1,000 tossed. With a repeating rifle she could make one ragged hole in the middle of a playing card, firing 25 shots in 25 seconds. Johnny Baker, another Wild West Show marksman, tried for 17 years to outshoot Annie Oakley and never did. "She wouldn't throw a match," he observed. "You had to beat her, and she wasn't beatable."

Annie used iron sights for exhibition shooting and favored Marlin lever-action rifles. At age 62, after an automobile accident badly crippled her, she could still shoulder a .22 and hit every one of 25 pennies tossed in the air. Sharing that era and following Annie

MISS ANNIE OAKLEY,
(LITTLE SURE SHOT.)
BUFFALO BILL'S WILD WEST.

Annie Oakley was born Phoebe Ann Moses. At age 16, the petite shooting prodigy married the exhibition shooter she'd beaten at a rifle match. Her exploits drew crowds at Cody's Wild West Show.

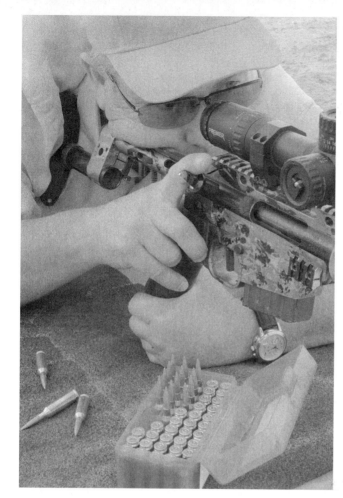

1,000 from 30 feet, the last 500 from 40. Ad became a showman. After firing at a washer tossed aloft, he'd tell onlookers the bullet went through its middle. The audience thought it knew better. But then Ad would stick a postage stamp over the hole, toss again— and perforate the stamp. He could, it was said, hit the bullet of an airborne .32-20 cartridge without tearing the brass.

TOP, PLINKY, AND THE GREAT HERB PARSONS

Winchester hired Adolph Topperwein, when the slim young man was about 27. There he courted Elizabeth Servaty, who worked in the company's ballistics lab. They married in 1903. To audiences, she became "Plinky," a fine shot in her own right. In 1916, she broke 1,952 of 2,000 clay targets with a Model 12 shotgun. She once ran 280 straight.

Ad would shoot for Winchester for 55 years. He preferred rifles to shotguns, which he didn't need to hit air-borne targets. Holding a Winchester 63 with the ejection port up, he'd fire, then nail the flying empty. He could riddle five tossed cans before any struck the ground. Ad used his artistic talents to profile Indian heads on tin with up to 450 .22 bullets, fired with precision at the headlong rate of a shot a second!

Topperwein's exploits drew competition. Exhibition shooter Doc Carver fired 11 Win-

into the spotlight was a tall, blue-eyed Texan who began his working career as a cartoonist. Adolph Topperwein, born in 1869 near New Braunfels, Texas, teethed while shooting aerial targets with a Winchester Model 1890 .22. He had little use for hunting or paper bull's-eyes. He replaced the 1890 with a Winchester 1903 autoloader, then with its successor, the Model 63. In 1887, Ad landed a job drawing cartoons, in San Antonio. He honed his marksmanship after hours and wound up shooting for a circus. In 1894, he used a rifle to break 955 of 1,000 2¼-inch clay disks tossed in the air. Dissatisfied with that score, he repeated twice, shattering 987 and 989. Clay shotgun targets proved too easy—he broke 1,500 straight, the first

Preston Pritchett, who builds super-accurate Surgeon rifles, can test them only when he can execute perfect shots. His concentration shows here, behind a Schmidt & Bender P/M scope.

chester 1890s in a 10-day stunt, 12 hours a day, to break more than 55,000 of 60,000 tossed glass balls. He ground out a second run and missed just 650 of the 2½-inch targets. B.A. Bartlett eclipsed Carver's marathon record, shattering 59,720 of 60,000 balls in 144 hours.

Ad Topperwein met those challenges, in 1907, at San Antonio's Fair Grounds, where he uncrated 10 Winchester 1903 rifles, 50,000 rounds of .22 ammunition, and 50,000 wooden blocks 2¼ inches on the side. The tosses began. After running out of blocks and ammo, Top got resupplied and resumed shooting. He stopped after 120 hours and 72,500 blocks. He'd missed nine. His longest straight: 14,500. Ad needed help, after his performance, to lower his arms! Topperwein's record stood until after World War II, when Remington salesman Tom Frye began firing at wood blocks with Nylon 66 autoloaders. Frye missed two of his first 43,725 targets. When he posted the eye-popping tally

of 100,004 hits for 100,010 targets, an aging Topperwein sent his congratulations. Ad died at age 93, nearly 18 years after losing Plinky, in 1945.

The shooter to pick up Topperwein's mantle was born, in 1908, to a farm family near Somerville, Tennessee. Herb Parsons got his first .22 at age seven. Unlike Ad, Herb loved to hunt. Shooting quail on the wing, he honed eye and hand. During the off-season, he shot walnuts and lumps of coal—airborne, of course. By the time Topperwein acceded to failing eyesight, in the early 1930s, Herb Parsons was working for Winchester as a salesman. Then he moved into Ad's spot. A stickler for realism, he refused to play the audience with make-believe shots. What you thought you saw Parsons do, Parsons did. During the 1940s, Herb gave 238 shooting demonstrations to soldiers at military bases. After the war, he tallied thousands of exhibitions for the public. The routines, most of his design, were marked by fast shooting and fast talking.

Herb would bend over, toss a handful of eggs between his legs, then whirl and break them all, one by one, with quick shotgun blasts as they fell. He'd toss oranges in the air pell-mell and pulp them with a stream of bullets from a .30-30. Grabbing a Winchester .351 self-loader, he'd empty the 10-shot magazine from the hip, dusting 10 clay targets standing on edge. "They're not hard to hit, folks," he'd laugh, deftly switching rifles and opening up on new targets, almost without pause, "just easy to miss!"

Parsons' most celebrated feat occurred at a racetrack near Blue Hill, Maine. A flock of crows cruised by in the distance, pepper specks to onlookers. "What's beyond those woods?" Herb barked. "More woods!" the audience boomed. Herb bolted a round into a .30-06, shouldered the rifle, and fired. A puff of feathers followed a second's delay, and a bird dropped. "Well," Parsons deadpanned. "That bullet had to go *somewhere*!"

Herb Parsons hunted with the biggest Hollywood names of his time, including Clark Gable, Roy Rogers, and Andy Devine. He did the stunt shooting for *Winchester*

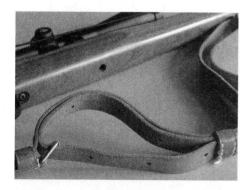

To shoot like a champ, you must steady the rifle! A shooting sling with an adjustable loop is a must in traditional rifle competition. Wayne has used a Brownells Latigo sling for 40 years on hunts.

'73, starring Jimmy Stewart. Herb collected many big-game trophies and urged others to take their children hunting. His extraordinary skills with a .22 rifle made him the man to beat on a trap range. In 1954, he won the professional division at the Grand American. Quail drew him afield often, but he also loved waterfowling. He commonly used smallbore guns like Winchester's Model 42, a .410. On one hunt, he dropped decoyed ducks so fast his partner never had a chance, until Parsons opened the little pump near day's end and grinned, "Your turn."

A guide once observed, "That man was a machine. He never missed. After the hunt, he'd toss up a cabbage, look over his shoulder, and ask how you wanted it chopped. Before it hit the ground, he'd grind it to bits!"

On July 19, 1959, Herb Parsons underwent surgery to repair a hernia. A blood clot caused a heart attack. Herb died four hours later, aged 51.

A ROUTINE TO BEAT ALL; OLYMPIC GOLD

Tom Knapp, a gifted shooter celebrated on video clips, is still active. He's done his most famous routines with Benelli shotguns. Like Parsons, he talks easily about shooting while blasting all manner of airborne objects to pieces. He nails some with the gun aimed from behind his back. Tom has broken nine clay targets before any hit the ground, one at a time. He's shattered seven with Benelli's Nova pump and emptied a magazine on ejected empties. "I should be familiar with the Nova," smiles Tom. "I fired 60,000 rounds testing it. Proofed it with turkey loads, too. I gave up on those after 3,800 shots because my wrists hurt."

True to the heritage of exhibition shooting, Tom is also a dead-eye with a rifle. Where conditions permit, he includes a .22 in his repertoire.

"I like the .22 Magnum (WMR). Those hollowpoints take things apart!"

He has used a rimfire rifle to hit a tossed golf ball as many as three times before it landed, clipping it low to keep it aloft. He has shot 13 consecutive hand-tossed aspirins. And he's hit BBs aloft.

"*I* can see the BB, Unfortunately, the audience can't. But when a .22 strikes a steel BB, the deformed bullet whines off into nowhere. You can *hear* that."

Aren't BBs hard to hit? Tom shrugs.

"I practice a lot."

Not all riflemen skilled with a .22 shoot fast or at aerial targets. Gary Anderson, a Nebraska farm boy, earned his place among accomplished marksmen at Olympic venues. At age 20, after just two years of competitive shooting, he joined the prestigious Army (USAMTU) team. That same year, 1959, he also made the U.S. team for the Pan American Games. He won silver and gold medals, then competed in the 1960 Olympics. He captured his first National Championship a year later. In 1963, he took both smallbore and centerfire gold at the Pan American Games. The next year, Gary set a new world record, winning his first Olympic gold in 300-meter free rifle competition. In 1968, he took another gold in that event. He has won 12 National Championships, seven World Championships, and set six world records. His book, *Marksmanship*, offers a synopsis of his rifle shooting technique. It's worth noting that the first nine of his 10 "Secrets of Shooting" have nothing at all to do with equipment (save the sling). They focus on how to best establish a position and control the body. The last chapter deals with zero.

No shooter has achieved more in rifle competition than Lones Wigger. The Montana native has won two Olympic gold medals and a silver. He has set 29 world records with a rifle (16 in team events, 13 as an individual). In the four international competitions in which international records are established, Wigger has shot his way to 111 medals. Like Gary Anderson, Lones got most of his practice with the U.S. Army Marksmanship Training Unit at Fort Benning, Georgia. There, he said, "Shooting was my job. I practiced three or four days a week, up to four hours a day. During a long session, I might fire 200 shots. After that I had to quit. Disciplined practice is hard work. When you're too tired to make a good shot, you'd best put the rifle down for a while. Shooting poorly in practice is practicing poor shooting."

Lones Wigger has much in common with early exhibition shooters who wielded fast-firing .22s as if they were wands, sweeping tiny targets from the sky.

"I shoot a lot. If you can't fire live ammunition every day, dry-fire. Get used to the rifle's weight and feel. Train your body to support it in every position. Shoot enough that the rifle becomes an extension of your body. And learn to put yourself at ease. I yawn a lot when I shoot, to relax."

Forty years ago, in Mishawaka, Indiana, I snugged my sling for a go at a spot on the U.S. Olympic Team. In the middle of the black bull's-eye that appeared as a dot at 50 feet was the real target, a 10-spot the diameter of a finishing nail surrounded by a nine-ring you could obliterate with one .22 bullet. Centering the black in the iron aperture, I'd rely on my much-practiced prone position to maintain that sight picture. Assuming it didn't change as I milked the last ounce from the trigger, my Anschütz 1413 and Eley Match ammunition would deliver 10s. To reach the finals, I'd have to put nearly every one of 60 shots on a spot I couldn't even see, with no error exceeding half the diameter of a .22 bullet. I thought, as we waited for the firing command, about Annie Oakley, Ad Topperwein, and Herb Parsons. I considered the exploits of my contemporaries, Gary Anderson and Lones Wigger. Theirs were tall shadows. I pulled a .22 cartridge from the block. And I tried in vain to yawn.

CHAPTER 37

IT'S ALL IN YOUR HEAD

Physical gifts aside, practice makes you a marksmen—assuming, of course, you can think straight.

The most important part of a shot happens behind your eyeball. Think the bullet to the target. Mind the sight picture and your breathing. Control your trigger squeeze. Follow through.

L ast fall, as I was in the middle of writing this book, a six-point bull walked out of my scope field at 280 yards. He vanished in an organic mesh of alder nine feet thick. I sighed, as others party to the event whispered, "… can't believe he didn't shoot … I'd have hammered that bull … won't get a chance like that again soon … ."

Counting me, we were four people—four times as many as needed to kill an elk or pass judgment on a shot. For better or worse, I made the only call that mattered.

"Most of my clients are comfortable with 300-yard shots."

It was my guide's diplomatic way of saying "What are you doing hunting elk, if you can't drop one at 300 yards?" As this fellow

was born 13 years after I'd shot my first elk, I cut him a little slack and replied gently that I had killed a couple of elk at 300, but that many factors, not just distance, determine where a bullet lands. "Shooting position, heart rate, light, wind, shot angle—they all matter."

"An elk's a big target," he said.

"I wasn't aiming at the elk."

He regarded me warily, the way 22-year-olds look at elders asking them about church attendance, retirement accounts, and commitment to higher education.

Truly, I had *not* been looking at the elk, but rather at a spot on its forward ribs. I'd envisioned a spot on the offside, as well, and the track between them, plus the curved path my bullet would have bored through the mountain breeze.

"Getting a bullet to an elk is easy," I said. "Killing elk every time you shoot at one is a thinking man's game."

That look again.

"Like, what do you mean?"

It had been explained to me long before all sentences came to begin with the word "like." People who could shoot very, very well emphasized that good marksmanship starts in your head. We pay a great deal of attention to accurate rifles and ammunition, but neither hardware nor routine can trump mental focus.

On a Michigan morning, in dry snow under sooty skies, my fingers wooden with cold, I bumped a fox from a brush pile. I triggered the old infantry rifle without aligning the sights on that red streak. But an eye blink before ignition, the picture of the bead in the notch and the blur of the fox coming to meet it froze in memory. The creature cartwheeled in a flurry of powder.

If you think that an accident, you might be right. If you assume it was a mindless poke, reflexive action used by the hand of Zeuss to nail Reynard for hen house transgressions, well, you'd be wrong. My head was *in* that shot, if briefly. Thinking needn't take long— indeed, much of it can happen before you see the target.

My first years of competitive shooting were tough. Often I came up against the time limit, though one shot per minute is a glacial pace. Invariably, I'd score badly on the final targets. Then, concluding the prone stage of a four-position match in some village now forgotten, I had an epiphany. My bullets were dutifully chopping big pieces from the 10-ring. Closing the bolt two shots

Take enough time for the shot—hurrying hunters miss! Waste no time getting into position. (You practiced that, didn't you?) Aim deliberately. Once the sight settles, squeeze right away, but gently.

from a clean target, I brushed the trigger accidentally with my little finger. The rifle fired. I'd barely sunk into position, had established *no* sight picture. The best I could hope was that the bullet had missed the paper, leaving no evidence. Any hole would be scored. Peeking through the spotting scope, I was astounded. Not only had the rifle found the correct target on a sheet of 11; it had centered the black disk—the equivalent of landing a .22 bullet in the mouth of a .22 case 50 feet away.

Now, any shot down the middle without help from sights is a great gift. But because I'd thought carefully about my position beforehand, the rifle pointed naturally at the target. You *must* do the same in the field when you plant your feet for an offhand shot or snug your sling from the sit. That rifle will point naturally—*somewhere*. Your position determines whether or not it points at the target.

"Center shots are made before they're punched," my first coach Earl Wickman told me long ago. He tapped ashes from a cigar long enough to holster. "But don't *over*-think. When you feel a good shot, let it go. Don't analyze it; don't tell yourself it's too good to be true; just give it permission to happen."

Unsupported offhand shots are a last resort. But part of your training should include them. Your effective range will be limited, but you can fire quickly and with little movement.

Some years later, on a Montana ridge, I snuck up to a small herd of elk and missed what I hope will be the easiest shot I ever miss at a bull. The animal all but filled the scope. Rather than let the bullet go, I refined my hold, held a tad forward to allow for the elk's step, and botched the chance.

TOO MUCH TIME IN THE SIGHTS?

The longer you aim, the more desperately you want to breathe normally again. The thump of your pulse becomes more pronounced, just when eye fatigue is burning a target image into your brain. Wobbles become shakes, as your muscles tire under the rifle's weight. Offhand, your entire body starts to sway. You can no longer distinguish between the actual target and the image that entered your brain while your eye was still keen. As the entire effort starts to unravel, you hurry the shot. And you miss.

Better to practice this routine:

Lay a foundation with a body position that makes full use of bone support (not muscles),

For deliberate shooting offhand, keep your left arm (for right-handed shooters) almost directly under the rifle. Keep your head erect, both eyes open. Holding too long will tire you. Accept acceptable wobble and squuueeeeeeze.

and that enables the rifle to point naturally toward the target.

As soon as you shoulder the rifle, find the target and begin your trigger squeeze. You will have breathed deeply a couple times and let the last breath about half-way out. Your lungs should lock about when the sight finds the target and your finger begins to pressure the trigger.

The shot follows—probably not in the first second, maybe in the third, certainly by the fifth. Hold longer than six or seven seconds, and odds of a good shot often drop. If that elk isn't diving for cover, start again, after a moment's rest.

"Believe that you'll hit and you will," said Earl. "Think you might and you might. Fear that you will miss and there's no hope. Beyond the mechanics of marksmanship, hitting depends on your mental readiness to hit. If missing is an option, hitting is less likely. But rather than add pressure by making a hit imperative, consider it the natural result of your shooting routine."

In a long-ago October, hunting deer on crags draped with new snow, I came upon a big mule deer buck. He spied me about the same time, leaped from his bed, and made off. The shot followed fast because it had to. The bullet caught a rear rib and exited between the shoulders. He tumbled. No time to think, but enough time to aim.

Watching film clips or tapes of exhibition shooters, you might assume they don't aim. Everything happens so *fast*! How could they find a relationship between sight and target? The top exhibition shooters do in fact aim. But they see *very* fast, and they don't dwell on sight pictures. A basketball player making a three-pointer at the buzzer doesn't take careful aim. He launches himself, arcs his hand. He looks at the basket, feels the ball, makes subconscious adjustments in an instant, because his body has been trained, by constant repetition, to know what it's supposed to do given the sight picture to the basket that he has. The thinking is over.

An exhibition shooter can't let the bead sit in the notch very long, if at all. Neither should you. If aiming longer doesn't improve your performance (and at some point it won't), maybe a faster shot will.

Given enough practice, you can hit remarkably well by pointing. Think front sight—even if you're not a handgunner, that's good advice. With the rifle's bead or the scope's reticle, focus fast and maintain that focus. Iron sights require alignment, too, but keeping your attention on the front sight helps you shoot faster without losing accuracy.

The level of accuracy you expect influences the speed of your shot. No one can hold a rifle still. The best you can hope for is an acceptable wobble, one whose speed and amplitude stay within bounds. *You* determine those bounds. They're tighter prone than offhand, tighter for a 300-meter competitor than for a hunter throwing down on a buck jetting for cover 30 feet off. One reason we don't shoot as well as we can in the woods is that *we demand too much precision*. When you're out of breath, or wind gusts tug the rifle, and especially if you must shoot without support, you'll have to accept more wobble! Insist on a perfect sight picture, and you'll hold the shot too long.

In practice, you're smart to measure wobble from various positions. Use paper at 50 yards. Take your time. Fire 10 shots to get an average and record it in minutes of angle. Do that for unsupported positions and with an improvised rest. Test yourself after you've sprinted to the firing line. If the cost of cartridges puts you off, use a .22. Get a realistic idea of what you can expect. When game appears, you'll know if wobble is too great to justify a shot; you'll also know to fire if the sight picture looks shaky but not *too* shaky. Learning to recognize acceptable wobble helps you shoot faster and better. Riflemen who shoot only from the bench take a long time aiming, as they're used to

placid sight pictures. In the field, you'll often have little time and no rifle support. The reticle may be gyrating like a barn fly on a hot window. Think *acceptable* wobble.

Shooting before the sight picture becomes still is best included in your practice routine—*get used to it*! When wobble unnerves you, you're apt to freeze or jerk the trigger. You see the sight pause in its dance, so you seize the moment. The result is a miss, because you moved the rifle as you triggered it. Get comfortable with a little wobble! Center it on the target, smoothly crush that trigger. The rifle is most likely to fire when the sight is *close* to the middle.

On a hunt, the shot can come at any time. Savvy shooters mind their step and the light, shot alleys, and their access to field rests. The rifle is always ready to hand.

THINK. BUT NOT TOO MUCH!

Beware of outside pressures. Block out distractions that can affect your judgment and focus. Once, after hitting badly an eland bull late in a Namibian afternoon, I was quite shaken. I'd fired from prone at modest range. Ordinarily, I could have hit a tennis ball under those conditions. But the bull had obviously caught my soft-point well behind his wash-tub vitals. At camp, I tried to make sense of the event, knowing my odds of finding the eland would be slim. That's when I noticed the windage screw on my scope mount was gone. Conclusion: I was not a bad shot, just a dunce for not periodically checking such things.

At dawn, a tracker joined me to follow the wounded animal. Hours later, I spied a horn

above the bush 80 yards ahead. The animal was on to us and trotted off, affording us only glimpses of its head. We dashed forward and by great good luck came upon a savannah. The bull, now 100 yards off and moving, gave me a brief look at the top of his shoulder. I had to fire offhand, quickly. No time for regrets, wishes, doubts. The bullet took the great beast down just as it reached taller cover. I'd done my thinking first, had recognized my only chance for what it was. Conditioned to take that shot, I acted.

Long pokes at game are typically less urgent. You've time to steady the rifle. Wobble matters less than bullet drop and drift. Still, drop and drift aren't the gremlins we make them out to be. Rather, they're functions of bullet flight. Know drop and drift, and hitting can be easy. As you put wobble out of mind when shooting fast, you must at some point decide your hold is correct for the long shot and concentrate on executing that shot. Remember, as you think the shot through in advance, that by zeroing you adjusted for some bullet drop.

Not long ago I watched a friend stalk a bighorn ram. Through my spotting scope a mile off, I could see John and his guide creep toward the bedded sheep, a band containing a dozen mature rams. High on a white rock the men set up for the shot, perhaps 300 yards across a gash to a green flat tilted so steeply it threatened to dump the creatures from the mountain's crest. After long minutes, the rams sifted enough to permit my friend a double-check on horn lengths

A big animal in the scope can bump your pulse. Keeping a calm focus on the shot gives you photographs like this.

In most cover, good rifle rests abound. Be aware of them always, and of places where you can flop prone. Wayne saw this limb before he caught sight of game and wasted no time getting there.

and a clear shot. Suddenly, the herd bolted, players from scrimmage cascading down the flat onto a ribbon of vertical rock. Three seconds later came the muffled *boom*. Then another. And another. I watched the rams single-file across the face.

"I must have aimed too high," grimaced John when he arrived, sweat-stained, at camp and swung off his packframe. "I tried to split the difference between reticle dots, should have used just one."

Indeed. With a 200-yard zero, his Remington 721 in .300 H&H would have held the 180-grain spitzer to seven inches of drop. Seeing air under a horizontal wire is usually a bad omen! More animals are missed high than low. Shooting over that ram, John did what I and many other hunters have done often. We forget that zeroing puts the barrel at an incline to the sight line, that every bullet leaves the rifle on an upward path. "Never hold off hair," Jack Atcheson told me once. "If you think the animal is so far off that you must see daylight under the wire, you're either wrong or need to move closer."

Thinking before you shoot far can also prevent misses due to wind. Once, bellied behind a log, I trained my .257 Weatherby on a distant deer—and almost shot too soon. The wind was puffy at about five miles per hour from two o'clock. Allowing for six inches of drop and that much for drift, I checked my squeeze when the deer stopped behind a bush. Light was failing, but I had to wait for a clear look. I used the delay to re-assess the drift, noting a hard lean to the tops of Doug-firs in the canyon between us. Protected by a bluff, I couldn't feel the true force of the westerly. When the buck came clear, I nudged the reticle a hand's width to windward and triggered the Mark V. The animal dropped instantly. Climbing to him, I found that even my revised drift estimate of nine inches was still shy of what it should have been. The TSX had lanced the lungs a bit to the rear, but my initial hold would have meant a paunched deer.

CHAPTER 38

OFFHAND AND FAST

When you haven't the time to get steady or squeeze slowly, you can still hit. Here's how.

T he snap of limbs, and then voices, told me the drivers were close. In minutes they were all but a pebble's toss away, boughs sloughing against canvas farm jackets. I relaxed. No deer in this pocket.

Then, suddenly, a whitetail buck popped free of the pines. He sunfished over a fence a few feet to my front, then rocketed straight-away. A .303 bullet caught him in the back of his neck. He tumbled, dead instantly. I couldn't remember lifting my rifle. Truly, sometimes muscle memory beats deliberate aim.

But such lucky shots aren't really. In-stinctive shooting depends a great deal on muscle memory. It leans, too, on hand-eye coordination, some of which you inherit. But cultivating good shooting form, then using it exclusively in practice, is not just training your muscles. It's refining coordination. Your

Rifles fired often from standing are best fitted with low-power scopes mounted forward in the rings. You'll naturally thrust your head toward the sight for a fast shot. Wayne shows good form with this .375—head erect but face forward, both eyes open, left hand well ahead on the stock.

body's routines, from walking and swimming to driving with a standard transmission, re-sult from repeated trials, mating one function with another *until the process is coordinate*d.

Accuracy is a measure of consistency. Anyone can score a bull's-eye once; five con-secutive center shots distinguish you. Such consistency breeds confidence. Confidence with practice brings improvement.

Shooting a rifle well starts at a bench. There, across sandbags or from a mechanical rest, you can focus on breathing, sight pic-ture, and trigger control, three fundamental aspects of marksmanship. Because the bench supports the rifle, you needn't fret about sight movement or fight tired, twitching muscles. But extended shooting from the bench can leave you thinking you're a marksman when you're not.

A clarification here: Competitive benchrest shooting tests riflemen who hone their skills *only* at a bench. If you think this to be easy shooting, you're right. It's much easier on your body than position shooting or lengthy prone matches. But benchrest accuracy standards are incredibly high. To place in a match, you'll have to shoot smaller groups than most hunters ever manage. "In the threes" means a group measurement of less than .4-inch—five shots, not three. At 200 yards. And that level of precision won't guarantee you anything more than a smile if conditions are good.

We judge hunting rifles and hunters more charitably. Three-shot bench groups under a minute of angle (1.047 inches at 100 yards or, for convenience, an inch), are considered very good. It's easy to shoot groups from the bench to match the potential of most production-class rifles, which, if I may paint with a broad brush, deliver 1½- to 2-minute accuracy. Most days, I can hold inside ¾-inch from a bench, if all is clicking, I'll keep the crosswire on a half-inch dot. Given a good rifle, good ammo, and a civil wind, I'll get groups that tempt me to stay on the bench.

That's not a good idea. You won't learn to shoot a hunting rifle well if you keep it on sandbags. While it's always a good idea to rest your rifle on the hunt, rocks, stumps, limbs and backpacks, aren't always handy.

Once, at a sight-in day on a shooting range, I asked hunters who'd just zeroed their rifles to take one offhand shot at a six-inch circle at 100 yards. Only five hits showed up. The backing paper, 22 inches square, had 30 holes. More than a dozen riflemen missed the *backer*. Few had practiced from the

Bone support is essential for good offhand shooting. Feet should be shoulder-width apart, torso comfortably straight with a slight forward lean into hard-kicking rifles, and left arm (for right-hand shooters) well underneath. Note the horizontal right arm here, the erect head for a straight look at the sights.

positions they would almost certainly have to use opening day in the hills.

"Stand up and shoot like a man" is bad advice. You'll shoot much better prone, sitting or kneeling because your center of gravity is lower and you have more ground contact. But if you must shoot quickly or over brush, standing may be your only option. Here's how to practice a position you'll try never to use, but one that could someday put venison on the table:

1. Before you lift the rifle, point your feet properly. Place them shoulder-width apart, with your weight evenly distributed. For starters, a line through your toes should cross your rifle's shadow at a roughly 30-degree angle. That will get you close to a comfortable position, but, if the sights are off target, adjust your body by first moving your feet. Find your natural point of aim: the direction in which the rifle naturally points. Do *not* force the rifle onto the target with your arms!

2. Grasp the grip firmly and pull the rifle's butt into your shoulder. Keep your left elbow (for right-handed shooters) nearly under the rifle and your right elbow almost horizontal. Your right shoulder will form a nice pocket for the buttpad. Raise the stock comb to your face; drop your face as little as possible for a firm contact with the comb. Touch the trigger with the first joint of your index finger.

3. Keep your head erect so you can look straight through the sight. Squint if you must, but try to keep both eyes open. If you must mount the scope so the lens housing extends more than an inch over the grip (beyond the rear guard screw), the stock may be too long for you. Your eye should be about three inches from the ocular lens when your face is as far forward as comfort allows.

4. Take two deep breaths, one as you shoulder the rifle, the other as you let it settle

This bear hunter on an Alaskan tidal flat has no clear shot from low positions. In hip boots and mud, reaching a tree stub can take longer than it appears. Almost every shot will be offhand.

on the target. Relax as you release the second breath; do not *forcibly* empty your lungs. Now the sight should be on the target, and your trigger finger should be taking up slack.

5. Apply trigger pressure when the sight is on target; hold pressure when the sight moves off target. The rifle should fire when the sight is where you want it. When you run out of air or if the rifle starts to shake badly, do *not* jerk the trigger. Start over. Resist the urge to "time" the shot, yanking the trigger as the sight bounces onto the target. Most often, you will miss.

6. Follow through, maintaining position as the rifle recoils. Call your shot—that is, tell yourself where the bullet hit before you look in the spotting scope or retrieve your target. An accurate call means you had your eyes on the target and knew where the sight was when the bullet left. That's important! Calling your shots is the first step in correcting problems with position, breathing, and trigger control.

In classic whitetail cover, this hunter swings a Mossberg .30-30 carbine. He would see more, and more clearly, if he didn't squint. He might control the rifle better with the left hand farther forward.

A PRACTICE ROUTINE THAT WORKS!

Use paper targets. They show exactly where bullets hit. Distance doesn't matter. Your goal is to master the fundamentals of marksmanship: position, aiming, trigger control. Before you load up, find the rifle's natural point of aim and adjust your *feet* to bring that point of aim onto the target. Don't pivot at the waist or force the rifle over with your arms. You *can't* hold the rifle still. Your goal is to hold it so its near-constant movement is centered on what you want to hit.

Tuning up for hunting season, I like to fire three-shot groups, one each prone, sitting, kneeling, and offhand. Then I rest.

Regular practice in small doses helps you more than does a long day at the range every two weeks. Keep your targets, assess your progress. As groups shrink, try to eliminate flyers. Dry-firing from field positions at home is a big assist.

Snap-shooting—the art of aiming quickly and shooting instinctively, almost without deliberation—comes easier with practice. It is all but nonsense if you've not first trained your body to execute a good shot. All components, from foot position to trigger squeeze and follow-through, must be second nature before you can expect fast hits. Shooting game quickly is more like shotgunning than sniping; to roll a buck jetting through the alders, you can't deliberate. But neither is snap-shooting a mindless response. A running deer is like a sporting clays target. You have an eye blink to map out a shot path, place your feet, bring

lead. Beyond 50 yards, depending on angle and speed, hold a grapefruit or two in front of the vitals. Up close and in tight places, most game looks jet-powered, and it's easy to get snookered into aiming too far forward. Remember, also, that a bullet is not like a charge of birdshot that forgives excessive lead by killing with the tail of a long pellet string. Your bullet must hit with its nose!

As a youth, I read too often about shotgunners firing at the first duck and hitting the last, about deer hunters splintering limbs behind departing bucks. It still happens, because hunters still stop their swing. But if you shoot with a moving rifle and as soon as the sight touches the shoulder, you'll hit vitals.

Anyone who can run a door latch can cycle a bolt-action rifle. Lift, pull, push, depress. Easy. But fast, uniform cycling takes practice. That's why Darrel Holland insists that students in his shooting school near Powers, Oregon, work the mechanisms on their rifles each evening. A hundred times. Still, repetition alone won't ensure quick follow-up shots. You must practice proper form.

The best way to operate many turn-bolt rifles is to hit the bolt knob with your trigger finger just aft of the low knuckle. As the handle reaches the top of its travel and unlocks the lugs, start pulling with that knuckle. Hooking your finger around the handle at the knob gives you more pull. An alternative is to lift with your trigger finger, but pull with the middle section of your middle finger. This method allows your trigger finger to ride over the knob, alongside a low scope, instead of getting squeezed between the receiver and the scope's ocular bell. Long, heavy bolts and sticky cases can require that you grasp the bolt. Don't practice one-finger retraction with an empty chamber if a fired case mandates aggressive grip!

the stock to your cheek, and swing the sight with the target. Already you've shifted your weight to power the swing from your thighs up through your torso. Your shoulders complete minor corrections to the sight picture, but every shot begins at ground level.

When a buck breaks for cover, don't delay! On the other hand, your best shot may come a split second *after* you're ready to press the trigger. Assessing the shot as you mount the rifle is a crucial first step. Fire as the buck changes direction or ducks a blowdown and you'll have squandered what may be your only chance. Convince yourself that a shot begins as soon as you see the target. Delay if you must, but don't lose your rhythm. Don't release pressure on the trigger; hold it until you can complete the shot.

A bullet gets there right away. Game must throttle back in thickets, and seldom will they cross at 90 degrees to your shot. So forget the arithmetic. Just swing and shoot. Imagine a grapefruit-size bull's-eye over the vitals. Up close, hold at its leading edge as you pivot. When swinging from behind, you probably have more than enough built-in

As the bolt nears the end of its rearward travel, move your hand straight forward, catching the knob with the heel or web of your hand. The bunched muscles at the base of your thumb should capture the knob and control it as you cam the handle down. Push forward and down at once as the bolt meets the end of its travel home. The bolt will rotate obediently—unless you try to separate closure into forward and down movements. Lose your momentum on the thrust, and you'll find the handle will refuse rotation. Camming requires a smooth transition from one direction to the next, constant pressure from your hand.

SPILL THAT BRASS!

Novice shooters—and even those of us who know better—commonly grasp the knob as if it were a cherry. We pick it up gingerly, then shift our grip for the rearward pull. I'm guilty of this from the bench when using a rifle with an aggressive ejector, so that I can keep the hull on the bolt face until I can pluck it. Bad form! In the field, you'll want that follow-up shot right away. Catching the brass before it hits the ground shouldn't be a priority if you're watching a bull elk spin on his heels and make for cover, or if the nostrils of a Cape buffalo are suddenly blocking your view of Africa.

Not long ago, at the FTW Ranch in the Texas Hill Country, I shot my way through a dangerous-game course that included life-size targets of surly beasts. Remotely controlled, they swung suddenly into view behind brush mere feet away, or came for me fast on rails. "Shoot!" screeched the fellow acting as my professional hunter. "Again! There's another! Kill it! Quick!" I'm cycling my rifle double-time. Empty! We're backing up, my fingers fumbling a pair of cigar-sized rounds into the Blaser's breech. "Load fast! They're on you!" *Bang! Bang!* And a pair of buffalo stop on the rail, a broomstick away. Whew!

Bring the rifle to your cheek, not vice versa. Keep both eyes open if at all practical. Keep your left arm well under the rifle, the right elbow (for right-handed shooters) horizontal as you pull the butt into your shoulder.

When it seems offhand is your only option, it may not be! This bull charged to a call and fell to a .30-30 in cover. But Wayne had sought a low shot alley and dropped prone to steady the rifle.

The straight-pull bolt of that Blaser R8 makes it a natural for fast follow-ups. It's quicker than a Mauser action big enough for the .458 Lott. On the other hand, Mauser 98s and Winchester M70s, Sakos, Remingtons, and Weatherbys can all be manipulated speedily by practiced hands. Recoil from full-power dangerous-game loads—and even from frisky medium-bore rounds popular among deer and elk hunters—bounces you off-target momentarily. A reasonable goal: trim cycling time to almost match recovery time.

Some turn-bolt guns are renowned for their speed. The SMLE is one, as the bolt kicks effortlessly rearward on opening. The silky Mannlicher-Schoenauers of my youth almost ran themselves. Bolt handle placement and knob design affect speed. David Tubb, the accomplished competitive rifleman from Texas, gave much thought to the handle on his "2000" rifle. You can cycle that short-action centerfire with one finger! "No need to get out of position," Tubb points out. "That helps immeasurably in making a fast follow-up shot."

A bolt knob shouldn't rap your knuckle on recoil, but it should hang low enough

for quick finger contact on the lift. It must be angled slightly away from the stock, to let your finger slip underneath, but without protruding so much as to impede handling or to catch on brush. Classic, straight-shanked Mauser bolt handles and the artfully swept pre-'64 M70s both appeal to me. Functionally, the correct angle for the handle depends on placement of the knob relative to the trigger. Checkering on the outside of the knob serves no purpose, other than cosmetic. It

Double-gun guru Graeme Wright shoulders a big-bore. A low line of sight makes these rifles point like shotguns. Keeping both eyes open, you get better depth perception as well as more field.

scars cases and scabbards and tears at your hand as you cycle the bolt. Checkering *underneath* can help you run a bolt in wet weather or when you're wearing gloves.

Whatever bolt rifle you own, and whatever bolt-cycling routine you prefer, practice running that bolt can bring you more game!

Recently, a pal and I were padding up a Land Cruiser track in the northern Namibian bush. We saw a couple blue wildebeest a couple hundred yards ahead and swung in a wide arc through the thorn. I bellied into the sand at 70 steps and crawled toward a shot alley. But the bull saw me and bolted. We scurried forward, in the event more of the shaggy creatures remained.

A herd, hidden by thick thorn, thundered off—then galloped in a circle and blasted from cover a few feet away as the wind reversed. I jammed the Sako ahead of the first animal. At the shot, it skidded on its nose. Cycling from the shoulder, I tugged the rifle back hard, swung again. A fat cow somersaulted with a broken neck. My next shot left too soon; a fourth broke too far back. More wildebeest streamed by, a black-and-brindle flood cascading through dense yellow dust. Magazine empty, I could only watch.

Now, 50 percent isn't a good score. What's useful here is the distribution of hits. The two fatal shots came right away, before I had a chance to think about aiming or wildebeests to come, before I could question the effects of bullets fired. My first shots were instinctive, the others unnecessarily complicated.

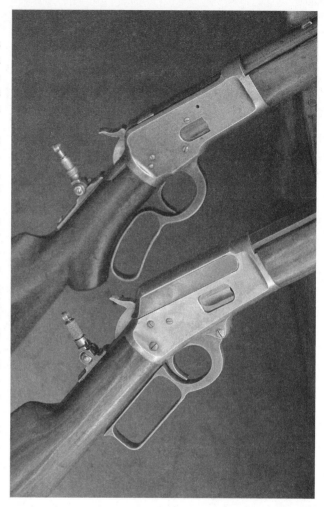

Winchester 92 (top) and Marlin 94 carbines were designed for offhand shooting. (Lever-actions are easiest to cycle from standing!) This pair has been fitted with tang sights for more precise aim. Both straight and pistol grips work well offhand but require different hand and wrist angles.

Getting my feet pointed right, cheeking the rifle so it pointed naturally at the leading edge of the first animal, and triggering that shot immediately worked in my favor. Those elements of your shooting routine can be practiced slowly. Practice them often enough, and your body will respond when you must shoot quickly.

CHAPTER 39

THE LONG POKE

Close is always better. Sometimes far is the best you can do.
Of course, you can always decline.

The foothills of the Rockies offer long looks at game—and may prompt long shots.

Had I stayed with Danny, I'd surely have killed the elk. Well, almost surely. What we think is often tempered by what we wish. No kill is certain until the eyes glaze.

I'd taken a parallel path a stone's toss downslope. Separated, we'd see more of the ridge. Alas, it was my lot that day to choose wrong. Danny's whistle brought me scrambling. Through the trees I spied him crouched, arm raised, motionless. I stopped, chest heaving. A screen of conifers hid the meadow from me. Danny hissed, "Right there!"

In fact the elk was 300 yards off. Ivory tips on six long tines finally caught my eye through the boughs. The bull was staring at Danny.

Prone, it was a makeable shot—heck, it was a cinch. But I wasn't prone and couldn't get prone or even sitting without losing the elk below the hump of the ridge. Offhand, the crosswire danced crazily. The decision was simple: fire offhand or try to reach Danny and a clear alley prone. I declined the shot and crept forward. The bull turned and was gone. I don't believe I've ever seen bigger antlers afield.

Long shots require precise shooting more than they beg powerful loads and optics. If you can't steady the reticle, shooting is simply an exercise in hope.

Because you alone determine where your

bullet goes, and because bullets cause lots of damage to anything they hit, shooting carefully makes sense. Indeed, it's your *imperative*. If you pull the trigger only *hoping* to hit, you'll miss and cripple more often than you'd like. Maiming animals takes little talent and brings few plaudits.

Among the variables that contribute to errant shots is distance. It's the one most talked about, but I've muffed many shots close enough for a field goal in a PeeWee league. Bad shot execution accounts for most misses; distance only puts the bullet farther off the mark. Then there's wind, shot angle, a flawed zero. And not aiming where you should. Just a few weeks ago I watched a young lady hit a big antelope in the shoulder. It would have been a good shot, had the beast been standing with its side squarely to her. But it was quartering sharply away. The bullet should have been driven from the middle ribs toward the off shoulder, bisecting the lungs. Instead, it mangled the shoulder, missed the vitals. A long chase ensued.

How far you can shoot effectively depends on your target's size, environmental conditions at the shot and your own ability, which in turn hinges on your shooting position. Prone, with a sling or bipod to assist or with the rifle over a pack, you can be bench-steady. Less stable positions shorten your reach. Ditto hard breathing and a heavy pulse, as when you crest a ridge and must shoot quickly.

Long shooting has something of a cult following these days and has spawned cottage industries in specialized hardware. Wyoming gunbuilder John Burns, with Coloradans Scott Downs and Don Ward, fashion GreyBull rifles for hunters who expect to shoot far.

Optics are a key component of GreyBull rifles. The firm contracts with Leupold to install its own reticle in Leupold's 4.5-14X VX III sight. It's essentially a Duplex with fine horizontal lines to assist with range estimation, and one-minute tics to help you

An adjustable objective—either as a front-bell sleeve (shown) or as a turret dial—lets you focus the target image and eliminate parallax error at the distance you specify.

shade for wind. The elevation dial is calibrated to be cartridge-specific, machined for the shooter's load and so marked. "You dial to the distance and hold center," Don told me, when I bellied into prone with a GreyBull-modified Remington 700. That was a few years ago. I've since been sold on the principle and the company's scope.

Adjusting windage dials, most hunters agree, is bad business. Wind is *always* changing, and you can easily get lost dialing off zero. So GreyBull's team gives you another option. Numbers scribed above distance marks on the elevation knob show minutes of lateral correction needed in a 10 mile-per-hour crosswind. You can thus see clearly how far into the wind you must hold. Testing these scopes, I've found yardage and windage marks accurate. Of course, a laser rangefinder is all but necessary to get the most from the elevation dial and to estimate drift.

"Calibrating a dial to match the arc of a bullet is a demanding job," John concedes. "We have to know starting velocity and 700-yard drop to calculate the ballistic coefficient and accurately mark the dial." GreyBull can supply scopes with dials for nearly any cartridge. "Ballistic coefficients in catalogs aren't always right, though," John adds. "If that C value is off a little, you'll eventually see bullets land where you don't expect. Not under 400 yards. But beyond that, you'll start to pick up error. The farther a bullet travels, the steeper its arc and the more important the accuracy of the data."

Don Ward builds in third-minute clicks to replace standard quarter-minute detents. That's so he can milk more distance from one dial revolution. "Then you won't get a full-rotation error. We program our scopes so you can click to any yardage, even beyond 1,000 yards." John and Scott have taken game at extreme range. "But that doesn't mean we shoot irresponsibly," says Don. "A hunter must know his limits and hew to them."

Where brush or hills prevent a low position, you can steady that rifle with a tripod. BogGear makes several good ones, easily adjustable so you can shoot kneeling or offhand.

LOADS TO MATCH THE OPTICS

Before you can benefit from a sight that tracks trajectory, you need ammo that delivers precision where arcs get steep. High-performance handloads help. John's aren't much if any faster than ambitious factory loads. However, VLD (very low drag) bullets retain velocity better than ordinary spitzers. That's crucial at long range. You need the highest ballistic coefficient practical. In other words, the bullet must be heavy for its diameter (high sectional density) and sleek in form. *Reducing rate of deceleration at distance matters a lot more than increasing muzzle velocity.* A 180-grain 7mm bullet lies at the heavy end of the weight range. So, too, 105-grain .243s. These bullets, driven by Hodgdon's Retumbo powder, shoot flat "and with enough precision for 1,000-yard hits," says John. Because distance saps velocity, terminal behavior (upset and penetration) from hollowpoint bullets can improve at long range, as impact energy diminishes.

Because long bullet ogives make seating a challenge in short actions, John prefers Remington's 700 long-actions, even for the .243. "Seating those 105-grain missiles out increases case capacity." John cuts relatively long throats in his barrels, because "short bullet jump hasn't delivered top accuracy for us. Besides, bullets seated into the rifling can become a problem in the field. One cartridge a tad long may stick the bullet when you close the bolt." Instead, GreyBull rifles sport lengthy throats "the thickness of a fly's wing" over bullet diameter.

GreyBull rifles wear 26-inch medium-heavy barrels from custom makers like Kreiger, Schneider, and Lilja. John floats the barrel and glass-beds actions in a synthetic, hand-laid stock he and his partners designed. It has a steep, full grip and ample fore-end. A special stud accepts a Stoney Point flexible bipod.

Like me, John and his crew think stiff recoil and harsh muzzle blast can offset benefits afforded by accurate loads, costly barrels, and sophisticated optics. "If you're afraid of a rifle, you won't shoot it well," he declares. A visit to the range confirmed just that. I watched several hunters fire powerful rifles. Softball-sized groups predominated. One shooter gingerly loaded his .338 Magnum for another try. As he yanked the trigger, he closed his eyes and pulled his face from the comb!

My first session with a GreyBull rifle in 7mm Magnum came at distance. "Dial up to 800 yards," Scott Downs told me, waving me off the gongs I could see with my naked eye. "There's a black dot just below the crest of yon hill. It's a 16-inch plate. The shot is actually 780 yards, so take a click off." I did and settled onto the bipod. A sharp wind quartered toward us at roughly 15 mph. "Give it 4 minutes left windage." At 780 steps, that's 30 inches! Lots of air gaped between the crosswire and the plate.

The two-pound Jewell trigger broke cleanly. A tiny puff of dust followed, lazily. "Two clicks more wind," Scott muttered from behind the spotting scope. I complied. Seconds after my next shot, we heard the distant pop of a solid hit. "See," he smiled. "You just have to trust the dial." He told me he'd coached a neighbor on the bench, "shooting that same gong. He hit high with the setting you used. I was perplexed until he admitted he'd *held* high. Of course, adding a few inches of elevation was absurd. Were it not for the *dialed* adjustment, he'd still have planted his bullets several feet *shy!*"

We don't advocate shooting at game half a mile off," John emphasized. The GreyBull team had been hit with that accusation. "But minute-of-angle precision at distance instills the confidence to shoot more accurately at normal distances. And you learn about wind."

AN INVISIBLE LEASH

My introduction to wind deflection, or drift, came in smallbore matches. When I

kicked at 3,000 fps from a .270 plows into a *2,000 mile per hour gale!* A 10 mile-per-hour headwind or tailwind is pretty small potatoes in comparison!

Even when wind comes obliquely from the side, most hunting loads show little deflection. Wind that picks up small dogs and rolls trash cans may have little effect on bullets when the angle is acute.

Because bullets spin, drift has a vertical component. Right-hand twists typically land bullets to 10 o'clock when they're pushed from the right, to four o'clock when nudged from the left (not to three and nine). You can ignore vertical displacement with hunting bullets at normal yardage.

Distance has a decided effect on drift. As a bullet's descent becomes steeper with distance, so the effect of wind becomes greater. A constant wind is like gravity. Bullets scribe a parabolic hook under the press of wind for the same reasons their trajectory is parabolic.

Double the wind speed and you double the drift. Halve wind speed and you halve the drift. Change the wind's angle from 90 degrees and drift diminishes proportionately. Change shot *distance*, however, and the math gets more complicated. Our 130-grain .270 bullet launched at 3,000 fps drifts less than an inch at 100 yards in a 10 mile-per-hour wind. At 200 yards, it is three inches off course—roughly *four times* as far! At 300 yards it drifts seven inches, at 400, 13. There's negligible drift at 100 yards, because the bullet gets there in just .1-second. Adding distance dramatically increases wind deflection for every bullet. In fact, drift for the .270 bullet at 500 yards is about 60-percent greater than drift at 400.

Downrange, bullets are moving slower, so wind has more time to work its mischief. Wind at the muzzle, though, has greater leverage. You can't afford to ignore either!

moved outside from enclosed ranges, I felt as if I'd been plucked from a hotel pool and dropped into the North Atlantic. Outdoors I had to dope wind. Flags and "windicators"—delicately mounted fans with tails that swung on ball bearings—showed its speed and direction. Both affect bullet flight. A "full-value" wind from three or nine o'clock is most troublesome, because it pushes at right angles to the bullet's path. Steeper angles reduce the effect. Wind from 12 o'clock or six o'clock has essentially *no* effect, unless it is very strong. A bullet fired at a distant target leaves nose up and *remains* nose up. Unlike an arrow, it does not "porpoise." Surface exposure due to the bullet's attitude does influence flight, but it's hardly measurable at hunting ranges. A bullet meets terrific resistance and friction even in still air. It generates its own fierce headwind. Indeed, a hunting bullet

Drift Example

	100 yards	200 yards	300 yards	400 yards
Actual drift (inches)	0.7	2.0	7.0	12.9
Rule of thumb drift (inches)	1	2	6	12

Many years ago, eyes a-water in a Wyoming gale that threatened to skid me, prone, into another cactus, I fought to keep my rifle still. During a brief lull, as the sling tugged the horizontal wire onto the antelope's back, I crushed the trigger. The buck sprinted, then stopped as I cranked in another cartridge. Doubling my wind allowance, I held the vertical wire into the sage, in front of the animal's nose. The 722 cracked again. Its 90-grain 6mm bullet arced the 400 yards in roughly half a second. Its path bent by that rush of high-desert air, it yielded a foot and a half to the right, lancing the buck's forward ribs

For popular big-game loads in a 10 mile-per-hour crosswind, you can assume an inch of drift at 100 yards, twice that at 200. Triple the 200 drift at 300, double the 300 drift at 400. How this rule works for a 180-grain .30-06 bullet at 2,700 fps is illustrated in the above chart.

In this case, the estimate stays within an inch of actual drift. The rule works for most pointed big-game bullets, no matter the chambering, between 2,600 and 3,100 fps.

Wind deflection also depends on bullet velocity and ballistic coefficient, or C. Bullets of similar C show about the same wind drift. Consider a quartet of Nosler Partitions: a 130-grain .270, a 140-grain 7mm, a 165-grain .308 and a 210-grain .338. All share a common form and similar C values—from about .390 to .440. Hurled at 3,000 fps, all drift about six inches at 200 yards in a 20 mile-per-hour full-value wind. Bullet weight doesn't matter. But trim C to .289 with a flat-

At very long range, you'll need lots of elevation adjustment to compensate for bullet drop. The increasingly popular 30mm tube allows more erector assembly tilt. Some makers replace standard quarter-minute elevation clicks with third-minute, to further boost elevation range.

nose bullet, and drift jumps 50 percent, to *nine* inches!

A bullet the shape of a soup can isn't very well adapted for flight. There's a lot of air pressure on the nose for a high rate of deceleration. But lightweight spitzers, like 70-grain .243s, also have low ballistic coefficients. Their low sectional density (ratio of a bullet's weight to the square of its diameter), acts like a blunt nose to reduce C. All else equal, fast bullets buck wind better than slow ones.

Note that, at 500 yards, the .300 Winchester bullet drifts only three inches less than that bullet from a .30-06, not much difference, considering the 380 fps disparity in starting velocities. Reason: the .300's bullet decelerates at a greater rate. Moving faster from the muzzle, it meets stiffer resistance. Speed must overcome that air resistance before it delivers the benefits of flatter flight and less drift.

Launched from a .30-30, a bullet of the same weight but with a blunt nose lags well behind the others and yields more readily to wind. Though its muzzle speed comes within 80 percent of the .30-06's, it drifts *more than twice as far* at 500 yards. Why? The .30-30 bullet has a dismal ballistic coefficient and decelerates much more rapidly. Its 500-yard velocity is only 40 percent of its launch

speed, while the '06 and .300 bullets retain about 60 percent at 500. Again, rate of deceleration trumps muzzle velocity.

READING (AND DRILLING) THE WIND

Bullet weight, ballistic coefficient, and velocity all affect drift because they all affect deceleration.

Sharp bullet tips have become popular of late, lending an aerodynamic shape to the missile. But ballisticians tell me the first .1-inch of the nose has little effect on trajectory or drift. The "ogive," the curve between tip and shank, is a bigger factor, accounting for a great deal of friction. Boat-tail bullets become an asset only at extreme range. A 30 mile-per-hour wind that shoves a flat-base 7mm bullet 17 inches at 350 yards moves a boat-tail bullet 15½ inches. The lesser drift afforded by that tapered heel at high wind speeds is academic, given how hard it is to estimate drift in a wind that strong, or to hold a reticle within a couple of inches at 350 yards. Also, *percentage* difference in wind deflection between these two bullets is about the same for a 10 mile-per-hour wind and a 30 mile-per-hour wind.

No matter how well your bullet resists wind, hitting consistently at distance can depend on your ability to predict drift. The

first thing to recognize is that wind where you are is not necessarily the same as wind at the target or in the bullet's path. The longer the range, the more varied the wind conditions can be. In competition,

Wayne uses a sling from the sit to steady this Savage rifle for a long poke. Distance magnifies all errors. If you can't hold the sight inside the vitals, you're not steady enough, or the animal is too far.

Wind Drift (10 mph, right-angled)

.30-30, 150-grain	0 yards	100 yards	200 yards	300 yards	400 yards	500 yards
Velocity (fps)	2390	—	—	—	—	1040
Drift (inches)	—	2	8	21	39	65

.30-06, 150-grain	0 yards	100 yards	200 yards	300 yards	400 yards	500 yards
Velocity (fps)	2910	—	—	—	—	1620
Drift (inches)	—	1	4	10	19	31

.300 Win., 150-grain	0 yards	100 yards	200 yards	300 yards	400 yards	500 yards
Velocity (fps)	3290	—	—	—	—	1810
Drift (inches)	—	1	4	9	17	28

I watched windicators at the line hum lazily, while my bullets jumped in and out of the 10-ring. Flags at 50 and 100 yards often showed downrange conditions unstable. Flags flapping briskly at 100 yards might belie conditions that left others hanging limp at 50. Windicators might spin furiously to the left, while mid-range flags lifted to the right and 100-yard cloth kicked left again! Bullets fired through gauntlets of strong currents may indeed chart a ziz-zag course!

Smart shooters make notes about wind on each range so they learn its idiosyncrasies. Spokane's range, where I often competed, hugs a riverbank. Wind typically angles across the firing line from seven or eight o'clock, then bounces off the bank and hits the targets from four o'clock. Alas, you won't have such data on a hunt, so you must learn to read the wind's effect on the environment.

Early in my shooting career, fellow marksman Dick Nelson (who helped Boeing design the first moon vehicle), took me aside. "Mind the mirage. It's your window to the wind."

Mirage, of course, is the distortion caused by heat waves rising from the earth's surface. If you don't see it, it isn't there. Mirage doesn't move bullets, but it shows you wind that does. Mirage can also "float" your target image in the direction the air is moving—so the deer you see is a virtual animal some inches away from the real deer. You can't see mirage at all distances at once.

To read the wind that most affects their bullets, competitive shooters typically focus their spotting scopes just short of the targets. Because riflescopes for hunting rifles have been set for sharp focus (and zero parallax) at 100 to 150 yards, you'll read mirage most clearly there. An adjustable objective lets you extend focus and read mirage far away.

Bumpy, slow-moving mirage indicates a light breeze. Mirage that's flat and fast shows stronger wind. When mirage disappears suddenly, it's often because the wind has picked up. Mirage that boils vertically indicates still air. But beware! A boil commonly precedes a reversal in wind direction. Many competitive shooters zero for prevailing breeze, then hold their fire during boils and reversals, shading as they shoot through pick-ups and let-offs.

In the field, you may seldom see mirage. Fall hunting seasons bring cold weather, which all but cancels mirage. To read wind then, you must rely on coarser signs, like nodding trees and grass. Leaves, snow, and mist also yield to wind. So does dust from bullet strikes. In the event you've doped the wind wrong or a last-minute shift has caught you, mind the drift from the miss! Remember that the dust you see as you come out of recoil may be well downwind of the actual bullet strike. If a miss is unexpected and the wind unreadable, maybe you'd best hold that next shot!

TOO LONG ISN'T ALWAYS FAR!

Many chancy shots come at modest range. Once, still-hunting through thick lodgepoles, I caught a wink of russet color. In the Leupold it became an elk ear, a pebble's toss uphill. I was not gulping air. The rifle steadied itself smoothly, reticle quivering in tight loops. Problem was, brush blocked the bullet's path to brain and spine. I could only guess where the shoulder lay. Seconds later, breeze kissed the back of my neck. The ear vanished.

No one can post a sure-kill distance for shots at big game, as no one can declare a safe maximum speed on a highway. Conditions matter. Arguably, sniping from afar diminishes the hunt (and the cynical might say a habit of shooting beyond point-blank range shows you're lazy). But neither long shooting nor fast driving is irresponsible of itself.

"Anyone who says he wouldn't take a risky shot at a big bull on the last day is a liar!" A reader sent me that note after I'd suggested that neither trophy value nor the likelihood of another shot should figure into a decision to fire. If your aim is to kill, only variables that affect the probability of a lethal hit matter. Wishing hard that you'll kill doesn't justify a shot any more than wishing earns you an Olympic medal or a PhD. Shooting when you're not sure of the shot is like poaching in this way: both events show you can't abide discipline. Hewing to standards in shot selection is like obeying game laws. You restrict yourself so that, whatever the outcome of a hunt, you will have acquitted yourself well.

Such high ground can be costly to hold. Pass a shot at a records-class animal and you may have passed the only one you'll ever have. No shoulder mount. No accolades from pals. No listing in the book. "Your one chance to be a celebrity, and you turn it down. Why? Because there's only a 50-50 chance of killing? Good grief! At least put a bullet in the air! If the shot's off the mark, no one else will know."

But *you* will.

Once, in Africa, I followed a tracker on the long trail of an eland bull. We were physically fit, but by mid-afternoon, the sun, sand, and thorn had exacted a toll. Then, suddenly, Kamati snapped his finger. The faint click of eland hooves sifted through the thorn. We crept forward. A huge bull appeared suddenly, 60 yards away. Slowly the crossed sticks rose. I slid my rifle into place, but branches screened my target.

"Shoot," hissed my companion. "Your bullet will get through."

I shook my head. A second later the eland vanished. We trekked back in uncomfortable silence. As luck would have it, I killed a fine eland later that week, dropping it with one bullet. All was forgiven.

Nice as my second chance was, you're foolish to count on them. Once, on assignment for an elk-hunting television episode, I fell on a rocky hillside—so quickly I couldn't save my rifle from a bruising. A freak event. Our party spotted an elk barely an hour later, quartering away in a small window in dense alder. Range about 300 yards. Ordinarily I'd have gone prone and fired. But there was no telling how my tumble had affected my scope. The alders wouldn't show a bullet strike. They'd surely prevent a follow-up. "Sorry," I said to guide, cameraman, and company. The rest of that week was an exercise in public relations, as no other elk appeared. The scope, by the way, had not lost zero. But it could have. A lucky hit from a risky shot means an animal died *in spite of* your judgment.

No matter how confident you are of a lethal hit, be ready to follow with another. Reaction to a hit in the paunch often mimics response to a heart or lung shot. Animals escape when hunters reload slowly or don't reload at all. Fast bolt work can give you a second hit. Shots at crippled game needn't meet a 90-percent standard of certainty. The time for deliberation is before loosing that first bullet.

MORE RIFLE WISDOM TO RELY ON

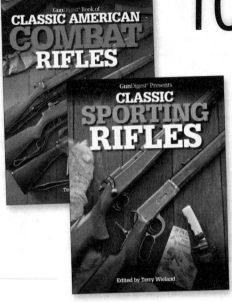

Gun Digest® Book of Classic American Combat Rifles

Explore the rich history of the greatest long guns in action during wartime, as told in feature articles written by top firearms writers.   W7942 • $24.99

Gun Digest® Presents Classic Sporting Rifles

Lessons about iconic rifles from the old school masters of gun writing.
W7930 • $24.99

Gun Digest® Book of the .22 Rifle

Learn how to put an old favorite, the .22, to good use for everything from target shooting and competition to varmint hunting.
Z8581 • $19.99

Gun Digest® Book of Long-Range Shooting

Techniques to hit the target 200, 500, 1,000 or more yards from wherever you are at.
Z0735 • $24.99